The New Testament: An Introduction

Volume IV

The Epistle to the Hebrews

The Epistles of James, I Peter, Jude and II Peter

The New Testament:
An Introduction

Volume IV

The Epistle to the Hebrews

The Epistles of James, I Peter, Jude and II Peter

Richard E.A. Rodgers

2021

The New Testament: An Introduction – Volume IV: *The Epistle to the Hebrews.*
The Epistles of James, I Peter, Jude, and II Peter — published by the Indian Society
for Promoting Christian Knowledge (ISPCK), Post Box 1585, 1654, Madarsa Road,
Kashmere Gate, Delhi-110006.

Online order: http://ispck.org.in/book.php

Also available on amazon.com

ISBN: 978-93-90569-55-7

Cover Credit: Internet Sources

Laser typeset at **ISPCK,** Post Box 1585, 1654, Madarsa Road, Kashmere Gate,
Delhi-110006.
Tel: 23866323, Fax: 91-11-23865490
e-mail: ashish@ispck.org.in • ella@ispck.org.in
website: www.ispck.org.in

Contents

Section I

The Epistle to the Hebrews

Chapter I

Introduction to the Epistle to the Hebrews

Chapter II

Contents

Section II

The Epistle of James

Chapter I

Chapter II

Chapter III

Section III

The First Epistle of Peter

Chapter I

Chapter II

Section IV
The Epistle of Jude

Section V
The Second Epistle of Peter

Section VI
Ecclesiology in the New Testament

OUTLINE OF THE SERIES

The New Testament – An Introduction

Purpose: The empowerment of the λαος (*laos* = laity) – the people of God.

1. To acquaint the reader with a brief geographical, historical and religious background of the New Testament in order to be familiar with the context in which the writings originated.

2. To provide an introduction to the books of the New Testament, and a short commentary, in order to give the reader a background from which to interpret texts while preaching or leading in Bible Study.

3. To provide beginners and laypersons with the basic tools required for an informed understanding and interpretation of the New Testament.

VOLUME I

Background and Synoptics

Chapter I: Background to the New Testament

Map: Palestine in New Testament Times

1. Historical Background

A. Diaspora in Assyria. Diaspora in Babylon. Rise of the Persian

Empire. Restoration under Ezra and Nehemiah. Rise of the Greek Empire under Alexander the Great.

B. Origin and Development of Hellenism. Jewish reactions to Hellenism.

C. The Maccabean Revolt. Rise of the Hasmonean Dynasty and its decline.

D. Rise of the Roman Empire. The administration of Palestine under the Romans.

E. Palestine under the Herods and Roman Governors.

F. Fall of Jerusalem A.D. 70, and destruction – A.D. 135.

G. Persecution of Christians under later Roman Emperors.

2. Social Background

A. Cities, Population, Common practices and beliefs

B. Wealth/Poverty/Slaves

C. Education

3. Religious Background

A. The Temple. Sanhedrin. The Synagogue.

B. Sectarian Judaism: Sadducees, Pharisees, Scribes, Zealots, Essenes, the Qumran Community and the Dead Sea Scrolls.

C. Jewish Messianism: hopes and restoration of the Kingdom of David. New Testament interpretation of a suffering messiah.

D. Emergence of Christianity – people, literature and emergence of doctrine.

E. Greek Influences: Greek Philosophies, The Mystery Religions, Gnosticism.

CHAPTER II

Formation of the New Testament Canon

CHAPTER III

Study of the Gospels

G. Form and Redaction in the Gospels.

H. Modern approaches to the study of the Gospels.

Select Bibliography

CHAPTER IV

The Synoptics

A. Why the first three gospels are known as "the Synoptics" and the Synoptic Problem.

B. Brief introduction to each of the Synoptics:

1. Matthew : authorship, date, place of writing, purpose. Brief analysis of and commentary on the text.

Select Bibliography

2. Mark : authorship, date, place of writing, purpose. Brief analysis of and commentary on the text.

Select Bibliography

3. Luke : authorship, date, place of writing, purpose. Brief analysis of and commentary on the text.

Select Bibliography

CHAPTER V

Selected Studies

Theme studies

Infancy Narratives – theological motifs

Parables – meaning, use and interpretation; value as teaching aids; use in preaching and teaching today

Miracles – meaning, use and interpretation. Value in preaching and teaching today

Kingdom of God – meaning, use and interpretation

Passion, death and Resurrection Narratives

Jesus and children

Jesus and women

Christian discipleship – the Sermon on the Mount.

Mission Perspectives

1. The Nazareth Manifesto – proclamation and participation

2. Confrontation with socio-religio-political powers/structures

3. Developments as Christianity spread from Palestine (Jewish) into the Hellenistic (Greek) world

4. Mission as promotion of peace and justice.

Eschatology and the Hope for the future. The universal reign of God

❋❋❋

VOLUME II

The Acts of the Apostles

A Study of Paul and the Pauline Letters

Section I

The Acts of the Apostles

Chapter I

Introduction to the Book of Acts of the Apostles. Authorship. Date. Place of writing. Purpose.

Chapter II

Birth and spread of the Church I (Acts chapters 1 – 14): Brief analysis and commentary on the text. Jerusalem. Persecution of the Church. Ethiopia. Introduction to Saul/Paul. Conversion of Cornelius. Spread beyond Judaism/Palestine. Church in Antioch. Paul's First Missionary Journey.

Chapter III

The Jerusalem Assembly (Acts chapter 15): Brief analysis and commentary on the text. The Jew-Gentile controversy and its resolution in Acts.

Chapter IV

Birth and spread of the Church II (Acts chapters 16 – 28): Brief analysis and commentary on the text. Paul's journeys. Paul's imprisonment and journey to Rome.

Chapter V

History and Theology in the Book of Acts.

Select Bibliography for Section I.

Section II

A Study of Paul and the Pauline Letters

Chapter I

General Introduction to New Testament Letters.

Chapter II

Paul's Life

Primary sources for information on Paul (his letters), secondary sources (Acts). The background of Paul. Conversion. His work.

Table of suggested Pauline chronology. Table of suggested chronology for all Pauline letters. Paul as interpreter of Christ to the Jews and Gentiles. Select bibliography.

Chapter III

An introduction to Paul's own letters: A. Romans B. The Corinthian Correspondence – I & II Corinthians C. Galatians D. Philemon

Founding of the community. Authorship/authenticity and integrity.

Date. Occasion and Purpose.

Brief analysis and commentary on the text of each of the letters.

Select Bibliography for each letter.

Chapter IV

An introduction to the deutero-Pauline letters: A. Ephesians B. Philippians   C. Colossians   D. The Thessalonian Correspondence – I & II Thessalonians

Founding of the community. Authorship/authenticity and integrity.

Date. Occasion and Purpose. Place of writing.

Brief analysis and commentary on the text of each of the letters.

Select Bibliography for each letter.

Chapter V

An introduction to the trito-Pauline letters – The Pastorals: A. I Timothy   B. II Timothy   C. Titus

The Addressees. Authorship/authenticity and integrity.

Occasion and Purpose. Date.

Brief analysis and commentary on the text of each of the letters.

Select bibliography for the Pastorals.

Chapter VI

Some issues in Pauline thought

A. Sin. Law. Righteousness. Salvation. Justification by faith.

B. Ἐν Χριστω (en Christo): Life in Christ. Individual and corporative perspectives.

C. The Church: Jews and Gentiles in the Church. The Body of Christ. Sacraments. Spiritual gifts. Γλωσσαλαλια (glossalalia) – speaking in tongues.

D. Eschatology and the summing up of all things in Christ.

E. The place and contribution of women in the Church. Women as partners in ministry.

F. Creation and ecological concerns (Rom. 8:18-25; Col. 1:15-20).

Select Bibliography

Chapter VII

The Relevance of Paul for Today

❊❊❊

VOLUME III

The Gospel of John

The Epistles of I, II, III, John

The Book of Revelation

Section I

The Gospel of John

Chapter IV Similarities and Dissimilarities between the Synoptics and John

1. Similarities: geography, John the Baptist, Passion and empty tomb.

2. Dissimilarities: chronology, ministry, cleansing the Temple, teaching of Jesus through discourses and "I AM" (ἐγώ εἰμι) sayings, eucharist, fewer miracle stories, fewer parables.

3. Theological differences: realized eschatology, Kingdom of God, mission and ecumenism.

Select Bibliography for Section I.

Section II

The Epistles of I, II, III John

A. Introduction to I John: authorship, date, place of writing, purpose.

B. Brief analysis and commentary on the text of I John.

C. Introduction to II John: authorship, date, place of writing, purpose.

D. Brief analysis and commentary on the text of II John.

E. Introduction to III John: authorship, date, place of writing, purpose.

F. Brief analysis and commentary on the text of III John.

Select Bibliography for Section II

Section III

The Book of Revelation

Chapter I An introduction to apocalyptic literature – a literature of hope.

Chapter II The background/context and date of the Book of Revelation; Authorship, Readers and Purpose.

Chapter III Approaches to the interpretation of the Book of Revelation.

❈❈❈

VOLUME IV

The Epistle to the Hebrews. The Epistles of James, I Peter, Jude and II Peter

Ecclesiology (Church Organization and Structure) in the New Testament

Section I
The Epistle to the Hebrews

Section II
The Epistle of James

Chapter I   General Introduction to the Catholic Epistles (James, I, II, III John, I, II Peter, Jude):   Reasons for naming these as "Catholic Epistles".

Chapter II   Introduction to the Epistle of James: background, authorship, recipients, date.

Chapter III   Practical Christian living: Analysis and commentary on the text of James.

A Liberation Theology Perspective.

Select Bibliography for Section II.

Section III
The First Epistle of Peter

Chapter I   Introduction to I Peter: background and purpose, authorship, date.

Chapter II   Ethical behaviour, persecution and suffering as marks of a true Christian: Analysis and commentary on the text of I Peter.

Select Bibliography for Section III.

Section IV
The Epistle of Jude

Chapter I   Introduction to Jude: background and purpose, authorship, addressees, date, and place of writing.

Chapter II   Jude: warnings against false teachings and heresies regarding the person and work of Christ, with special reference to Christ's second coming.

Insistence on sound doctrine. Analysis and commentary on the text of Jude.

Section V
The Second Epistle of Peter

Section VI
Ecclesiology (Organization and Structure) in the New Testament

Acknowledgements

Any writing work requires one to put aside other things and bring to bear time and concentration on the writing. This means that the burden of household chores and social obligations falls on others in the family. In this case my wife, Sunita, has taken over my responsibilities in addition to her own commitment to the home and willingly foregone her own interests so that I could have time to complete this series. In a time of retirement when we both should be finding relaxation and joy in each other's company, I have been on the computer and unable to hear and see anything other than the images of Hebrews, the end of the world pictures of Jude and II Peter, and the false teachings of the Catholic Epistles! There are no words that can express my gratitude to her for her love and sacrifice. Thank you, dear wife, for making it possible for me to devote time to writing and for putting up with ill-temper and crankiness!

Other members of our family – our children Rahul, his wife Neha, and our grandson, Jared, my mother Mrs. Lillian Rodgers (*it is sad that my mother passed away before the publication of Vol. IV. Vol. II of the series was co-dedicated to her*), my sisters Geraldine and Chrystal, my brother Norman and their families, my mother-in-law Mrs. Primrose RadhaKrishan, my sisters-in-law, Usha, Asha, Saroj, and their families – have all shared in the intrusion into family life and the priority that these writings have taken. All of them, and many loving friends, colleagues and former students, have been supportive and encouraging and are still cheering along the track waiting for each volume as it crosses the finishing line! My heartfelt thanks to each of them.

The Board of Directors of Leonard Theological College, Jabalpur, and the Delhi Regional Conference of the Methodist Church in India, were gracious in granting me a year's sabbatical leave (2015-2016) during which time I should have completed this work, but was unable to do so. My grateful thanks to the College and Regional Conference authorities.

To the many students, who may find themselves reflected in these pages, my grateful thanks to each of you for your interactions and interventions, and for keeping me focused.

The publishers and distributers, ISPCK, Delhi, Dr. Ashish Amos the General Secretary, Ms. Ella Sonawane the Associate General Secretary, and all the Staff involved in printing and publication, have been most gracious in their handling of my text of all the four volumes, making suggestions for improvement, and overall technical input in printing especially in handling the Greek script, for the cover design of the series, and the many times they accommodated me in the corrections to the text. Their enthusiasm that these books will make a contribution has been a great encouragement. My grateful thanks to the General Secretary and the whole team at ISPCK.

I must acknowledge my gratitude to my student who has risen to heights of leadership in the church – the Most Rev'd. Dr. P. C. Singh, Moderator of the CNI Synod and Bishop of the Jabalpur Diocese, President of the NCCI, President of the Bible Society of India, and Chairperson/member of many Boards and Governing Bodies of institutions. The unfailing recognition that he accords to his teacher is both a humbling experience and an encouragement. My grateful thanks to him for permission to release each of the volumes in a church service and for taking time off from his very busy schedule of travel, meetings, demands of Synod and Diocesan administration, to be present and to release each of the four volumes.

The Christ Church Cathedral, CNI, Jabalpur, has been our family's place of worship for over four decades and since these volumes have been written for the laity, I wanted the books released in a church service where the laity were present and would participate. My grateful thanks to the presbyters of the Cathedral, Rev. Bruce Thangadurai and Rev. Subba Venkataram, and to the Pastorate Committee, for permitting the release of the first volume at the inaugural function of the Cathedral's celebration of 175 years of glorious service, and the other three volumes during worship services.

The New Testament writings covered in this volume were particularly concerned with the on-going mission of the church as it came face to face with issues that threatened its existence, and to give the church direction for the future; in other words these writings were not just for the concerns of that time, but more importantly for the 'gen-next'. So, in keeping with this concern to encourage faith and faithfulness, this volume is dedicated to the 'gen-next' – to our beloved children Rahul and Neha and our precious little grandson, Jared Philip (our *Bundoo – little insect!*).

Richard E. A. Rodgers
Jabalpur, M. P., India

Kingdomtide
2020

Preface

This series of four volumes on introductory material to the New Testament, and a short commentary on each book, has at least three reasons for their origins.

1. When I joined Leonard Theological College, Jabalpur (LTC), for my BD studies, the only model of ministry that was before me was the pastoral ministry. My family and I had been greatly helped by a loving, caring pastor at Centenary Methodist English Church, New Delhi; he and his wife were my role models, and now more than 50 years later, I still think of them as my parents in the ministry because it was their example that was the deciding influence in my decision to join full-time church work (Vol. I of this series was dedicated to them in gratitude). During the course of studies, I felt a shift in my understanding of ministry, and slowly, but surely, I came to realize that my calling was to the teaching ministry – theological teaching. Further, under the guidance and influence of excellent teachers, my focus narrowed to the field of New Testament studies. After the required time spent in pastoral ministry at my home church in New Delhi, and having been ordained, the Bishop was pleased to grant me study leave for my M.Th. (Senate of Serampore) in New Testament at the United Theological College, Bangalore (now Bengaluru). On completion of that, an invitation was received from LTC to serve on the faculty; I was excited at the thought of going back to my *alma mater* which I had come to love. The request was sent from

LTC to my Bishop in Delhi who was again pleased to release my services to LTC (for the next 37 years, consecutive Bishops released my services to LTC). The paradigm shift that I had experienced and dreamt about was becoming a reality. The ease with which all of this happened (no red tape and pulling of strings and playing politics!) convinced me that God was indeed calling me to the teaching ministry. As I submitted to this understanding of ministry, I felt at ease within myself, and the love affair with the College which began on the day I entered it as a student, opened up new avenues for flowering and flourishing in teaching, research, and in preparing students for responding to the endless possibilities of ministry to which God had called them. This does not mean that the 'pastoral' aspect of ministry totally gave way to the 'academic'. Over the 37 years of teaching/academics/administration at LTC, I know that dealing with staff and students who are hurting and confused and need a healing touch, has been an exercise of pastoral ministry – reaching out to them in love and caring yet with a sense of discipline. I do earnestly hope that God has blest those efforts of pastoral care as much as God has blest my efforts at being a faithful teacher.

So, my first reason is to acknowledge the love and care that I have received all along the journey; the encouragement, through letters and constant communication from my pastor, church leaders, teachers, colleagues, friends and students. In a very small way, may this be an acknowledgement, from a grateful heart, of all that I have received from them.

2. Over the years of teaching, I have always been intrigued by the unquestioning acceptance with which people, and especially my students, approached the New Testament. In my own experience, throughout the years of religious education (Sunday school, youth groups etc…), I had always been taught to ask questions, to rationalize, and to try to reckon how, in the Bible, people understood God as speaking to them, and how we understand God as speaking to us today. The unquestioning acceptance is often described as

"blind faith", "simply believe", "God's will" etc.…. It has always been my endeavour to inculcate in my students a questioning mind – to approach the text with critical questions, to bring to bear on the text their knowledge from history, sociology, religions, anthropology, language, literature, various other sciences etc…. Or in technical terms, to use the methods of modern historical-critical studies. It has never been my intention to undermine my students' faith or to question what has been deeply implanted in their psyche, but to get them to understand their faith and beliefs in a more informed way rather than through "blind faith" often bordering on superstition. The first few classes of any course was usually spent in an unlearning process so that the class was open to new approaches and fresh understandings of God's word which would strengthen and undergird the faith. This was never a one sided exercise; no matter how many times I taught a course, each time I learnt, unlearnt, and re-learnt how God speaks to us through God's word; a hermeneutical exercise that led to a greater appreciation of the New Testament both as literature and as a document of faith. However, I was also aware that such an approach could have ended in a negative way leading to destruction of faith and beliefs. Therefore, a very careful handling of the critical approach had to be nurtured. This resulted in a challenge to me regarding the content and presentation of my lectures, and now to reshape my lectures into books/literature that would lead to a deepening of faith and greater appreciation of God's word through this critical approach. Books/literature were not always available, even in the best stocked libraries, because most books are too expensive for individuals, and also most books assumed a certain level of critical understanding which was difficult to find in our rather conservative religious ethos.

So, my second reason was to develop literature/books/guidelines as a "primer" before the student/seeker could go on to more complicated theories and hypotheses in advanced commentaries. However, the pressures of work (church, university, personal interest involvements), preparation for teaching-corrections-thesis guidance, and the administration of a college did not permit the time to devote to this task. Now, in retirement, I rely on the many, many files of notes made over the years of teaching and on personal insights gained from the constant interaction with the text. This series is offered as a small contribution to the onward journey of faith and of being interpreters of God's word in today's world.

3. The third reason arises from a concern to provide the church with literature which could be used by the layperson – literature that would help the layperson to grapple with issues, but at the same time would avoid the hassles of plunging into academic niceties such as ponderous references, credits in footnotes and bibliography which are absolutely fatal for the beginner! (these should be left to professional courses and research papers); technical language will be largely avoided, or further explained when its use is unavoidable; important words will be found in transliteration. The intention is to lead the person into a critical understanding of scripture even in the absence of a professional such as a theological teacher/theologically trained person. For several years I had wanted to give time, thinking and efforts to this concern which would undergird the theological foundations of Christian doctrine. As Principal of the College, I had even proposed that Leonard Theological College, Jabalpur – its resources in terms of library, faculty, and the structure of the College's School of Research – could be the locus for this endeavour with an on-going programme for constantly producing literature for the church. But this was not to be (except for the publication of the Bishop and Mrs. S. K. Parmar Lectures of which I edited the first six volumes). Giving expression to this concern of mine is now my retirement project!

So my third reason is that I should bring together my concern for developing easily available resources, at least for the New Testament, which could be used by laypersons, and students in external study programmes, in their devotions and study, especially those who are also entrusted with pastoral and preaching responsibilities and who have no access to a theological library. It is hoped that these books will fill some of the gap that exists when laypersons seek guidance in the interpretation of the New Testament.

Finally, I hope that this series will make a contribution to theological literature that is available for the layperson, especially in various programmes developed for empowering laypersons through external studies, as a token of my own concern and work in this area of preparing persons for ministry in the church.

Outline of the series

I.   Volume I : General Introduction to the New Testament. Formation of the New Testament Canon. Study of the Gospels. The Synoptic Gospels.

II. Volume II : The Acts of the Apostles. A Study of Paul and the Pauline Letters.

III. Volume III : The Gospel of John. The Epistles of I, II, III John. The Book of Revelation.

IV. Volume IV : The Epistle to the Hebrews. The Epistles of James, I Peter, Jude and II Peter. Ecclesiology in the New Testament.

There are many outlines and introductions to the New Testament, each with their own perspectives and approaches, and while I am aware that the above is not the usual outline for studies in the New Testament, I have developed this approach over the years of teaching, and I hope to show in the course of the series, and below, that there is some logic in the grouping of books for the purpose of historical and theological continuity. A detailed discussion on the salient points will be given when dealing with each book, but for the sake of perspective and introduction, the following points are to be noted:

1.   Vol. I: A General Introduction is always necessary before coming to the text itself. This helps to place the text within a context, to understand the forces that impacted the text, and to understand

how and why writers responded to situations, and expressed themselves, in the way in which they did.

The Synoptic Gospels (Matthew, Mark, Luke) are studied first as they outline the story and presentation of the understanding of Jesus, the central figure of the New Testament, in a way that indicates that they have a common perspective (synoptic: συν ὀψσις = seeing together). Studies about Jesus therefore forms the base from which other New Testament writings can be understood.

2. Vol. II: The Acts of the Apostles purports to tell the story (history and theology) of the early movement which became the church – its formation, mission, the spread of the Gospel, issues faced etc…It takes the message of the good news a step further than the Gospels – from Jesus, Judaism and Palestine into the Gentile Hellenistic/Greco-Roman world. It also sets the stage to understand Paul and his writings which are an interpretation of Jesus and the implications of Jesus' message including instructions to regulate community/congregation life, to understand and develop approaches to everyday situations/ relationships in the light of the new faith in Jesus, to warn against false teachers, and to provide guidelines for church order – part of the development of Christianity in the Pauline and post-Pauline eras. So taking the two together (Acts and Paul) brings about a logical step from the beginnings of the community to the development of its theological expressions that emerged from various life situations and later became the scriptures and doctrines of the church.

3. Vol. III: The Gospel of John, though also a part of the story of Jesus, has a different perspective from that of the Synoptics and has to be approached in a different way in order to appreciate its message, and so treated after the Synoptics, Acts and Paul. Further, writings related to the Johannine school of thought/ Johannine community – I, II, III John and the Book of Revelation – are also taken up together so that they can be grouped as

originating from a common Johannine community/circle of thought.

4. Vol. IV: The remaining letters – Hebrews, James, I Peter, Jude, and II Peter – address situations towards the end of the first century-beginning of the second century (James, I & II Peter, I, II, III John and Jude are most often grouped together as the 'Catholic Epistles'). The various communities/congregations being addressed seem to be more settled in their thinking and life-style, and earlier concerns about conversion, Jew-Gentile relationships etc… are not touched upon, instead the concerns are for practical living, an apologetic for suffering and persecution, warnings against false teachings etc….. Each writing/letter has its own concerns and context, but this overall generalization helps to keep them together for the purpose of study. The last chapter in this Volume will deal with the development and concerns of ecclesiology – church organization and structure in the New Testament – a study which provides significant insights and directions for the church and church leaders today. Since this is the last volume in the series, a summary of the introductory material to each book is given as an Appendix.

It is important to note three points in the methodology followed:

1. the sections on analysis and commentary of the texts is to provide the reader with tools for interpretation; the analysis and commentary will not go into homiletics, i.e. the development of the text into a sermon. Each reader is in a different context and should use the background and tools of interpretation provided here for their own homiletic development and to suit their own contexts.

2. each writing/book is studied in and by itself. No attempt is made to present a unified/comprehensive/compendium of thought as though there is only one picture and one theological expression in the New Testament. This approach, used here, results in different formats being used to present the studies. It is hoped that these different formats/

numbering/arrangement etc… will only help the reader/student to appreciate the variety of the material in the New Testament that show that these writings cannot be squeezed into one mould.

3. in dealing with Paul and the Pauline letters, a different method is used in Vol. II: the letters are grouped into three categories (Paul, deutero-Pauline, trito-Pauline), and the compilations are taken in the order of chronological development (e.g. see the Corinthian Correspondence consisting of seven letters; Philippians; Pastorals). Similarly, the Gospel of John, the Epistles of I, II, III John, and the Book of Revelation are grouped in Vol. III. The remaining writings of Hebrews, James, I Peter, Jude, and II Peter are grouped in Vol. IV. These groupings and order of chronological development are based on my years of study, research and teaching in the New Testament and are somewhat different from the usual approaches.

In this way, it is hoped that the 4 Volume series is not just a compilation, but will also make a contribution to New Testament studies and research.

All biblical quotations are from the Revised Standard Version (1952) and are given in italics. Where a quotation is from the section under discussion, only the text is given in italics; other texts have references mentioned. The reader is advised to constantly refer to the biblical text. Several quotations are given in Greek (from The Greek New Testament, edited by K. Aland, M. Black *et al.*, Third Edition, United Bible Societies, 1975) for the more advanced student who can appreciate the Greek idioms/ phrases/vocabulary that have come to be associated with a particular writer/author both in theological understandings and in a meaningful expression and usage of the original language.

It is hoped that this overly simple explanation of the rationale for the series will suffice for the moment and that the readers will be in a better position to appreciate the outline at the end of the series.

Readership

The concern for theological writings for laypersons has been mentioned earlier in the Preface and must be stressed again. The series has been written to fill the need for a basic introduction to the books of the New Testament which would not require professional expertise/lectures. The readership kept in mind is the person in the pew who would like to know more about scripture and have guidelines for its interpretation. Therefore, the accepted norms of detailed references and footnotes, and an extensive bibliography have been avoided; also after years of lecturing on the subject one is not quite sure of what is one's own and what is borrowed! I hope I may be forgiven if sometimes in my 'borrowings', that have been so long appropriated, I have forgotten that they are borrowings! The series is not intended to take the place of a formal study of the New Testament undertaken in a theological college; those preparing for theological degrees need to be familiar with much more advanced material even if they find some of the basics in this series to be helpful and which open up the possibility for further study and research. The advanced student will be able to identify the sources on which this series has relied; my students will find a similarity to my class lectures. I hope that all who engage in Bible study may find in this series some material which will help to light up the New Testament and that this will serve the purpose of stressing how important it is for the New Testament – a vital part of our scripture and theological formulations – to be constantly studied and interpreted in order to build up the faith and to help in an informed and relevant proclamation of the gospel.

Richard E. A. Rodgers
Jabalpur, M. P., India

Kingdomtide
2020

Section I
The Epistle to the Hebrews

CHAPTER I

Introduction to the Epistle to the Hebrews

Authorship, Date, Addressees and purpose. Jewish background and interpretation of the person and work of Christ as the High Priest.

In the New Testament, Hebrews appears as one of the most carefully constructed writings and ably written in quality Greek. Yet Hebrews also presents a puzzle: there is little or no clue about its author, its locale, and its addressees. Almost all this information has to be extracted from an analysis of the text supplemented by early traditions in the Church. One scholar puts it thus: *Hebrews begins like a treatise, proceeds like a sermon, and closes like an epistle!* This would indicate the difficulty in placing Hebrews into one particular category. It may be best to start with considering Hebrews as the written text of a sermon, or the written text of a collection of sermons on various topics, supplemented/expanded by lengthy explanations/discussions/exhortations which may not have been possible in a sermon, and finally an epistolary ending being attached when it was circulated as a written document. Hebrews was traditionally associated with Paul and owes to that association its reception into the Pauline collection of writings as the 14th epistle and then into the New Testament canon. However, today, no scholar would accept that Hebrews originated with Paul and hence it is treated here separately from the Pauline epistles.

It is recognized that there is a literary relationship between Hebrews and the writings of various Alexandrian scholars/leaders including Clement of Alexandria (mid to end of 2nd century), however, nothing further can be drawn from the relationship. The inscription *to the Hebrews* (προς ᾽Εβραιους) is a later attestation and gives rise to the tradition that Hebrews was written to Jewish Christians. In the history of the New Testament canon, Hebrews was regarded as Pauline in the Eastern and Syrian churches and hence there was no question of its canonicity. In the Western churches, it was included among the Pauline letters and placed after Philemon (i.e. before the personal letters to Timothy and Titus); however, in one early canonical witness, Hebrews stands after Romans and before the Corinthian correspondence. In the Muratorian canon (reflecting the Western position at the end of 2nd century), Hebrews is missing; its place was only assured in the 4th century when it was mentioned in Athanasius' 39th Festal (Easter) letter (A.D. 367) which contained the list of writings accepted as canonical (see Vol. I of this series for the History of the Canon). In the period of the Reformation (16th century), Luther separated Hebrews from the Pauline letters and placed it with three other writings at the end of the canon, holding that these four books (Hebrews, James, Jude, and Revelation) did not meet his criteria of canonicity. In response, the Council of Trent in 1546 reaffirmed 27 books in the New Testament canon and included Hebrews among the Pauline letters.

Authorship

The early attestation of Hebrews among the Pauline letters, and the reaffirmation by the Council of Trent, tended to imply that Hebrews was written by Paul. However, during the period of the Enlightenment, biblical scholarship was freed from church constraints to explore critical studies and in the early 19th century it was shown that Hebrews could not have come from Paul. Since then, Protestant, Catholic, and Orthodox scholars have accepted that Paul could be acknowledged as the apostolic authority behind the writing even though, in its present form, Hebrews may not have originated from Paul but by someone in the Pauline school of thought writing at a later date after the lifetime of Paul. The position that Hebrews does not originate with Paul is taken on the following grounds:

A. The literary structure of the writing is not the same as the other letters of Paul, or the deutero or trito Pauline writings. As a rule, the Pauline epistles have a proper epistolary opening, a main section dealing with doctrine, questions and controversial issues, concluding with a hortatory section, followed by greetings and a blessing. This format is not found in Hebrews; the main section is constantly interrupted by longer and shorter exhortations; it conforms to a letter pattern only in four verses at the end.

B. The style, language/vocabulary/grammar, and mode of expression are quite different from that of the Pauline letters; only in the concluding section is there some affinity with the Pauline letters. Its literary style shows much dependence on Greek rhetorical writings, and is, in fact, one of the best Greek writings in the New Testament coming close to a classical style unlike the more 'common' (*koine* κοινη) style of Paul.

C. The theology of Hebrews is not Pauline. There are places where there is an echo of Paul, but whether it reflects a dependence on Pauline thought or just the general ideas prevalent in the church at that time is not certain. The dominant major idea of Hebrews – the high-priesthood of Christ after the order of Melchizedek – is completely lacking in the main Pauline epistles. The theological concepts of covenant, sacrifice, Sabbath rest as a synonym for salvation, the wandering people of God, etc… are also ideas that are developed in a completely different way in comparison, if they appear in Paul.

D. The historical setting of Hebrews seems to be closer to Alexandrian Judaism represented by Philo and his writings, which may also account for the writing being well known by Clement of Alexandria and other Alexandrian leaders – a style of interpretation that does not pay much attention to the context and exegesis of a text but simply makes a link to a text because of a common vocabulary, and prefers to interpret the text in an allegorical manner (a method applied a great deal in interpreting the parables), and characterized by typological exegesis (e.g.

Melchizedek as a type of high priest on which the high priesthood of Christ is modeled). In many ways, Hebrews may reflect the type of preaching and teaching that was carried on in Hellenistic synagogues.

It can therefore be said that though there are some affinities with Paul, by and large Hebrews diverges decisively from Paul and the Pauline writings to the extent that authorship by Paul can no longer be defended nor is it proposed in scholarship today. There is a reference to Timothy (13:23) which is the only tenuous link to the Pauline circle and from which no conclusion can be drawn. Further, the lack of an epistolary form indicates that it is more of an expanded discourse with an epistolary ending added to probably facilitate circulation and acceptance. Many have tried to associate Hebrews with the author of Luke-Acts, or James, the head of the Jerusalem community (see Acts 15) which represents a Jewish style of Christianity, or Clement of Rome, or Apollos (a scholar from Alexandria who was well versed in Greek rhetoric – Acts 18:24ff.; I Cor. 1:12), or Barnabas, a Levite from Cyprus (Acts 4:34, 9:27, 11:22), but none of these hypotheses have carried much weight. Like the description of Melchizedek (7:3), the author of Hebrews, must remain without father or mother or genealogy! However, from the sophisticated rhetoric and quality of Greek and knowledge of Hebrew scriptures (whenever there are quotations, the author quotes from the Septuagint, the ancient translation of Hebrew scriptures into Greek that was produced in Alexandria, Egypt), the author must have come from a Jewish Christian background with a good Hellenistic education which would have included knowledge of Hellenistic philosophical systems not normally used in Judaism; it would suggest that the author's theological outlook was similar to that of Hellenistic Christianity which had a much freer attitude toward the Jewish cultic observances/heritage. The only conclusion, therefore, to the authorship of Hebrews is that it is no longer possible to determine the identity of the author, so it must be acknowledged that **Hebrews stands among the anonymous writings of the New Testament**, or as Origen (he placed Hebrews among the "doubtful" writings, i.e. not fully accepted as canonical), as far back as the mid-3rd century put it: *God only knows who wrote Hebrews!*

Date and place of writing

Since Hebrews builds upon the Jewish priestly, sacrificial systems and cultic traditions, the question of whether the Jerusalem Temple was still standing is raised, but Hebrews provides no answer. A date before A.D. 70 is also ruled out as then there would have been reference to a close association with Paul. On the contrary, the references to persecution (10:32-34) and the traditional association with Luke-Acts, point to a date later than A.D. 70; also the author seems to be a second or third generation Christian (2:3: *...it was attested to us by those who heard the Lord...*). A date after the 70s would also account for the emphasis on the replacement of the Jewish feasts, sacrifices, priesthood and earthly place of worship due to the destruction of the Temple and the cultic system in A.D. 70. The link with Clement of Rome (about A.D. 94-96) would mean that the writing was in existence by the mid 90s and the reference to Timothy (13:23) would mean that he was still alive. **In all probability, therefore, the writing as a collection of sermons had its origin between A.D. 80 and 90.**

As to the place of writing, there have been many conjectures. Since it stands close to the Alexandrian style of interpretation of texts, Alexandria is often proposed as the place of writing. But just as strong are the arguments that since the writing uses Jewish liturgical imagery, it probably originated in Jerusalem. The affinity to the writings of Luke-Acts and Clement of Rome have led to the suggestion that Rome could be the place of origin (the greetings in 13:14 – *those who come from Italy greet you...* could mean that the letter was written from outside of Italy where there were several Italians sending greetings to Rome, or it could mean that the letter was written from within Italy – Rome – and greetings were being sent to those outside; in either case, the arguments are inconclusive). Hence, without a definite name for its authorship, **the place of writing/origin remains a matter of speculation.**

Addressees and Purpose

The purpose of the writing would be closely connected with the readership. The earliest understanding of Hebrews was that it was written to Jewish Christians and therefore relied heavily on interpretation of texts from the Hebrew scriptures, Jewish religious/sacrificial rites, and understandings of the priesthood. There is also the theological apologetic concerning the superiority of the new covenant over the old and therefore the superiority of Jesus over Moses; similarly, the arguments concerning the high priesthood of Jesus as being superior to the high priesthood of Aaron. These references pointed to the readers being sought among the Jews, and especially among Jewish Christians, to convince them of the superiority of the new faith over the old Judaism. However, none of this is clear from the text; it can only be derived by interpretation and therefore is open to a variety of interpretations.

Most scholars would feel that the writing was not addressed to the Jerusalem community: the Jerusalem community was poor and needed to be helped (see Vol. II of this series for the Pauline mission to raise funds for Jerusalem in Acts and I & II Corinthians), whereas the recipients of Hebrews had on several occasions helped others (6:10); the descriptions/ characteristics given in 2:3ff. and 13:7 do not fit the Jerusalem community; the persecution mentioned in 10:32ff. does not coincide with the periods of suffering in Jerusalem as known from Acts. Therefore the hypothesis that the readers, and the purpose of the writing, were Jewish Christians in Jerusalem is not a convincing argument. The question of whether the readers could have been Jewish Christians in another city is also not answered in the writing. The author calls the letter *my word of exhortation* (13:22) in order to encourage the readers to hold fast to their faith, not to give up their belief in the efficaciousness of Jesus' self-sacrifice, and to focus on heavenly things. **Probably the best answer while seeking the purpose of Hebrews is that the readers were Christians seeking to understand their faith, and the context of their faith, in terms of the background from which that faith emerged.**

With such general terms of reference, it is **not possible to identify the location of the readers**; the writing could have been addressed to any of the centres of Christianity in the early years – Antioch, Corinth, Ephesus, Colossae, Cyprus, Alexandria, and/or even Rome.

Jewish background and the interpretation of the person and work of Christ as the High Priest:

The major contribution of Hebrews is the Christology of the High Priest – a unique method of presenting the person and work of Christ using a Jewish background. The style of writing/expression stands close to Alexandrian Judaism, especially Philo, which interprets the Hebrew scriptures without reference to the historical context, but rather tries to get to deeper meanings using the allegorical method, i.e. for every character/item in the text, there is a corresponding reality which has to be exposed by interpretation – by introducing the author's own ideas (4:3), by interpretation of names (7:2), by relating as many texts as possible to a particular idea regardless of the context of those texts (1:5, 2:5ff., 10:5ff.), by allegorical exposition attributing a secret meaning to the text which is related to the present (11:13ff., 13:11ff.), by typological exegesis, i.e. setting a person/character/event from Hebrew scriptures over against those/that in the New Testament in which they find their corresponding fulfilment, e.g. Melchizedek as the type of true New Testament high priest (ch. 7), the earthly tabernacle being but a shadow of the heavenly tabernacle (8:2, 5). Hebrews refers in new ways to the opposition between shadow and reality, earthly and heavenly (9:23ff., 8:1ff.), between created and uncreated (9:11), between present and future (9:1ff., 13:14, 2:5), between transitory and enduring (7:3, 24, 10:34, 12:27, 13:14); it is as though the author wants to convince the readers that only the heavenly things constitute reality (6:4ff., 10:1, 11:1, 16, 12:22). This approach stands close to Philo's works, but more than that, it reflects a strong influence of the Hellenistic literature and teachings in Hellenistic synagogues. Among these interpretations of Jewish background proposed by Hebrews, is the idea of Christ as the ideal High Priest – the main Christology of Hebrews.

The high priesthood of Christ emphasized by Hebrews is somewhat of a contrast to the Gospels where Jesus is usually critical of the Temple procedures and treated with hostility by the Temple priesthood. Hebrews seems to attempt an understanding/interpretation to explain this contrast by attributing Christ's high priesthood to Melchizedek – a legendary figure – and not to the Aaronic (Levitical) priesthood followed in the Temple in Jesus' day.

The presentation of Christ as **the** High Priest is prefaced by the understanding of the superiority of Christ: He is the final revelation of God (1:1-4) written from a Jewish perspective where God has revealed Godself in many ways and through many messengers. Christ, the son, is the heir of all things (6:12, 17); the coming of the son in the "last days" indicates that for the author, the eschatological hopes have been fulfilled, i.e. the "last days" have been entered. Since the son, in his coming, has fully revealed God, there is no need for further revelation, thereby also signalling the "last days". In the death and exaltation of the historical Jesus, God's salvation has been accomplished and Jesus' unique relation to the Father as the son has been revealed. The son stands as superior to all other beings – angels (1:5 - 2:9); Moses (3:1 - 4:13) – the son also brings the fulfilment of "the rest" promised to the people of God, but which was not fulfilled under Moses (3:6 - 4:13) – here "the rest" is not entrance into the promised land, but foreshadows the eschatological rest that takes place at the end – a 'rest' that brings creation to completion (...*God rested on the seventh day from all God's work... which God had done in creation...* – Gen. 2:2-3) . All of these concepts – the superiority of the son, the final revelation of God through the son, the rest into which the people of God enter – are taken over from a background of Judaism and re-interpreted in the light of Jesus Christ as the son (detailed comments in the Analysis and Commentary, below). Further, all of this Jewish background leads into the presentation of the main argument, that of Christ as the High Priest.

In this central aspect of Hebrews' Christology, the author compares and contrasts Christ's work with that of the Levitical priesthood. Like the Levitical priests, Jesus is also human so he can sympathize with human weaknesses (4:14-16); like the Levitical priests are appointed by God to act on behalf of people, offering gifts and sacrifices for sins, so Christ is appointed by God and offers a sacrifice (5:1ff.), but the difference lies in the fact that the Levitical priest, as a sinful human being, has first to offer a sacrifice for himself and then for the people, whereas

Christ, though human, is yet without sin (4:15) and so does not need to offer a sacrifice for himself. Aaron and the line of Levitical priests were appointed by God, but Christ is self-appointed (5:5-6) because he is not as a servant in the master's house, but as the son and heir. The quotation from Ps. 2:7 – *you are My Son, today I have begotten you* – in the context of the discussion of Christ's priestly role shows that Jesus as the Messiah also exercises a priestly role. This is further affirmed by the quotation from Ps. 110:4 – *you are a priest forever after the order of Melchizedek* – which identifies Jesus as both Messiah and Priest, and therefore far superior to the Levitical priesthood (ch. 7).

Although Hebrews is the only writing in the New Testament to stress the priesthood of Christ, there was already a strain in Judaism that identified the Messiah as coming from a priestly line, especially in the texts from Qumran which expected the Messiah in the line of Aaron. Matthew's Gospel brings out the point of Jesus' priesthood in the gifts offered by the magi – the gift of frankincense (Mtt. 2:11) – which is used in the liturgy and which symbolizes the priesthood. Hebrews makes it clear that Jesus came from the tribe of Judah *from which no one has ever served at the altar* (7:12ff.), but nevertheless Jesus has become a High Priest, *not according to a legal requirement...but by the power of an indestructible life* (7:15-16), and that *when there is a change in the priesthood, there is necessarily a change in the law as well* (7:12); so although Jesus comes from the tribe of Judah, he can still be a priest. Also the Levitical priests hold office only during their lifetime (7:23ff.), but the priesthood of Christ is *permanent because He continues forever.* In this way, the author justifies the presentation of Christ as the High Priest and does away with any Jewish objections based on genealogy or tradition, or pertaining to the theology of Judaism.

A further explanation of the superiority of Christ's priesthood over the Aaronic priesthood is brought out through the understanding of the priestly and high priestly roles in the Jewish sacrificial system: *...every high priest is appointed to offer gifts and sacrifices* (8:3)....*they go continually into the outer tent performing their ritual duties...the high priest once year...taking blood which he offers for himself and the people...*

(8:6ff.); *every priest stands daily at his service, offering repeatedly the same sacrifices...*(10:11ff.). But Christ enters with his own blood, which he offered *once for all when He offered up Himself* (5:7-10; 7:23-28; 9:11ff.; 10:12ff.), and so Christ has obtained a more excellent ministry (8:6) and *is the mediator of a new covenant* (9:15ff.).

Thus through a method of interpretation common in the author's day (perhaps unacceptable and questionable today), the author seeks to establish the superiority of Melchizedek over Abraham and the Levitical priesthood which was descended from Abraham, and then the superiority of Christ as *the* High Priest after the order of Melchizedek. The rhetoric used would have been seen as impressive to a first century reader, but to later readers, the argument sounded, and still sounds, strange. But the basic point being made, and the distinctiveness of the message in Hebrews, is that Christ as *the* High Priest replaced the old system by which humans approached God and that the new approach through Christ is superior in every way.

In a time (last quarter of 1st century) when there was still confusion regarding the relationship with Judaism, and when a formal position on several doctrinal matters had not as yet been formed (the period of 'Early Catholicism' when theological and liturgical positions were still being worked out), the writing known as the Epistle to the Hebrews would have brought a definite direction – a re-interpretation of the Jewish origins of Christianity and its hope of God's salvific activity as the final goal – thereby justifying and substantiating the faith and the hope of early communities, *looking to Jesus the pioneer and perfecter of our faith* (12:2), a faith that is *the assurance of things hoped for, the conviction of things not seen* (11:1).

CHAPTER II

Analysis and Commentary on the Text

The earlier chapter on introductory issues indicates the difficulty of drawing up a systematic outline of the writing; however, several scholars have attempted outlines based on genre, literary structure (matching beginnings and endings; beginning of one section as connected to the end of the previous section etc...). The structure is complicated by the fact that the exposition begins without an epistolary opening followed by a hortatory section which does not come at the end as in most letters; it is only at the end that an epistolary ending appears. Although the author would have had an outline in mind, the arrangement cannot be readily discerned, as a result, there are several suggestions. Given below is an outline which is a combination of several suggestions made by scholars with sub-sections added under each main section:

I. 1:1-3 Introduction

II. 1:4 – 4:13 Superiority of Jesus as God's Son (Eschatology)

III. 4:14 – 7:28 Superiority of Jesus' priesthood (Ecclesiology)

IV. 8:1 – 10:39 Superiority of Jesus' sacrifice (Sacrifice)

V. 11:1 – 12:29 Faith and Endurance (Ecclesiological paraenesis)

VI. 13:1-19 Injunctions/Justice, Faith and Practice (Eschatology)

VII. 13:20-25 Conclusion, blessings, greetings.

Although the above seems a feasible working hypothesis, it would probably be better to study – analyse and comment – on the text chapter by chapter, or sometimes a block where the topic/theme continues, and in so doing, the text itself may suggest its own outline and train of thought; this will be the methodology followed in this study.

1:1-3: Introduction

In many and various ways (πολυμερως και πολυτροπως) *God spoke of old...but in these last days* (ἐπ᾽ ἐσχατου των ἥμερων τουτων) *God has spoken to us by a Son...* The writer immediately connects the present with the past, i.e. there is a continuity with the past that is being stressed with the present being seen as the 'last days'.

...a Son...whom God appointed the heir of all things, through whom also God created the world... Again the stress on connecting the past and the present: the Son as the agent of creation (past), and also as the heir (present and future).

...He reflects the glory of God and bears the very stamp of God's nature... an emphasis on pre-existence.

...when He had made purification (καθαρισμον – cleansing, purging) *for sins, He sat down at the right hand of the Majesty on high....* An affirmation of Christ's salvific work.

Comments

a. The writing begins without an epistolary opening formula of the identity of the writer and to whom the writing is addressed, nevertheless, the opening verses form an impressive prologue introducing topics that will be taken up in detail as the writing proceeds.

b. The writer seems to have been influenced by the thought of Hellenistic Judaism (Philo) of the divine wisdom (λογος - *logos*) being the creative principle. But like John's Gospel and Ephesians-Colossians, the divine creative principle of *logos* is equated with Jesus Christ. This emphasizes both Christ's pre-existence and Christ's role in creation.

c.   However, the introduction ends, not with cosmological speculation about the origin and end of creation, but with an interest in the purpose of creation as revealed in the accomplishment of salvation through the work of the Son. It could almost be said that creation has reached its completion only in the work of redemption; this comes close to the affirmation in Romans – *for creation waits with eager longing for the revealing of the children of God...creation itself will be set free...and obtain the glorious liberty of the children of God...the whole creation has been groaning in travail...until the redemption of our bodies* (Rom. 8:18-25).

d.   The finality of God's revelation is spoken of in two senses: 1. In an eschatological sense – the 'last days' have been entered/started. 2. In a philosophical sense – the Son has fully revealed the nature of God and reflects the glory of God; the Son bears the very stamp of God's divine nature. The title 'Son' itself suggests a unique relationship with God using a well known Hellenistic allegory with a play on the words 'son'/'sun' : just as the rays of the sun reflect the very essence of the sun without diminishing the source, so the 'Son' reflects the very essence of God.

e.   The reference to *purification for sins* and Christ's having *sat down at the right hand of the Majesty on high* are the essential and crucial points which will be further expanded in the writing. The writer sees these as the accomplishment of God's act of salvation in the death of the historical Jesus and the Son's exaltation to heaven.

1:4-14: Superiority of Jesus as God's Son

...having become as much superior to angels... The chapter deals with showing that the Son is superior to angels or heavenly beings. Seven quotations from Hebrew scriptures are given in support of the author's point: Ps. 2 (a psalm used during the enthronement of a King), and II Samuel 7:14; Deut. 12:43 (quotation from the Septuagint); Ps. 97:7; Ps. 104:4; Ps. 45:6-7; Ps. 102:25-27; Ps. 110:1. The rabbinic style used here is to give as many quotations as possible as an attempt to prove one's point, but not necessarily to pay attention to the context of the quotation.

Comments

a.   The writer elaborates Christ's superiority to all other beings, starting with angels. Passages from the Hebrew Scriptures are used to support the writer's arguments. The Hebrew Scriptures are being used/referred to as prophecies which look forward to, and find their fulfillment, in Christ. The style of interpretation of the Hebrew Scriptures shows influences of the Alexandrian style – rabbinic and allegorical styles of interpretation having little or no regard for the context just as long as a connection can be made by using a related word or idea.

b.   The quotations from the Hebrew Scriptures are used to stress that God had called Christ "Son" whereas no angel had ever been called by that name/title; in fact, the angels had been commanded to worship the Son. In the Jewish understanding, angels were next to God in the heavenly hierarchy, so to place the Son above angels is to put the Son almost on equality with God. The writer uses an enthronement psalm (Ps. 45 – used in the liturgy of enthronement of Israel's kings) to show Christ as the anointed, righteous ruler of God's kingdom. This makes Christ a Messiah-King and all enemies of righteousness will be put in subjection to him. In contrast, angels are not to be served, but are to serve those who are receiving salvation.

c.   The practical point of showing Christ's superiority to angels is made clear in the opening section of the next chapter.

2:1-4 : Exhortation

…we (ἡμᾶς) *must pay the closer attention to what* ***we*** *have heard…how shall* ***we*** *(*ἡμεῖς*) escape if* ***we*** *(*ἡμεῖς*) neglect…* The use of the first person plural pronoun, "we", shows that the author is included in the reference.

Comments

a.   As is frequent in Hebrews, and as the case here, a doctrinal/descriptive section leads into a section of exhortation. The author has shown Christ as superior to angels and here the point being made in the exhortation is that the salvation offered by Christ is superior to the message of the Law given through angels (the rabbinic understanding that the Law was given by God to Moses through angels as the messengers); therefore the exhortation is to pay close attention to the work of Christ which is superior to the message of angels. To pay attention to *what we have heard* is a reference to the Law and the Prophets; in Hebrews, both point to God's salvific work in Christ.

b. *What we have heard* is also a reference to the proclamation of the message of the Gospel. It would seem to place the writer not with the first generation eye witnesses, but among those who have heard from others – perhaps second or third generation.

c. Since salvation is given only through the work of the Son who is superior to all other heavenly beings, the writer asks how those who hear can escape judgement if they neglect to pay attention to so great a salvation. This salvation was first declared by Jesus, then by the eye witnesses (apostles), and then by others who heard from the apostles, among whom the author is included (by use of the first person personal pronoun, "we").

d. By insisting on *what we have heard* the author is firmly grounding his/her message in the teaching and preaching of the early church (*kerygma*); the author is remaining true to what has been received both in content and intent. The normality of the contents of the *kerygma* is a sign of Early Catholicism.

e. *If the message declared by angels was valid and every transgression or disobedience received a just retribution....* This would be a reference to the Law which demanded that justice meant punishment. But this is contrasted with the salvation that is offered – not punitive/ retributive justice – but forgiveness, and if this offer is neglected, then it would be impossible to escape punitive/retributive justice.

2 : 5-18 : The incarnation and salvation through suffering

...it was not to angels that God subjected the world to come, of which we are speaking.... The author insists that there is a person superior to angels and that angels are not the final inheritors of the world to come.

...what is the human being that Thou art mindful of them....putting everything in subjection under their feet... A quotation from Ps. 8:5-7 which talks of the majesty of God and yet God's relationship with human beings who are part of God's creation and whom God has exalted: *God left nothing outside of human control.*

...we do not yet see everything in subjection to humans... The practical situation that there is still suffering and evil in the world.

...we see Jesus, who for little while was made lower than the angels... The equation of Jesus with created human beings, giving the author the freedom, in rabbinic style, to assume that the Psalm is a reference to Jesus.

...He was crowned with glory and honour because of the suffering of death...He might taste death for all... The author emphasizes the exaltation of Christ only because of suffering and death which was on behalf of all human beings.

...God made the pioneer of human salvation perfect through suffering... Christ referred to as having been made perfect through suffering therefore justifying human suffering which will lead to perfection. Since Jesus and human beings pass through suffering, they become related to each other: *He is not ashamed to call them brethren (relatives).* Two quotations are used to substantiate the author's point – Ps. 22:22 and Is. 8:17-18.

...He Himself partook of the same nature....He was made like His fellow human beings in every respect.... The author brings out the complete identification of Jesus with created humanity – an understanding of the incarnation unique to Hebrews.

...a merciful and faithful high priest... The Christology of the High Priest, taken up in greater detail in later chapters, is here introduced. The introduction shows Jesus in complete solidarity, and identified, with humanity – *it is not with angels that He is concerned but with the descendants of Abraham...in order to make expiation for the sins of the people.*

...because He Himself has suffered and been tempted, He is able to help those who are tempted. The complete identification with humanity leads to Jesus' ability to empathise with human beings in their suffering and temptations.

Comments

In Heb. 2:5-18 there is a Christology combining both lowliness and exaltation. The author uses Ps. 8:5-7 which speaks of *human beings made a little lower than God, but crowned with glory and honour and given dominion over all the works of God's hands...* The Psalm is normally interpreted to refer to the creation of human beings, but here, the author of Hebrews, using a rabbinic style of interpretation, assumes that 'human being' refers to Christ – a new way of understanding/interpreting Ps. 8. *We see Jesus, who for a little while was made lower than angels...* the author uses the Psalm and the reference, in the singular, to a male, thus emphasizing that the Psalm is being interpreted to refer to Christ and not human beings in general.

To a community that is despondent because of hardship, the author emphasizes that God' plan for humanity is exaltation through suffering. Christ's suffering serves as an example and his suffering made him the pioneer of salvation; through his death he destroyed the power of death; his death was not on behalf of angels, but on behalf of humanity.

In claiming a relationship to humanity, the author emphasizes that Jesus too shared in this humanity – since therefore the children share in flesh and blood, *He Himself likewise partook of the same nature ...he had to be made like them in every respect.* This shared humanity will lead to Jesus being *a merciful and faithful high priest in the service of God...For because He Himself has suffered and been tempted, He is able to help those who are tempted.* Jesus becomes the model for human beings; the understanding of Jesus as high priest, which will become the major focus in later chapters, is here introduced. Seen from this perspective, Hebrews makes a great contribution to the understanding of the incarnation of Jesus.

3:1-19: Superiority of Christ over Moses

...Jesus, the apostle and high priest of our confession (᾿Ιησους, τον ἀποστολον και ἀρχιερεα της ὁμολογιας)*...* An example of the high Christology used in Hebrews.

*...He was faithful to Him who appointed Him, just as Moses who was also faithful in God's house. Yet Jesus has been counted worthy of as much more glory than Moses...Moses as a servant...but Christ as a Son...*The comparison with Moses which will bring out the superiority of Jesus over Moses.

...Today, when you hear His voice...they shall never enter my rest... A quotation from Ps. 95:7-11 pertaining to Israel's wilderness wanderings, their doubts and their testing of God/rebellion against God at Meribah and Massah provoking the wrath of God (Ex. 17:7; Num. 20:13, 27:14; Deut. 9:22, 32:51, 33:8; Ps. 81:7).

...those who left Egypt under the leadership of Moses...they were unable to enter because of unbelief. The comparison with Moses continues in that Moses' leadership did not bring the people into the promised 'rest' although it was the people's unbelief that prevented their entry; the 'rest' still remains to be entered into as a response to Christ's call.

Comments

Jesus is to be considered as *the apostle and high priest of our confession* – an example of the superlative titles used of Jesus. Probably the only place in the New Testament where Jesus is referred to as an 'apostle'. The Greek ἀποστολος has the meaning of one who is sent with the commission and authority of the sender (God), and is here coupled with the title of 'High Priest' which gives it an added meaning. On the Day of Atonement (see 'Religious Background' in Vol. I of this series), the High Priest entered the Holy of Holies as an apostle of the people and represented them before God. Later in Hebrews, the discussion of Christ as the High Priest will again raise the point, hence it can be considered here as an introduction to a later discussion.

The superiority of Christ over Moses is illustrated by the greater glory of the builder over the house building (3:1-6) and of the Son over the servant (3:5-6); Moses was only a foreshadow of what Christ was to say and do; since Moses was only a foreshadow, then the author's argument is that Christ is superior to Moses. The believer is part of the Son's house provided the believer holds fast to *confidence and hope.* This was probably written as an encouragement during a time of persecution.

There seems to be no connection between the discussion on the superiority of Christ over Moses and the quotation from Ps. 95:7-11 which deals with the exodus tradition of the disobedience of the Israelites. The only common factor is the name 'Moses' which is related to the exodus event and the discussion in chapter 3. The author is using a well-known rabbinic interpretation that held that the people did not enter the promised 'rest' under Moses, and that the 'rest' is something that is still awaited and will be fulfilled in the Messianic time. The 'rest', in rabbinic theology, is also the rest that God entered after God completed creation, but further rabbinic thinking was that creation could never be complete and God could never rest, and so this 'rest' remains to be completed by the Messiah – salvation/redemption is the completion of creation.

In the exhortation that follows, the believers are encouraged to remain faithful and not to fall into disobedience (3:12-19) like *those who left Egypt under the leadership of Moses, and with whom God was provoked forty years.* This disobedience is counted as 'sin', *and they were unable to enter because of unbelief.* The 'rest' still remains and the people are encouraged to respond to Christ's call, *today, when you hear His voice, do not harden your hearts as in the rebellion…*(3:15). The word 'today' is used in an eschatological sense – i.e. today is actually foreshadowing the day into which Christ has called the true household into existence, and does not refer to the time of the exodus. The readers are exhorted to respond to Christ's call and remain faithful members of the household of God (the Church).

4:1-13 : A 'rest' for the people of God

...while the promise of entering His rest remains, let us fear lest any of you be judged to have failed to reach it... At the end of chp. 3, the author showed that the 'rest' for the people of God remains. Chp. 4 begins with the exhortation to enter into that rest.

...As I swore in my wrath...never enter my rest... The quotation from Ps. 95:11 to show that 'the rest' still remains.

...God's works were finished...God rested on the seventh day...they shall never enter my rest... The interpretation from rabbinic sources that God rested after creation; yet divine, creative activity continued even during 'the rest' as creation/creativeness belongs to the very nature of God.

...today, when you hear His voice, do not harden your hearts... The quotation from Ps. 95:7-8, where 'today' is used in an eschatological manner, i.e. foreshadowing the day in which Christ brought about salvation and foreshadowing the day on which the believers heard about this salvation. This is an exhortation to respond positively to the salvific activity of God in Christ.

...whoever enters God's rest also ceases from labours as God did... A reference to God's act of salvation. Creation is complete, and God can rest only when God's creation enters a relationship of salvation.

...the word of God is living and active, sharper than any two-edged sword... (ζων γαρ ὅ λογος του Θεου και ἐνεργης και τομωτεπος ὕπερ πασαν ῥαχαιραν διστομον...). A very famous passage from Hebrews describing the nature of the word of God which is able to divide what is normally thought of as indivisible: *soul and spirit...joints and marrow...thoughts and intentions of the heart.* Such a sharp division leaves the believer completely open and vulnerable to the judgement of God.

Comments

The 'rest' promised to the Israelites was entrance into the Promised Land with peace and prosperity, but because of disobedience, none of those in the generation that came out of Egypt entered the Promised Land; they wandered for forty years until the generation had passed out of existence. Therefore, 'the rest' still remains. However, here the author sees 'the rest' as foreshadowing a better promise, i.e. entering a heavenly rest or salvation. The 'rest' of the wilderness wanderings is being used as an allegory for salvation.

The interpretation/exegesis of 'my rest' is taken from Jewish rabbinic sources based on Genesis 1:1ff. that when God had finished the creation, God rested. However, in Jewish theology, it was impossible that God had rested, i.e. ceased divine activity. Philo held that 'rest' was a symbol of God's continuing effortless divine activity of creation; some rabbinic interpretations hold that God's 'rest' refers to the completion of creation which ends in judgment and salvation; all of these interpretations were related to the Sabbath which commemorated creation (cf. John 5:10ff. where there is a Sabbath controversy which ends with *My Father is working still, and I am working…and the Jews sought all the more to kill Him…* Jesus' work on the Sabbath had put Him on equality with God whose divine activity of creation (birth), judgment (death) and salvation did not cease on the Sabbath which was otherwise a day of rest for God and creation). Therefore, *there remains a Sabbath rest for the people of God.*

Entering into the Sabbath rest is the true rest, and so at the beginning of chapter 4, the writer turns to exhortations centered on 'the rest' which remains from the exodus and which was also mentioned at the time of creation. The disobedient Israelites failed to achieve the goal of entering 'the rest' and so it remains for those who remain faithful. Christ has already entered this rest having been perfected through suffering. It is this rest that the people of God are exhorted: *strive to enter that rest, that no one fall by the same sort of disobedience.* To fall short of that 'rest' is to come under the judgment of *the word God which is living and active, sharper than any two-edged sword, piercing to the division of soul and spirit, of joints and marrow, and discerning the thoughts and intentions of the heart.*

4:14 – 5:10 : Introduction to the theme of Jesus as High Priest

...we have a great high priest...Jesus the Son of God...(ἐχοντες οὐν ἀρχιερεα μεγαν...Ἰησουν τον υἱον του Θεου...). The opening verse of the section states the theme that will be stressed in the next few chapters – the theme of Christ as ***the*** High Priest which is the main contribution of Hebrews to the Christology of the New Testament.

...we have not a high priest who is unable to sympathize with our weaknesses, but who in every respect has been tempted as we are, yet without sinning... The understanding of a high priest who is human, yet able to rise to the level of the divine.

...let us then with confidence draw near... An exhortation after a faith affirmation.

...every high priest chosen...offer gifts and sacrifices for sins... An outline of the duties of the high priest with special mention that the high priest does not place himself in that role, but is chosen to act on behalf of people/represent people before God. In Jewish tradition, there was a strict genealogical line and other qualifications that had to be met in order to qualify a person to be chosen as high priest.

...he can deal gently with the ignorant and wayward...he is called of God, just as Aaron was... The pastoral task of the high priest is outlined but because he is a human being, he *is bound to offer sacrifices for his own sins as well as for those of the people.*

...Christ did not exalt Himself to be made a high priest but was appointed by God who said to Him...Thou art My Son...Thou art a priest forever... There is a stress on the ***appointment*** of Christ and a quotation from an Enthronement Psalm to show that Christ is God's Son (Ps. 2:7) and another quotation regarding Christ's priesthood after the order of Melchizedek (Ps. 110:4).

...in the days of His flesh, Jesus offered up prayers and supplications, with loud cries and tears...He learned obedience though what He suffered... He became the source of eternal salvation... An emphasis laid on the incarnation and the identification with humanity – suffering as the means by which he accomplished the work of salvation.

Comments

a. This section introduces the Christology of the High Priest which will be dealt with in later chapters and in greater detail.

A. Jesus is referred to as **the great High Priest**. The image of the High Priest is taken from Judaism where the High Priest presided over the Jewish court – the Sanhedrin – and all other administrative matters; among the religious duties, the most important function was to enter the Holy of Holies once a year, on the Day of Atonement, taking the blood of the sacrificed lamb which was applied to the four corners of the altar on behalf of the people for the forgiveness of sins (for further details on High Priest, Day of Atonement etc…, see Background Studies in Vol. I of this series).

However, the contrast here is that Jesus did not enter the Holy of Holies, but ascended into heaven and entered the presence of God. Yet this *great high priest* also identifies with other high priests:

B. *Identification with humanity*: Here there is an introduction to the humanity of Jesus – one who can sympathize with humanity because he was fully human, having weaknesses and being tempted. The difference in Jesus' humanity was that he remained without sin. This would be of particular encouragement to the original readers who were going through a difficult period.

C. *Identification with the high priest*: Here Jesus is compared to the high priest after the order of Aaron: the similarity being that just as the Aaronic (Levitical) high priest having fulfilled certain qualifications was appointed by God so Jesus too was appointed by God. But here the similarity ends: Jesus is the Son and appointed under the order of Melchizedek, a superior order to that of Aaron.

D. *Identification with the pastoral task*: Like the Levitical priests and high priest, the pastoral task is to deal gently with the people and to offer gifts and sacrifices on their behalf. As human beings, the Levitical priests and high priest have to first offer sacrifices for their own sins and then for the sins of others. However, while Christ can deal gently with people so identifying with the pastoral task, he is without sin and so does not have to offer sacrifices for himself.

b.   In identifying Jesus with humanity, there is also the stress on Jesus, though the son, learning obedience through suffering – by this reference the author shows familiarity with the passion narratives – the agony of Gethsemane and the suffering of the cross which accomplishes salvation – and thus Jesus becomes the source of eternal salvation.

5:11 – 6:20 : An exhortation

...we have much to say...you have become dull of hearing (νωθροι γεγονατε ταις ἀκοαις - slow of understanding or sluggish)...*by this time you ought to be teachers, but you need someone to teach you... you need milk...for you are a child...but go on to solid food which is for the mature...to distinguish good from evil...leave aside the elementary doctrines...* The section on exhortation begins with a reprimand of the readers who seem not to have matured in their faith but who are constantly going over elementary teachings again and again.

...impossible to restore again to repentance those who have once been enlightened... The issue seems to be how to deal with apostasy – deliberately repeating what has been repented of.

...land which has drunk the rain...brings forth vegetation useful to those for whose sake it is cultivated, and receives a blessing from God...but if it bears thorns and thistles, it is worthless....its end is to be burned... The reprimand is very severely expressed through the agricultural allegory of cultivated land.

...we feel sure of better things...for God is not so unjust to overlook your work...and the love which you showed... After the reprimand, the author gives the readers encouragement and a basis for future hope.

...when God made a promise to Abraham...God swore by Godself... Since there is nothing greater than God, God swore by Godself – *through two unchangeable things, in which it impossible that God should prove false:* God's promise and God's oath. The stress is on the absolute assurance of God's promise.

...we have this as a sure and steadfast anchor of the soul...enters into the inner shrine behind the curtain...Jesus has gone as a forerunner on our behalf...after the order of Melchizedek... The affirmation that the intercession of Jesus, as high priest officiating at the altar, is effective and a source of surety and assurance.

Comments

There is again an exhortation in this section – reprimanding the readers who still act as babies feeding on milk when they should be like adults eating solid food. The author mentions six elementary doctrines/teachings (a *foundation of repentance from dead works, faith toward God, instructions about ablutions, laying on of hands, resurrection of the dead, eternal judgement*) which should not be constantly repeated but the believer is expected to go on to maturity. Apostasy was the concern that needed maturity in thinking and practice (6:4-8) – *impossible to restore again to repentance those who have once been enlightened,* i.e. deliberately repeating those things of which the believer has repented (cf. the unforgivable sin against the Holy Spirit – Mtt. 12:31 and parallels – see Vol. I of this series). The reprimand becomes more severe in the section from verses 4 to 8 ending with the warning that compares them to cultivated land but if they *bear thorns and thistles, they are worthless and near to being cursed; its end is to be burned* (6:7-8).

God's unchanging nature and the assurance of God's promises being fulfilled would have been a source of comfort for the readers who were going through difficult times and who needed the reassurance of God's presence and protection.

However, after the severe reprimand with the warning that they could be burned for being useless, the author hopes that the readers' good works will not be overlooked by God (6:9-12), because God is faithful to God's promises which is the guarantee of the effectiveness of Christ's intercession before the heavenly court, as the high priest (6:13-20).

One of the functions of the high priest is stressed – the function of interceding for God's people. The imagery is taken from Judaism and especially the liturgy of the Day of Atonement where the high priest enters behind the curtain of the Temple with the blood of the sacrifice on behalf of himself and the people. Through Jesus who enters behind the curtain, and who intercedes for people, the separation from God has been removed and there is now direct access to God.

7:1-28 : A High Priest after the order of Melchizedek

...Melchizedek, King of Salem...i.e. King of Righteousness and King of Peace... The translation of the name, Melchizedek, associates him with heavenly/divine qualities, and not with a geographical location. *Salem* is derived from *shalom* – the Hebrew word for peace and well-being.

...he is without father or mother or genealogy...he continues a priest forever... The attempt to show the divine origins of Melchizedek and the reason for his continuation as priest. This places Melchizedek above the Levitical (Aaronic) priesthood.

...this man...received tithes from Abraham and blessed him who had the promises...the inferior is blessed by the superior... The author shows the superiority of Melchizedek over Abraham when Abraham was returning from battle (Gen. 14), and Abraham gave Melchizedek *a tithe/tenth of the spoils.*

...if perfection had been attainable through the Levitical priesthood...what further need would there have been for another priest to arise after the order of Melchizedek...where there is a change in the priesthood, there is necessarily a change in the law as well... The author justifies the priesthood of Jesus after a superior order since the Aaronic (Levitical) priesthood did not achieve the desired purpose. The law demanded that the priests should be from the tribe of Levi

(*...a legal requirement concerning bodily descent...*), but Jesus was from the tribe of Judah (David's line, *...in connection with that tribe Moses said nothing about priests*), so a change in the line of priests necessitated a change in the law – a change for the better as it is raised to a superior order.

...Thou art a priest forever after the order of Melchizedek... Psalm110:4 is quoted several times here (verses 11, 15, 17, 21) and in earlier chapters (5:6, 10; 6:20) to stress the superiority of Jesus' priesthood – a permanent priesthood.

...he is able for all time to save those who draw near to God...He always lives to make intercession for them... The task of the permanent priesthood is outlined.

...it was fitting that we should have such a high priest...a Son who has been made perfect forever. The superiority of Jesus' high priesthood is shown through the example of the priests making repeated sacrificial offerings, whereas Jesus offers himself as the sacrifice and only once – a once and for all perfect offering.

Comments

The whole of chapter 7 of Hebrews is given over to developing the superiority of the priesthood after the order of Melchizedek possessed by Jesus over the Levitical priesthood. The cultic issues of chapters 7-10 could be taken together but it would be better to study the chapters separately.

There were groups within Judaism that expected a priestly Messiah, especially the Essenes at Qumran as known from the Dead Sea Scrolls. However, that expectation was linked to the Levitical priesthood (i.e. line from Aaron), whereas Hebrews, by quoting various Psalms, links Jesus' priesthood to the Davidic line, but since that is not the line for priests, the author of Hebrews goes further back and links Jesus' priesthood to the mysterious Melchizedek, a heavenly figure mentioned in two passages in the Hebrew scriptures – Genesis 14:18-20 and Psalm 110:4ff..

There are several points which speak of the superiority of Melchizedek: he has neither beginning nor end; since Abraham paid him a tithe, and he blessed Abraham, therefore he is superior to Abraham; by implication, Levi (the ancestor of the priestly tribe) who was not yet born, but a later descendant of Abraham (...*Levi was still in the loins of Abraham...*), paid tithes to Melchizedek, whereas Levites (priests) now receive tithes from the people; perfection was not achieved under the law (Aaronic/Levitical priesthood), therefore a new order had to arise which was not under the law – the order of Melchizedek – which set aside the old order and brought about change in the law, this was confirmed by God's oath; the Levitical priesthood was marked by many priests each taking their turn in office and replaced after death, but Jesus holds the priesthood permanently because he continues forever.

The qualities of Jesus are listed which make him a better high priest: *holy, blameless, unstained, separated from sinners, exalted above the heavens. He has no need to daily offer sacrifices on His own behalf and then on behalf of the people; he did this once and for all when He offered up Himself... The law appoints men in their weakness as high priests, but the word of the oath... appoints a Son who has been made perfect forever.*

The implication of this is that *this makes Jesus the surety of a better covenant.* The old covenant involved the law and an ever-changing priesthood in which one priest succeeded another, but Jesus continues forever. Thus he is a constant intercessor on behalf of the people.

8:1-13 : The superiority of Jesus as high priest - I

...a minister in the sanctuary and the true tent which is set up not by humans but by the Lord... The idea that Jesus is a high priest leads to an understanding of a heavenly tent/tabernacle. The reference is to the tent/Tabernacle that was erected by the people of Israel and which they moved with them during the exodus and wilderness wanderings.

...when Moses was about to erect the tent, he was instructed by God... Moses built the earthly tent/tabernacle based on the model God showed him of the heavenly tabernacle (Ex. 25, 9, 40; 26:30).

...Christ has obtained a ministry which is much more excellent than the old...if the first covenant had been faultless, there would have been no occasion for a second. The affirmation that Christ's ministry is far superior to that of the Aaronic/Levitical priesthood as his sacrifice is unique – he offered himself – and since the 'old' has proved insufficient, there is need for a 'second'/new covenant.

...the days will come...when I will establish a new covenant... Verses 8-13 are a quotation from Jeremiah 31:31-34 showing the necessity and character of the new covenant; whereas the old covenant admitted only the children of Israel, the new covenant includes all humanity – all the children of Adam *from the least to the greatest.*

...in speaking of a new covenant God treats the first as obsolete... what is obsolete and growing old is ready to vanish away. The affirmation is that the first covenant has failed to achieve its purpose and is being replaced.

Comments

The author has established the superiority of the order of Melchizedek and so Melchizedek passes out of the argument; instead, a new and superior high priest leads to the idea of a new tabernacle and a new covenant. The author goes back to the tabernacle erected by Moses and the people of Israel and which moved with them throughout their wilderness wanderings; it was based on the heavenly model. This may be based on the Platonic scheme in which the heavenly tabernacle set up by God is true and the earthly tabernacle is a copy or shadow; the author uses the words "copy" and "shadow" (8:5; 9:23, 24; 10:1) in contrast to "true" and "perfect" and "real" (8:2; 9:11, 14; 10:1).

The Aaronic/Levitical priesthood serves in the copy or shadow; Christ serves in the heavenly tabernacle and so his ministry is superior. It is interesting that throughout the discussion on the tent/tabernacle the author refers to the tent/tabernacle set up in the wilderness and not the Temple in Jerusalem planned by David and built by Solomon. Possibly the author felt that the Jerusalem temple was too geographically localized whereas the message had now gone far beyond Jerusalem and so a movable, non-localized reference seems more appropriate. It might also be that the localized Temple in Jerusalem had been destroyed (A.D. 70) by the time Hebrews was written.

Further, Christ ushers in a new covenant superior to the old covenant. The quotation from Jeremiah 31:31-34 is used to illustrate that the new covenant that was promised by God is now mediated through Christ. This is the point of the discussion regarding the tent/tabernacle – that the true high priest, Jesus, serves at the heavenly sanctuary and has mediated a new covenant. The old covenant which has become obsolete was based on obedience to the law; the new covenant is wider in scope, based on God's grace, and will bring about a forgiveness of sins – *I will be merciful toward their iniquities, and I will remember their sins no more* (8:12) – restoring and bringing about a new relationship between God and humans.

9:1-28 : The superiority of Jesus as high priest – II

...the first covenant had regulations for worship and an earthly tent.... the Holy Place ... the Holy of Holies ... cherubim of glory overshadowing the mercy seat (ἱλαστηριον) *... A short description of the worship setting in the Tabernacle during the wilderness wanderings, and then of the Solomonic Temple in Jerusalem.*

...the priests go continually into the outer tent, performing their ritual duties...into the second, only the High Priest goes...once a year, and not without taking blood which he offers for himself and for the errors of the people... A description of the rituals carried out by the priests, and the ritual of the Day of Atonement performed by the High Priest.

...the Holy Spirit indicates that the way into the sanctuary is not yet opened...gifts and sacrifices are offered which cannot perfect the conscience

of the worshipper... This shows the ineffectiveness of the old covenant and the pattern of worship.

...when Christ appeared...a more perfect tent not made with hands... He entered once and for all...taking not the blood of goats and calves but His own blood thus securing an eternal redemption...how much more shall the blood of Christ purify your conscience from dead works... This brings out the superiority of Christ's ministry as the High Priest.

...a death has occurred which redeems them from transgressions under the first covenant...without the shedding of blood there is no forgiveness of sins... The first covenant – Law – required a sacrifice, i.e. a death had to occur. Here that requirement is fulfilled in the death of Christ.

...necessary for the copies of the heavenly things to be purified...but the heavenly things themselves with better sacrifices...Christ has entered, not into a sanctuary made with hands, a copy of the true one, but into heaven itself... The use of Platonic thought that the earthly is a copy (shadow) of the heavenly.

...nor was it to offer Himself repeatedly...but He appeared once for all... A reference to the death of Christ, indicating that His death was a superior sacrifice.

...Christ ...will appear a second time...to save those who are eagerly waiting for Him... An affirmation of future hope which is brought about by the work of Christ as the High Priest.

Comments

There is a description of the earthly sanctuary (Tent, Temple), the daily priestly rituals, and the annual High Priestly ritual on the Day of Atonement when the High Priest entered the Holy of Holies with the blood of a bull which he offered for forgiveness of his own sins, and then he applied the blood of a goat to the four corners of the altar, asking for forgiveness for the people; this is described in Greek as the ἱλαστηριον (*hilastarion*) – the place of expiation. forgiveness, *the mercy seat.* This annual Day of Atonement ritual was a high-point in Jewish worship (Lev. 16). The description is taken from Ex. 15ff.; 25:9, 40; 26:30 which are references to God showing Moses the heavenly model on which the earthly tabernacle was built, a later priestly writing but which is placed back to Moses as descriptive of the requirements for worship under the Law.

The author is not interested in describing the whole worship setting and rituals (9:5), but only with the two tents (spaces) for worship. The first, or outer tent, the Holy Place, was accessible by all priests, not the people, to perform the daily sacrifices and rituals, and since these had to be repeated, the author's comment was that these did not really purify the people; the second, or inner tent, the Holy of Holies (Most Holy Place), was entered into only by the High Priest once a year on the Day of Atonement; again this was a ritual that had to be repeated annually signifying that it was not effective for all time. The point that the author was making was that the sacrifices required under the Law could only serve as ritual purification and not purification of the conscience (9:10). The 'outer tent' is a symbol of the present age and as long as it stands, then entering into the 'inner tent' by the High Priest does not really allow for entry into the presence of God.

Christ has entered the 'inner', heavenly sanctuary *not made with hands* and stands in the presence of God ushering in the "new age" (9:11ff.), taking his own blood as the sacrificial offering, once and for all. The superiority of this sacrifice is that: 1. it purifies the conscience from dead works (Law?); and 2. it was a single non-repeatable sacrifice. It marked the end of the old age and the beginning of the new age in which sin was forgiven by Christ's sacrifice.

The allegory of how a person comes into inheritance through the validity of a will is given to show that the will can only be implemented on the death of the person who made it (9:16). In a similar fashion, when Moses delivered the Law, the blood of calves and goats was sprinkled on the book of the Law signified that the Law had been ratified – *the blood of the covenant* (9:20). Similarly, Christ's death and blood signify the ratification of the "new covenant" (see Vol. I for the interpretation in the Gospels of the Eucharistic cup being the blood of the new covenant – Mtt. 26:26-29; Mk. 14:22-25).

Through this comparison with the earthly Tent (Tabernacle, Temple) and *the sanctuary not made with hands*, the author shows Christ's sacrificial death and ministry as High Priest as being superior to the Levitical priesthood and the requirements under the Mosaic Law. Possibly the Platonic concept in which the heavenly is true and the earthly is a copy or shadow has influenced the author therefore the heavenly is superior to the earthly.

The eschatological hope of the culmination of Christ's ministry is not lost sight of: Christ, *having been offered once to bear the sins of many* (9:28), *now appears in the presence of God on our behalf* (9:24), *... will appear a second time, not to deal with sin but to save those who are eagerly waiting for Him.* Thus chapters 8-9 and the first half of chapter 10 deal with the superiority of the High Priesthood of Christ over the Levitical priesthood and earthly High Priest.

10:1-18 : The superiority of Jesus as high priest – III

...the law has but a shadow of the good things to come... it can never make perfect...it is impossible that the blood of bulls and goats should take away sins... The author brings out the inefficacy of the Law indicating that a superior system has to be put in place.

...consequently when Christ came into the world... The superiority of Christ's sacrifice is brought out through a quotation of Psalm 40:5-9 using a rabbinic style of interpretation especially brought out in 10:8-10.

...for by a single offering...there is no longer any need for offering for sin... The perfection of Christ's sacrifice is brought out by quotations from Jeremiah 31:33-34 and Isaiah 26:11.

Comments

The author insists that the repeated daily offerings and sacrifices performed by priests *can never take away sins* (10:11). The superiority of Jesus' sacrifice, made with his own blood, is re-iterated – *Christ had offered for all time a single sacrifice for sins* (10:12). Having accomplished this, the eschatological hope that *His enemies should be made a stool for His feet...* is repeated. Jesus' sacrifice has *perfected for all time those who are sanctified* (10:14) therefore there is no further need of sacrifices. This shows the superiority of Jesus' sacrifice over the daily rituals.

The author emphasizes that God prefers obedience to multiple sacrifices – *sacrifice and offerings Thou hast not desired...;* the obedience of Jesus (10:5-9) is emphasized in the quotation from Ps. 40:7-9, ending with *behold I have come to do Thy will, O God...* In the obedience of Jesus *He abolishes the first covenant in order to establish the second* (10:9); this also contributes to his superiority over the Levitical priesthood and the earthly High Priest.

10:19-39 : Exhortation to avail of Jesus' high priestly service

...therefore, since we have confidence to enter the sanctuary by the blood of Jesus... let us draw near with a true heart in full assurance of faith... let us hold fast to the confession of our hope...stir up one another to love and good works... The exhortation to avail of the benefits of Jesus' priestly and high priestly service with the implication that the community has to be built up.

...the Day drawing near... The exhortation to perform as the end-time is near; an exhortation that includes eschatological hopes.

...if we sin deliberately after receiving the knowledge of the truth...there no longer remains a sacrifice for sins, but a fearful prospect of judgement.... The warning that there is no second chance for forgiveness where sin is a deliberate/conscious action.

...a person who has violated the law of Moses dies without mercy at the testimony of two or three witnesses...how much worse punishment... deserved by the one who spurns the Son of God... A reference to the Mosaic Law (old covenant) under which two witnesses were sufficient for conviction of the death penalty (see Deut. 17:6-7), and a warning that far worse punishment will be accorded to those who reject Jesus (new covenant).

...recall the former days... The author makes an appeal to history and how the readers showed compassion and accepted persecution. The exhortation to remain faithful and endure suffering, with reference to Habakkuk 2:3-4, ending with the author's affirmation of trust and assurance in the readers.

Comments

This section continues the pattern of making an exhortation after a doctrinal/theological discussion. Here the exhortation is for individuals to avail of the benefits of Jesus' services, with the exhortation that in doing so, the whole community should be included (10:19-25) meeting together *to build/encourage one another to love and good works.* Added to this is the eschatological hope of the *Day drawing near.*

The exhortation recalls the background of the readers and how they endured suffering and persecution when they were first converted. But if they deliberately fall back, their punishment would be severe as *there no longer remains a sacrifice for sins.* It would seem that apostasy was a major problem probably because suffering and persecution for the faith were not attractive options. This is probably a reflection of the "unforgivable sin" mentioned elsewhere (6:4-6; 10:26. See also Mk. 3:28-30 where the "unforgivable sin" is to attribute Jesus' works to an unclean spirit rather than to the Holy Spirit). The exhortation ends with a stern warning that *it is a fearful thing to fall into the hands of the living God* (10:31).

Verses 32-39 indicate that a situation of persecution either exists or is shortly expected, hence the exhortation to remain faithful and the expression of the author's assurance that the readers would remain faithful and persevere: *we are not of those who shrink back and are destroyed, but of those who have faith and keep their souls* (10:39).

11:1-40 : The roll call of the examples of faith

...faith is the substance of things hoped for, the conviction of things not seen (ἐστιν δε πιστις ἐλπιζομένων ὑποστασις, πραγματων ἐλεγχος οὐ βλεπομενων...)... A definition of faith using a Platonic

approach that there is a perfect, true world that exists of which the present world is only a shadow therefore faith is that which is hoped for and a conviction that things not seen nevertheless exist.

...the world was created by the word of God...made out of things which do not appear... The Platonic understanding that the true world has come into existence by the mind (νους, *nous*), or by reason (λογος, *logos*). However this is also a reference to the Genesis 1 creation story in which the world was created out of nothing (*creatio ex nihilo*) – *the earth was without form and void...* An example of something visible being created from that which is not visible.

*...Abel...Enoch...Noah...Abraham...Sarah...Isaac...*the examples of faith – a trusting response to God's word – from the Hebrew scriptures and Jewish history.

...Moses...Gideon, Barak, Samson, Jephthah, David, Samuel, and the prophets...women... the examples of faith as a patient endurance.

Comments

Chapter 11 is one of the best known passages in Hebrews – the roll call of examples of faith from the Hebrew Scriptures. The author starts with a famous definition of faith – the only explicit definition in the New Testament – *the substance of things hoped for, the conviction of things not seen.* The author relates this criteria/ definition to the creation of the world – it was created by things that do not appear/exist – *creatio ex nihilio*, out of nothing. The concept reflects Hellenistic thought, especially that of Plato that the material world is a shadowy mage of the heavenly which cannot be seen but which exists – *by faith Abraham looked forward to the city which has foundations, whose builder and maker is God* (11:10). Later apocalyptic thought of the heavenly Jerusalem is added to the picture of the world of reality (12:22). Earlier the author had spoken of the heavenly sanctuary, the true tent, the Holy of Holies etc... so all the heroes of faith move towards this heavenly reality *not having received what was promised, but having seen it and greeted it from afar, acknowledging that they were strangers and exiles on the earth…they deserve a better country, a heavenly one… God has prepared for them a city* (11:13-16). The author affirms that through faith – *the conviction of things not seen* – that the readers understand the existence of such a world, a transcendent order beyond this material world of time and space.

In calling the roll of heroes of the faith, the author stresses another aspect of faith, perhaps more popular a definition than the philosophical one described above – faith as a trusting response to the word of God and the promises contained therein, so a list is given – Abel, Enoch, Noah, Abraham, Sarah, Isaac. A whole section (11:13-17) is given over to the story of Moses and how every event in his story was an act of faith. An interesting inclusion in the list of heroes is the reference to Rahab the prostitute (Josh. 2:1-21, 6:22-25) who is presented as one who had an insight into God's plans for Israel and as an instrument of God – her faith saved her and her family when Jericho fell (interesting that a socially despised woman is acknowledged as playing a part in God's plan and mentioned as a hero of faith!). The author interprets these heroes as seeking more than a partial fulfillment of the promises: it was really the city of God to which they were all heading though at times they did not know the way. Here 'faith' comes close to being interpreted as 'hope' – faith/hope for entrance into the city of God.

In 11:23-38 faith has yet another meaning: that of patient endurance. In the list of names which covers a major portion of Israel's history, the men and women involved risked their lives, suffered, and died a martyr's death in obedience to God's word and as an assurance that in patience they were awaiting the fulfillment of the promises which God revealed and fulfilled in Christ (11:39-40). At the end of the list of heroes of faith, the author contrasts the old and the new: that the old did not receive what had been promised, *for God had foreseen something better for us, that apart from us they should not be made perfect* (11:39-40). Therefore the author sees the heroes of Israel's history and the readers as being in continuity: all moving towards and awaiting in faith the fulfillment of God's promises in

Christ – *the substance of things hoped for, the conviction of things not seen.*

Thus with three sets of examples, the author illustrates the various aspects/approaches and definitions of faith, not in an abstract sense, but through the examples of real people from history who exhibited *a conviction of things not seen, a trusting response, a hope, and a patient endurance.*

12:1-29: Exhortation to live with perseverance and patient endurance

...therefore since we are surrounded by so great a cloud of witnesses... let us run with perseverance the race that is set before us, looking to Jesus...seated at the right hand of the throne of God... The author uses the examples of faith to exhort the readers to live with perseverance and patient endurance following the example of Jesus, *the pioneer and perfecter of our faith.*

...consider Him who endured from sinners such hostility against Himself...you have not yet resisted to the point of shedding your own blood... A recollection of the passion and death of Jesus which should serve as the motivation for resistance even to the point of death.

...do not regard lightly the discipline (παιδειας) *of the Lord...* A quotation from Proverbs 3:11-12, where 'discipline' is education and obedience. The idea of suffering as a means of education leading to obedience is being developed (12:7-11).

...lift your drooping hands and strengthen your weak knees...strive for peace with all... An exhortation to inculcate maturity through suffering.

...you have not come to what may be touched, a blazing fire...so terrifying was the sight...but you have come to Mount Zion and to the city of the living God... A contrast with the situation at Mount Sinai when Moses received the Law and the people, and beasts, were not allowed to even touch the mountain (Ex. 19), and the heavenly mountain where God meets the people with forgiveness.

Comments

The examples of faith in Israel's past history, and the example of the suffering and obedience of Jesus, serve as exhortations for the present readers to persevere in faith with patient endurance for they too must expect to undergo the discipline of suffering. The Greek word (παιδείας) translated as 'discipline' literally means 'education' (related to the word for 'child' - παιδίον); the author develops the thesis found in Jewish Wisdom Literature (as the quotation from the Book of Proverbs indicates) that it is through the discipline of suffering that God educates God's people in righteousness. Stoic philosophy also held that suffering is part of a person's education leading to maturity. Using this background of Proverbs 3:1-12, the author holds that Christians realize their relationship to God, even as Christ did, through suffering (12:7-10).

A further exhortation is that Christians who endure the present pain will gain *the peaceful fruit of righteousness* (12:11), *therefore lift your drooping hands and strengthen your weak knees...* lest under affliction and pain they fall into sin from where there is no forgiveness (12:16-17: using the example of Esau who sold his birthright and then could not get a blessing even when he wanted one) for they do not have to do with the covenant mediated by Moses, awesome as that was, but with the covenant mediated by Christ (12:18-24). So Christians can look forward to *a kingdom that cannot be shaken,* and in response *let us be grateful* and *offer to God acceptable worship* (12:27-28).

In the last section of the chapter (12:25-29), the example of those who failed to escape after disobedience to Moses is given as a warning and an exhortation to the readers: they are to offer an acceptable worship to God, not just through reverence and liturgical acts, but through good deeds (13:15). Failure to worship in spirit and truth will result in invoking God's wrath – *our God is a consuming fire* (12:29).

13:1-25 : Final exhortation and blessing

...let brotherly love continue...hospitality to strangers...remember those who are in prison...those who are ill-treated... The exhortation for love to hold the community together and for this love to be exhibited in concern and care for those beyond the community: *do not neglect to do good and to share what you have...*(13:16).

...let marriage be held in honour... Adultery seemed to have been a major concern and the exhortation to be faithful to one's partner.

...keep yourself free from money...be content with what you have... The exhortation to avoid the love of money and power with the assurance that God will provide for all needs: *I will never leave you not forsake you* quoting Psalm 118:5-7.

...remember your leaders...imitate their faith... Those who were leaders/teachers are to be held in high honour as examples after whom to model one's life.

...Jesus Christ is the same yesterday and today and for ever (Ἰησους Χριστος ἐχθες και σημερον ὅ αὐτος και εἰς τους αἰωνας)... After mentioning those of the past who are models, the author mentions the permanent, unchanging model of Jesus Christ.

...do not be led away by diverse and strange teachings... The warning against false teachings and heresies.

...we have an altar...sacrifice for sin are burnt outside the camp...so Jesus also suffered outside the gate...let us go forth to Him outside the camp...for we have no lasting city, but we seek the city which is to come... The author's final comparison of Jewish rituals/liturgical practices with the work accomplished by Christ and the readers' participation in that work, combined with the eschatological hope of the city to come summarizes the whole thrust of the writing.

*...obey your leaders and submit to them...they are keeping watch over your souls...*The exhortation to live within the community's regulations and respect the hierarchical system.

...pray for us... The identity and context of the writer is not mentioned, but it would seem that the writer was well known to the readers, hence no name was necessary.

...now may the God of peace...blood of the eternal covenant... The benediction given in terms of the death and resurrection of Jesus expressed in the language of the Jewish covenant, which would again remain true to the whole thrust of the writing.

...hear my word of exhortation...written to you briefly...Timothy has been released...those who come from Italy send you greetings... The final verses o the writing are the only place that contains any personal information bringing the writing into an epistolary/letter format. The context of Timothy's imprisonment and release are not clear neither is the reference to *those who come from Italy* – whether the writing is *from* somewhere outside, or whether from somewhere outside *to* Italy.

Comments

The writing concludes with a series of specific admonitions and exhortations regarding treatment of those inside and outside the community (hospitality), marriage, money, respect for elders, and concerns about false teaching (13:1-17); the admonitions and exhortations cover social, private, religious and political life. These were areas of concern in every city of the empire, so a specific place cannot be deduced. These ethical and practical injunctions come closest to the Pauline style, but are entirely different in language and conceptual world. The personal references to *Timothy* and *those who come from Italy* are equally enigmatic and do not support any concrete solutions to either the author, the place of writing, or the addressees.

There are two well-loved and eloquent affirmations which appear in this concluding chapter: the first is the appeal for considering leaders/elders/teachers of the past – people who come and go even when they make a great contribution – when compared with the permanence of Christ, *the same yesterday, today and for ever* (13:8). The affirmation provides an assurance of continuity and stability.

The second is in the context of the benediction – the readers are in the care of the *great shepherd of the sheep* (a description used for Yahweh in Ps. 23:1; Is. 40:11; Jer. 31:10) who will provide them with strength and encouragement (13:20-21). Both these texts would have served as an encouragement in a stressful situation and would have brought hope to other Christian communities as well thereby accounting for the acceptance of the writing.

The concluding section (13:22-25), is the only place which follows the epistolary format, and even then, not too closely; it is more like a postscript to the writing. The reference to Timothy is difficult to place from other writings in the New Testament – where was he in prison, where did he go after release etc… Similarly the reference to *those from Italy* does not answer the question as to whether it refers to a place inside Italy or to a place outside Italy; the interpretation could go both ways. Therefore, the conclusion has led scholars to believe that Hebrew was actually a sermon, or a collection of sermons on various topics written down later, with a some semblance of an epistolary ending (see Introductory issues above).

The continuing relevance of Hebrews: The place of Hebrews in the New Testament canon has a chequered history but was finally accepted as a Pauline writing (see History of the Canon in Vol. I of this series, and the introductory issues to Hebrews, above). In the period of the Reformation, Luther raised the issue of the place of Hebrews in the canon on the theological grounds that the writing stresses the impossibility of a second repentance, and placed the writing after what he called "the really certain chief books of the New Testament". As the reader goes through the writing, many of these issues come up again, especially the issues of the writer's heavy dependence on the Jewish cultic practices and concepts: its sacrificial and priestly system, the Sabbath rest, the Tent/Tabernacle etc…and Platonic/Hellenistic philosophy of reality and shadow – all of which question the writing's relevance for the modern day. However, the writing would have had a particular appeal for Christians of the 1st century who lived in a time of social and religious confusion, as if they were *strangers and foreigners* looking for a savior and a place of safety, *a heavenly home, a Sabbath rest.* Added to this, the references to the forgiveness of sins with Christ as both the sacrifice and High priest, the Hellenistic dualism of the heavenly and the shadow, made the writing very appealing and meaningful.

The theological issue of no possibility of a second repentance has to be understood in the same light as the *unforgivable sin against the Holy Spirit* in the Gospels, i.e. a conscious turning away from the gift that had been accepted and then deliberately rejected. At a time when the community was looking for direction, the author's presentation of a great *cloud of witnesses* gathered together in suffering and journeying towards *the heavenly city* would have been very stirring. This, coupled with the interpretation of Jewish elements of theology, worship and sacrifice in terms of fulfillment in Christ provided a firm grounding in the continuity of the faith and God's salvific acts; today these elements provide for an example of an early exercise in indigenization.

Above all, the portrayal of *the great pioneer and perfecter of faith* as a historical person, not a mythological figure, provided for the readers, and 1st century Christians, a clearer image of the God whom they had worshipped from afar. In this sense, the writing to the Hebrews continues to have a relevant message and to inspire Christians in all ages and therefore justifies its place in the canon of the New Testament.

***

Select Bibliography for Section I

Brown, R. E. *An Introduction to the New Testament.* Bangalore: Theological Publications in India, 2000.

__________. *The Message of Hebrews.* The Bible Speaks Today, Downers Grove: Inter Varsity Press, 1982.

Bruce, F. F. *The Epistle to the Hebrews,* New International Commentary on the New Testament. Grand Rapids: Eerdmans, 1996.

Evans, L. H. *Hebrews.* Waco, Texas: Word, 1985.

Hering, J. *The Epistle to the Hebrews.* London: Epworth, 1970.

Hughes, P. E. *A Commentary on the Epistle to the Hebrews.* Grand Rapids: Eerdmans, 1977.

Kasemann, E. *The Wandering People of God.* Minneapolis: Augsburg, 1984.

Kee, H. C. and F. W. Young. *The Living World of the New Testament.* London: Darton, Longman & Todd, 1966.

Kummel, W. G. *Introduction to the New Testament* (Revised Edition). translated by Howard C. Kee. London: SCM Press, 1975.

Varghese, B., "Hebrews" in Brian C. Wintle (General Editor), *South Asia Biblical Commentary.* Udaipur, Rajasthan: Open Door Publications, 2015, pages 1708-1729.

SECTION II

The Epistle of James

CHAPTER I

General Introduction to the Catholic Epistles (James, I, II, III John, I, II Peter, Jude)

Reasons for naming these as "Catholic Epistles".

The Christian church was born in the midst of conflict: Jesus carried out his mission in conflict with Jewish authorities which finally ended in conflict with the Roman Procurator; the early movement found itself in conflict with Judaism and Judaizing Christians; there was conflict with Hellenistic religions and philosophies, and individuals (e.g. Paul) and communities found themselves in conflict with Rome; within communities there were conflicts regarding doctrinal and practical issues of daily life (e.g. Corinth). The conflict with Judaism slowly faded and finally came to an end in the 4th-5th centuries, but the communities' conflict with Roman authorities intensified into severe persecution which went on into the middle of the 2nd century, and false teachings within the community (Church) continued till most of the controversies were settled in ecumenical councils by the end of the 5th century. These conflicts had a profound effect on the Christian community wherever it spread giving rise to literature that addressed the issues.

A general response to this conflict from within and without was to produce a literature (which would later become scripture) that would speak to the specific situation being faced as well as which would provide a guideline for other places/cities that faced similar situations. One type (genre) of writing were the Gospels which set out to trace the development of Christianity from the time of its inception – the time of Jesus[1]; the Acts of the Apostles sought to show the further development of the movement taking it beyond the boundaries of Judaism and Palestine[2]; the Pauline letters to specific recipients addressed doctrinal and practical day-to-day issues in the midst of critical contexts[3]; another literary response was that of the Apocalypse[4] – the Book of Revelation – which saw in the present age the signs of the end-times and also envisaged a glorious future giving hope in the context of persecution and suffering. There was yet another literary response, though included in the other writings, which specifically sought to tighten doctrinal positions/teachings in order to preserve tradition and what was held to be 'true/orthodox teaching' and 'sound doctrine'. When the early Christian community had opened its doors to the Gentiles and thus to Hellenistic influences, then these 'false teachings' began to infiltrate and pose a danger to various communities and hence they had to be sternly corrected. By the end of the 1st century, the church was faced with a number of 'false teachings', which if allowed to grow unchecked, would have submerged the essential truth of the Gospel under popular Hellenistic thought. The identification of these 'false teachings', and the stern corrections, often led to discord within the communities and the danger of breakaway groups. A number of New Testament writings show evidence of this struggle, especially the later writings – evidence that the leaders were forced to scrutinize and reaffirm their fundamental beliefs, not entering into any profound theological discussion, but simply reiterating what they believed to be the truth and to condemn any teaching that deviated from this position, either directly or by implication.

The primary vocation of the early church was to proclaim the message of Jesus – salvation – to the world. The message emphasized that in Christ was the final revelation of God and therefore, by implication, the message was a judgment on all other ways of thinking about God, human beings and creation. Yet the church had to adopt the language and concepts of these 'other ways' – the world – in order to proclaim its message relevantly without at the same time perverting or distorting it. The church was driven to find theological and ethical expressions of the faith whereby it could share the proclamation of the new life and at the same time preserve its unique qualities. This task was heightened, became more urgent, with the conversion of the Gentiles whose ethical views were radically different from those of Christianity (a Christianity which, in the first instance, was influenced by the Judaism from which it emerged). In this task, the church drew on five main sources that can be identified in the New Testament:

> The Hebrew scriptures – the sacred writings of Judaism – which the church also used as its scriptures and quoted freely from these writings;

> The ethical tradition of various Jewish apocalyptic sects that were looking for the appearance of the Messiah as a sign of the end time;

> The teachings of Jesus preserved and circulated in early oral tradition; the written Gospels came later which is probably why New Testament writers do not give direct quotations from the Gospels;

> The theological/ethical teachings of Hellenistic Judaism especially used in Hellenistic synagogues for instructions to proselytes which included Hellenistic philosophical concepts;

> The ethical teachings of various Hellenistic philosophical schools of thought which formed the background of the Gentile converts.

New Testament writings consciously or unconsciously reflect these sources though it is difficult to ascertain when the borrowing was direct and when it was mediated through the general thought patterns/ expressions of the day. The writings that show most clearly the influence of these sources are the seven 'Catholic Epistles'.

In the New Testament there are 7 letters which fit the description of the concerns mentioned above and which mention the name of the author in the superscription: James, I & II Peter, I, II, III John (the self-designation of the author is "the elder") and Jude. The letter to the Hebrews was considered in this category but, though anonymous, was eventually attributed to Paul and included among the Pauline writings. Eusebius (Bishop of Caesarea, A. D. 314, a historian of the canon. See Vol. I of this series) was the first to speak of these as the "seven Catholic letters". The word *Catholic* in the term *Catholic Epistles* has been a convention dating from the 4th century. At that time, that word simply meant 'general', and was not specifically tied to any denomination, i.e. referring to what would later become known as the Catholic Church. Nevertheless, to avoid any confusion, alternative terms such as 'general epistles' or 'general missionary epistles' were used. In the historical context, the word *Catholic* signified that the letters were addressed to the general church, and not to specific, separate congregations or persons. However, II John and III John appear to contradict this view, because they are addressed respectively to the "elect lady", speculated by many to be the church itself, and to "Gaius", about whom there has been much speculation but little in the way of conclusive proof as to his identity. Earlier, I John was the first to be called a "catholic epistle" which was by way of describing the breadth of its address (although it is not possible to identify the specific addressees). However, the title "Catholic Epistles" was soon used to describe all 7 letters intended for general (catholic) readership. Among these letters: II & III John have specific addressees/readers, either an individual or a community (see Vol. III of this series); I Peter is addressed to a geographic region; James, II Peter, and Jude are addressed to all Christians.

In terms of authorship, three of the seven letters are anonymous (I, II, III, John). These three have traditionally been attributed to John the Apostle, the son of Zebedee and one of the Twelve Apostles of Jesus. Consequently, these letters have been labelled as the Johannine epistles, despite the fact that none of the epistles mentions any author (for details see Vol. III of this series).

Two of the letters claim to have been written by Simon Peter, one of the Twelve Apostles of Jesus. Therefore, they have traditionally been called the Peterine epistles. However, most modern scholars agree that they were probably not written by Peter, because they appear to have been written in the late 1st or early 2nd century, long after Peter had died, therefore they are classified as pseudonymous writings.

In one epistle, the author only calls himself James. It is not known which James this is supposed to be. There are several different traditional Christian interpretations of other New Testament texts which mention a James, brother of Jesus. However, most modern scholars tend to reject this line of reasoning, since the author does not indicate any familial relationship with Jesus. A similar problem presents itself with the Epistle of Jude: the writer claims to be a brother of James, but it is not clear which James is meant. According to some Christian traditions, this is the same James as the author of the Epistle of James, who was allegedly a brother of Jesus; and so, this Jude should also be a brother of Jesus, despite the fact that he does not indicate any such thing in the text. Both these epistles come under the category of pseudonymous writings.

The Table given below summarizes the overall view (details for I, II, III John are given in Vol. III of this series; details for James, I Peter, Jude, and II Peter are given in this Volume) :

Traditional name	Author according to the text	Traditional attribution	Modern consensus
Epistle of James	"James, a servant of the Lord Jesus Christ"	James, brother of Jesus	An unknown James. Pseudonymous. Date: end of 1st century Place: Jerusalem?
First Epistle of Peter	"Peter, an apostle of Jesus Christ"	Simon Peter	Not Simon Peter. Pseudonymous. Date: A.D. 85-95 Place: Rome?

First Epistle of John	No name mentioned	John, son of Zebedee	Unknown. Anonymous. Date: A.D. 100-110 Place: Ephesus?
Second Epistle of John	"the elder"	John, son of Zebedee	Anonymous. Date: A.D. 100-110 Place: Ephesus?
Third Epistle of John	"the elder"	John, son of Zebedee	Anonymous. Date: A.D. 100-110 Place: Ephesus?
Epistle of Jude	"Jude, a servant of Jesus Christ and brother of James"	Jude, brother of James/Jesus	An unknown Jude. Pseudonymous. Date: A.D. 100-120 Place: unknown
Second Epistle of Peter	"Sim(e)on Peter, a servant and apostle of Jesus Christ"	Simon Peter	Not Simon Peter. Pseudonymous. Date: A.D. 120-140 Place: unknown

The seven Catholic epistles were added to the New Testament canon, reaffirming the criterion followed by the early church leaders to include anonymous/pseudonymous writings if they could be attributed to, or traced to apostolic origins, and to attribute the epistles written by people with the same name as having apostolic roots/connections.

The inclusion of these writings in the canon of the New Testament also reaffirmed the doctrinal standards adhered to by the early church even when there were no formal decisions taken on the theological expressions of the faith. The insistence that these were the true/ orthodox teachings from which there should be no deviation, along with supportive writings, recognition, and acceptance from influential church leaders, ensured that the Catholic Epistles found a place in the New Testament canon and served as a corrective, and as an expression of the true/orthodox faith, for the whole church.

CHAPTER II

Introduction to the Epistle of James

Background, Authorship, Recipients, date.

Background: Canonical, theological, and literary issues:

In the textual and literary history of the New Testament, and the history of the canon, the Epistle of James has always raised questions concerning its origin and character, time and value. The letter is missing from the Muratorian canon (see Vol. I of this series for history of the canon) and is not mentioned or quoted by church leaders until after A.D. 200. The writing was reviewed after that time and more serious attention was paid to it since the tradition began that it was written by the Lord's brother. However, the writing still underwent critical survey and it was not until Jerome's translation of the Vulgate in the 5th century that the Epistle was finally included in the Western canon; the Eastern churches continued the debate until the 11th-12th centuries. In the 16th century, Luther compared the position on *justification by works* in James to Paul's insistence on *justification by faith,* and declared that James was a "right strawy epistle" and that it did not preach Christ because it makes no explicit reference to the death, resurrection, or divine sonship of Jesus, therefore he felt that it cannot be considered to be apostolic, so he placed it at the end of the canon among the 'disputed' writings. The Council of Trent in 1546 re-iterated the place of the Epistle of James in the canon where it is accepted by churches today.

In the 19th century, it was felt that James was a Christian revision of a basic Jewish writing by the introduction of the name of Christ in two places (1:1 and 2:1). In the 20th century, James was thought of as early Christian paraenesis (exhortation/encouragement/advice) or wisdom literature (e.g. 1:5 || Matthew 7:7 – petition for wisdom) like Proverbs since it consists largely of moral exhortations and precepts without any definite historical connection: just a collection of paraenetic tradition and general ethical admonitions and since there is no readily discernible over-arching literary structure, many felt that the epistle may not be a true piece of correspondence between specific parties but an example of Jewish wisdom literature, formulated as a letter for circulation.

Understanding the circumstances of James' writing helps in better understanding James' organization of the letter. The epistle is viewed as having a legitimate purpose for its composition: a response to the suffering of its recipients. Some explore a violent historical background behind the epistle and offer the suggestion that it was indeed written by James, the brother of Jesus, and it was written before A.D. 62, the year James was killed. The 50s saw the growth of turmoil and violence in Roman Judea, as Jews became more and more frustrated with corruption, injustice and poverty. It continued into the 60s and four years after James was killed war broke out with Rome (A.D. 66-70) and would lead to the destruction of Jerusalem and the scattering of the people. The epistle is renowned for exhortations on fighting poverty and caring for the poor in practical ways (1:26–27; 2:1-4; 2:14-19; 5:1-6), standing up for the oppressed (2:1-4; 5:1-6) and not being *like the world* in the way in which one responds to evil in the world (1:26-27; 2:11; 3:13-18; 4:1-10). Worldly wisdom is rejected and people are exhorted to embrace heavenly wisdom, which includes peace making and pursuing righteousness and justice (3:13-18). This approach sees the epistle as a real letter with a real immediate purpose: to encourage Christian Jews not to revert to violence in their response to injustice and poverty but to stay focused on doing good, staying holy and to embrace the wisdom of heaven, not that of the world.

There was a powerful appeal of Judaism that lingered on into Christianity, not the rituals, but the moral law. The letter of James exhibits this thoroughly Jewish ethical appeal using examples from Hebrew scriptures and without any developed teaching about the role of Christ.

The content of James is directly parallel, in many instances, to sayings of Jesus found in the gospels of Luke and Matthew, i.e., those attributed to the hypothetical Q Source (see Vol. I of this series), e.g. *Do not swear at all, either by heaven...or by the earth....Let your word be 'Yes, Yes' or 'No, No'; anything more than this comes from the evil one* (Mtt. 5:34, 37) and *...do not swear either by heaven or by earth or by any other oath, but let your 'Yes' be yes and your 'No' be no, so that you may not fall under condemnation* (James 5:12). According to James Tabor, an acknowledged authority, the epistle of James contains "no fewer than thirty direct references, echoes, and allusions to the teachings of Jesus found in the Q source" (Q source is teaching material common to Matthew and Luke but not found in Mark. See Vol. I of this series). However, it must be noted that these parallels/references do not imply a copying from the Gospels (there is no literary dependence), but are more like recollections of the oral tradition of the story of Jesus.

The debate, started by Luther regarding the letter, on Paul's theology of *justification by faith* versus James' *justification by works* has moved from whether James knew Paul and his theology: whether it was written before Paul so making it the earliest Christian writing, or whether the teaching of James is a corrective to a misunderstood Paul thus placing the writing in the later apostolic period closer to the end of the 1st century. The writing contains the following famous passages concerning faith and works:

> *What good is it if someone says they have faith but does not have works? Can that faith save them? If a brother or sister is poorly clothed and lacking in daily food, and one of you says to them, "Go in peace, be warmed and filled," without giving them the things needed for the body, what good is that? So also faith by itself, if it does not have works, is dead. (2:14-17)*

> *But someone will say, "You have faith and I have works." Show me your faith apart from your works, and I will show you my faith by my works. You believe that God is one; you do well. Even the demons believe—and shudder! Do you want to be shown, you foolish person, that faith apart from works is useless? Was not Abraham our father justified by works when he offered*

up his son Isaac on the altar? You see that faith was active along with his works, and faith was completed by his works; and the Scripture was fulfilled that says, "Abraham believed God, and it was counted to him as righteousness"— and he was called a friend of God. You see that a person is justified by works and not by faith alone. And in the same way was not also Rahab the prostitute justified by works when she received the messengers and sent them out by another way? For as the body apart from the spirit is dead, so also faith apart from works is dead. (2:18-26)

These passages have been cited in theological debates, especially regarding Paul's teaching on justification and James' teaching on works. Some scholars even hold that passages such as these are a response to Paul, taking the view that James is a response to a misunderstanding of Paul. Paul was dealing with one kind of error while James was dealing with a different error. The error with which Paul was dealing was with people who said that works of the law were needed to be added to faith in order to help in earning God's favour. Paul countered this error by pointing out that salvation was by faith alone apart from deeds of the law (Gal. 2:16; Rom. 3:21-22, 28; 5:1). Paul also taught that saving faith is not dead but alive – faith working through love (Gal. 5:6). James was dealing with those who said that if they had faith they did not need to show love by a life of faith (James 2:14-17). James countered this error by teaching that faith is alive, showing itself to be so by deeds of love (James 2:18,26). James and Paul both teach that salvation is by faith and also that faith is never alone but shows itself to be alive by deeds of love that express a believer's thanks to God for the free gift of salvation by faith in Jesus.

The main issue of the debate which concerns faith and works suggests the period immediately after James (died in A.D. 62) and Paul, in the last third of the first century. A fitting conclusion to the debate is to agree that James and Paul are two sides of the same coin and that one side defines the other in the Christian life. Indeed, James has its place in the canon when a person who has already heard the message of Jesus and Paul has his/her vision expanded to include the work that grows out of faith – a message contained in James. With the 20th century concern for social morality – faith is unacceptable without works, clothes for the poor, food for the hungry – the message of James became important in the light of liberation theology and a corrective to what was considered to be a socially insensitive Christianity.

The letter is written within an overall theme of patient perseverance during trials and temptations; James writes to encourage his readers to live consistently with what they have learned in Christ; he wants his readers to become mature in their faith in Christ by living what they say they believe; he condemns various sins, including pride, hypocrisy, favouritism, and slander; he encourages and implores believers to humbly live by godly, rather than worldly wisdom and to pray in all situations.

The characteristics that make the letter distinctive are: 1. its unmistakably Jewish nature; 2. its emphasis on vital Christianity, characterized by good deeds and a faith that works (genuine faith must and will be accompanied by a consistent lifestyle); 3. its topical style organization; 4. its familiarity with Jesus' teachings preserved in the Sermon on the Mount; 5. its similarity to Hebrew wisdom writings such as Proverbs; and 6. its excellent Greek.

Authorship

The letter claims to have been written by *James, a servant of God and of the Lord Jesus Christ* (1:1); the issue is to identify the person. The New Testament mentions 5 men with the name of 'James' :

James, the son of Zebedee, a disciple of Jesus (Mk. 1:19, 3:17 & par., Acts 12:2);

James, the son of Alphaeus, a disciple of Jesus (Mk.3:18 & par.);

James, the brother of Jesus, son of Joseph and Mary (Mk. 6:3 & par.; Acts 12:17, 15:13, 21:18; I Cor. 15:7; Gal. 1:19, 2:9; Jude 1);

James, the younger, son of a Mary (Mk. 15:40 & par., 16:1);

James, the father of the apostle Judas (Lk. 6:16; Acts 1:13).

The author cannot be an unknown person as he does not need to provide a reference other than that he is *a servant of God and of the Lord Jesus Christ.* The New Testament does not give information about James son of Alphaeus, James the younger, and James father of Judas; James the son of Zebedee was martyred in A.D. 44 (Acts 12:1-2) which was probably much before the date of the letter; thus James son of Joseph and Mary and brother to Jesus and Jude is the only person left to be considered, and since the mid-3rd century his name was associated with this letter as the author. He was the only person of this name who occupied so significant a place in early Christianity that he did not need an extensive introduction; he had risen to a position of prominence in, and eventually became the head of the church in Jerusalem (the Orthodox Church regards him as the first Bishop of Jerusalem) and earned a position of respect throughout Christendom.

The following information about James, and the position of respect that he held, can be extracted from the tradition of the early church:

James was one of several brothers of Jesus, probably the oldest after Jesus since he heads the list in Mt 13:55. At first he did not believe in Jesus and even challenged him and misunderstood his mission (Jn. 7:2–5). Later he became very prominent in the church;

He was one of the select individuals to whom Christ appeared after his resurrection (1 Co 15:7);

Paul called him a "pillar" of the church (Gal 2:9);

Paul, on his first post-conversion visit to Jerusalem, saw James (Gal 1:19);

Paul did the same on his last visit (Acts 21:18);

When Peter was rescued from prison, he told his friends to tell James (Acts 12:17);

James was a leader in the important Council of Jerusalem (Acts 15:13);

Jude could identify himself simply as *a brother of James* (Jude 1:1), so well known was James.

He was noted for his adherence to the Law and his sense of justice (Acts 15 as an example), so earning the name of *James, the Just*. As explained by Eusebius, James the Just was a Nazirite (ascetic) totally dedicated to God and praying so often and for long periods in the Temple, that his knees became as calloused as that of a camel. He was martyred in A.D. 62 by being stoned to death, outside the Temple, on the orders of the High Priest, Ananus II, who had the Sanhedrin accuse James of blasphemy for proclaiming Jesus as Son of God and Messiah.

In support of this James as the author of the letter, there are two considerations:

The simple self-designation is of a well known person;

The close contacts with important ethical teachings in the Gospels.

Given the above background of James the Just, it is not surprising that the letter that purports to bear his name echoes traditional Jewish belief and piety.

But there are weighty arguments against the authorship by James, brother of Jesus:

The cultured language is not that of a simple Palestinian;

It is difficult to conceive of a person who was faithful to the Law, and who demanded obedience to the ethical demands of the Law even to the extent of demanding that the Gentiles observe ritual/ceremonial purity making it possible for them to have fellowship with Jewish Christians (Acts 15), thus it is unlikely that such a person could refer to another law as the *perfect law of liberty*... (1:22ff.) or of giving expression to the Law solely in ethical demands (2:11ff.) without concern for Jewish rituals;

The debate in 2:14ff regarding faith (Paul) and works presupposes a considerable distance from Paul, whereas James died in A.D. 62; the lack of knowledge of Pauline thought can hardly be accounted for when there were several meetings between Paul and James, especially on Paul's last visit to Jerusalem, about A.D. 57/58 (Acts 221:18ff.);

Would the brother of Jesus really omit all reference to Jesus?

The history of the canon shows that this letter was not readily accepted in the church, thus there does not seem to be an old tradition associating the letter with James, the Lord's brother; the tradition comes only from the mid-2nd century.

In the light of the above, modern scholarship holds that **the Epistle of James was written by an unknown Jewish Christian writing under the authority of James, the respected leader of the Jerusalem community, and therefore it must be considered as a pseudonymous writing.**

Recipients and date

The Epistle of James is addressed to *the twelve tribes which are scattered abroad* (1:1). These were the Jews who were living outside of Palestine, often referred to as the *Diaspora*, a word which means *dispersion*. If this epistle was sent to all of the cities where there were Jewish Christians in the first century, it may have been read in such diverse places as Italy, Greece, Turkey, Syria, Lebanon, Palestine, Egypt, Cyprus, and Crete. Since the epistle is addressed to *the twelve tribes which are scattered abroad*, it is likely that it was written after the 60s, for the Christian communities outside of Palestine did not begin to develop significantly until then when the Pauline missions began to take effect as established communities.

Some hold that the expression, *twelve tribes scattered among the nations* refers to Christians in general, but the term "twelve tribes" would more naturally apply to Jewish Christians. Furthermore, a Jewish audience would be more in keeping with the obvious Jewish nature of the letter (e.g., the use of the Hebrew title for God, κυριον σαβαωθ, *Lord Almighty* (5:4). **It is clear from 2:1 and 5:7-8 that the recipients were Christians, so it has been plausibly suggested that these were believers from the early Jerusalem church who, after Stephen's death, were scattered as far as Phoenicia, Cyprus and Syrian Antioch** (see Acts 8:1; 11:19). This would account for the references to trials and oppression, the intimate knowledge of the readers and the authoritative nature of the letter. As leader of the Jerusalem church, 'James' wrote as pastor to instruct and encourage his dispersed people in the face of their difficulties.

Many scholars consider the epistle to have been written in the late 1st or early 2nd centuries based on the following:

> The author introduces himself merely as *a servant of God and of the Lord Jesus Christ* without invoking any special family relationship to Jesus;

> The cultured Greek language of the Epistle could not have been written by a Galilean/Jerusalem Jew. Some scholars argue for a primitive version of the letter composed by James and then later polished by another writer;

> The epistle was only gradually accepted into the canon of the New Testament;

> Some see parallels between James and 1 Peter, 1 Clement, and the Shepherd of Hermas (early Christian writings) and take this to reflect the socio-economic situation Christians were dealing with in the late 1st or early 2nd century.

Other scholars suggest an early dating for the Epistle of James based on the following:

> The Letter of James is among the earliest of New Testament compositions. It contains no reference to the events in Jesus' life, but it bears striking testimony to Jesus' words. Jesus' sayings are embedded in James' exhortations in a form that is clearly not dependent on the written Gospels. Therefore it must be dated before the first of the written Gospel tradition – i.e. before A.D. 65-70, the date for Mark's Gospel.

> If written by James the brother of Jesus, it would have been written sometime before A.D. 62, the traditional date for his martyrdom.

> Its distinctively Jewish nature suggests that it was composed when the church was still predominantly Jewish.

> It reflects a simple church order—officers of the church are called *elders* (5:14) and *teachers* (3:1).

No reference is made to the controversy over Gentile circumcision.

The Greek term συναγωγη ('synagogue' or 'meeting') is used to designate the meeting or meeting place of the church (2:2).

However, in view of the issues regarding authorship, above, and especially the theological debate on faith and works which would demand a conceptual distance from Paul to account for changes in the meaning of words ('faith' = a dynamic 'trust' in Paul; 'faith' = a static acceptance of 'belief' in James), the consensus is that the **date of the writing is towards the end of the 1ˢᵗ century.**

The place of writing could be Jerusalem (the traditional locale for James the brother of Jesus, and the place where he was venerated as the leader of the Jerusalem community) or it could have been written from anywhere, and to anywhere in the Empire where Christians spoke Greek – a truly 'Catholic Epistle'.

CHAPTER III

Advice for Practical Christian Living

Analysis and Commentary on the Text of James.
A Liberation Theology Perspective.

1:1: Opening Formula/Greetings

James... see introduction, above, for discussion on the identity of the person. Just the name with no further connections is indicative of a well known person.

...servant (δουλος) *of God...* The Greek word is for slave – totally submitted to God and Jesus Christ.

...to the twelve tribes in the Dispersion (ἐν τῃ διασπορᾳ)... The *diaspora* meant places outside of Palestine. Here there seems to be a direct reference to Jews – *twelve tribes* – living outside Palestine.

...greetings... Most versions translate the Greek word χαιρειν (*chairein*) as 'greetings', but its basic meaning is 'joy' from the Greek χαρα (*chara*).

Comments

The discussion on the authorship issue showed that the author was unknown (pseudonymous writing) but writing in the name of James, to give the impression that the writer is James, the brother of Jesus and the leader of the Jerusalem community. This accounts for the simple introduction where there was no need for an extensive elaboration of the writer's credentials.

The description of the writer as *a servant (slave) of God and of the Lord Jesus Christ* places the writing in a Christian framework. Various characters in the Hebrew scriptures (Abraham, Moses, prophets) were called *servant of God*, so the title seems to have been taken over to refer to Christians (see also Rev. 1:1) and is a designation of modesty as commanded by Jesus (Mtt. 23:8-12). This is the only writing in the New Testament, other than Paul, to use the term 'servant' to describe the writer's relationship with Jesus. In describing himself so modestly, James reflects Gospel tradition without directly quoting a text (perhaps because there was no written Gospel?).

The reference to the *twelve tribes in the dispersion* would make the writing sound very much like it was addressed solely to Jews living outside Palestine. However, Christians considered themselves to be the successors/inheritors of God's promises and therefore the new Israel (I Pt. 1:1). The use of descriptions from the Jewish background would not necessarily exclude the Gentiles, but would probably indicate that the addressees were Christians who were strongly influenced by the Jewish heritage and sought to re-interpret that heritage in terms of Christianity. The *tribes in the dispersion* would also indicate that people were forced out of their homeland and so lived in a situation of oppression/exploitation. I Peter (1:1) is the only other writing in the New Testament to use this phrase to refer to Christians living scattered all over the Empire (see comments, below, on I Peter which may have been written to dispel the feeling of alienation in a foreign land). The use of 'joy' in the opening greeting is an emphasis repeated in the Epistle bringing hope and encouragement to a troubled community.

1:2-27: Faith, humility, temptations, trials, and marks of true religion

...count it all joy...when you meet various trials...the testing of your faith produces steadfastness...blessed is the one who endures trial...they will receive the crown of life which God has promised to those who love God...

This may be a reflection of Matthew. 5:11-12: *blessed are you when they revile and persecute you...rejoice and be glad.* The author realistically faces a situation of *trials* but responds theologically with a reference to *faith* and the outcome of patient endurance.

...the person who doubts is like the wave of the sea that is driven and tossed by the wind...a double-minded person is unstable in all their ways... The admonition and encouragement to have faith without doubting; faith expressed as complete trust. Ask with faith and without hesitation (Mtt. 21:21).

...let the lowly boast in their exaltation, and the rich in their humiliation... The social concern for overcoming the difference between the rich and the poor is brought out. The illustration of the *flower of the grass* and the withering of the grass echoes Jesus' teaching (close to the Lucan beatitude, 6:20, 24). *...let no one say "I am tempted by God"; for God cannot be tempted...and tempts no one...each person is tempted by their own desires...desire gives birth to sin...and sin brings death...* The teaching on temptation and the outcome of giving in to temptation is brought out.

...let everyone be quick to hear, slow to speak, slow to anger...put away all filthiness and rank growth of wickedness...be doers of the word and not hearers only...if anyone thinks they are religious and does not bridle their tongue, their religion is in vain...Religion that is pure and undefiled before God is this: to visit orphans and widows in their affliction, and to keep oneself unstained from the world... The marks of true religion is here identified in term of social behaviour/concerns. *Slow to anger – see Matthew. 5:22.*

Comments

After the opening formula, there are no greetings as is normal in the letter format, instead the author immediately starts a series of exhortations, much of it echoing the teaching of Jesus in Q material – Mtt. 5-7 and scattered in Luke (especially in Lk. 6). There is much Gospel teaching on testing and trials (Mtt. 5:11, 48; 24:9-13), as well as the issue is addressed in other New Testament writings as well, hence the exhortation to accept testing as a means of strengthening one's faith was a commonly accepted axiom.

The social emphasis regarding the rich and the poor comes close to the teachings of the Sermon on the Mount (Mtt. 5-7 and scattered in Luke) especially the beatitude/blessing for the poor and woes for the rich. The emphasis here is not to give importance to the temporal/perishable things but to concentrate rather on values that up build and contribute to development. Other passages in James also attack the rich (2:1-9, 5:1-6), so this seems to be a major concern of the author. If the author is James, the leader of the Jerusalem community, then the images of that community having things in common and of the injunction to share goods would account for the concern (see Acts 2:44-45, 4:34-37, 5:1-11, 6:1, Gal. 2:10), and the fact that the community was finally impoverished and Paul had to raise support for them (Acts 24:17; Rom. 15:25-27; II Cor. 8 & 9).

The first insistence that works must accompany faith or that faith must be expressed through works comes out in the famous saying, *be doers of the word, and not hearers only* (1:22; see also Mtt. 7:24 – hearers and doers of the Word), i.e. Christians must manifest in their lives the practical working out of their faith. This leads into the marks of true religion which is measured by the care of, and concern for, *orphans and widows* and avoiding worldly attractions. This would be characteristic of a person who was stable in their faith rather than a person who is unstable and does not know what they believe or how they should express their beliefs.

2:1-13: Warning against partiality

...show no partiality... The practical socio-economic gap between the rich and poor is addressed.

...has not God chosen the poor in the world to be rich in faith and heirs of the Kingdom... A reflection of the beatitude/blessing on the

poor from the Sermon on the Mount in Matthew (Mtt. 5:3ff.), and the Sermon on the Plain in Luke (Lk.6:20).

...if you show partiality, you commit sin... The author insists on equal treatment for all.

...judgment is without mercy to one who has shown no mercy; yet mercy triumphs over judgment... After examining the Law and it observance, the author comes back to the crux of the Gospel: *mercy triumphs over judgment.* See also Matthew. 5:7 – *blessed are the merciful....*

Comments

The picture at the beginning of chapter 2 is that Christian communities that gather for worship (2:2) tend to receive the rich with special considerations while neglecting or even ignoring the poor. James is reminding the communities of the teaching regarding the poor inheriting the Kingdom – a reference to Jesus' teaching but without giving an exact quotation from the Gospels. The situation seems to be such that the rich are going to court against the poor who ultimately have no resources to defend themselves and so are oppressed (cf. the situation in Corinth – I Cor. 6:1-8).

James 2:8-10 is a re-iteration of the summary of the Law and commandments: to love one's neighbour (Mtt. 22:39-40. Also Mtt. 5:19). Any offence on this point, or on any one point of the Law, renders the person guilty of breaking the whole Law. The expression *law of liberty* poses a challenge between the ethical demands of the Law and freedom. Would the author, who seems to be steeped in traditional Jewish understandings, really have made this distinction between Law and freedom unless the understanding is that the stage is being set for the gospel message of grace – *mercy triumphs over judgment.*

At the end of chapter 1, James had spoken of the marks of true religion; in chapter 2, James finds practical expression of true religion – there is to be no favouritism, partiality or nepotism. If the wealthy are treated with partiality, then the communities are reminded that the Kingdom belongs to the poor. In fact, the behavior of the rich brings dishonor to the name of the Lord and the community.

2:14-26: The classic debate between Faith and Works

...what does it profit a person who says they have faith (πιστιν) *but has not works* (ἐργα)*...faith* (πιστις) *by itself, if it has no works* (ἐργα), *is dead...* This is the opening statement in the debate between faith and works. Both 'faith' and 'works' are used as nouns, indicating the acceptance of a set body of beliefs.

...some will say, "you have faith and I have works". Show me your faith apart from your works, and I by my works will show you my faith... faith apart from works is barren...Abraham our father justified by works... faith was active along with his works...you see that a person is justified by works and not by faith alone...faith apart from works is dead... The author's affirmation that faith and works must go together; they are not mutually exclusive; Illustrations of this combination are given from the stories of Abraham and Rahab.

Comments

The debate begins in the diatribe style, i.e. the author addressing an imaginary audience/person and answering the question/ proposition. The point that is being made is that faith and works must go together. Possibly the insistence on faith in Paul led to a misunderstanding in later times that faith need not be supported by expressions of works (this would require a distance from Paul, affecting the dating of the letter, as discussed above). James stresses that actions must match what is claimed to be believed.

The author often cites the combination of faith and works in examples from Hebrew scriptures: the story of Abraham offering Isaac (Gen. 15:6 and 22:16-17), and the story of Rahab and her assistance to the Israelite spies (Jos. 2; she is also praised in Heb. 11:31 among the host of witnesses to the faith).

The discussion shows that James 2 is not a rejection of the Pauline insistence on salvation by faith, but a pointing out that faith without works is insufficient. In Paul's time this insistence on faith only for salvation was necessary to counter the Jewish understanding of salvation by works of the Law. James, written at a later time, brings about a correction that both faith and works are needed; James does not go back to the Jewish understanding of works of the Law only, but brings about a combination of faith and works.

The Pauline position is stated clearly in these two texts: *a person is not justified by works of the Law but through faith in Jesus Christ…because by works of the Law shall no one be justified* (Gal. 2:16), and *a person is justified by faith, apart from the works of the Law* (Rom. 3:28). The position in James is stated thus: *a person is justified by works and not by faith alone* (2:24). Both use the example of Abraham in Gen. 15:6 to support their point. Most scholars would not agree that Paul was a reaction to James, so it would seem that James is a corrective to a misunderstanding that Paul would divorce faith and works. Paul was not arguing against works (there are many sections on ethical behavior in Paul, e.g. faith working through love: Gal. 5:6; I Cor. 13:2; Rom. 2:13), but against the understanding that the ritualistic works of the Law would lead to salvation; James on the other hand was arguing that only faith would not lead to salvation, but that faith must find expression in works (2:14-17) – translating belief into practice. Thus the debate/issue is not faith versus works, but to see faith and works as two sides of the same coin, each side bringing out a perspective of, and a correction to the other."

3:1-12: Control of the tongue

…let not many of you become teachers…we who teach shall be judged with greater strictness… This shows that teachers occupy a role in the structure of the community and that possibly the later church organization reflected in the Pastorals is not yet in place. See Matthew 23:8-12 on the desire to be called a teacher.

…bits in the mouths of horses…ships guided by a very small rudder…a great forest is set ablaze by a small fire… The intention is to show that small things control behavior patterns, directions and cause great destruction.

...the tongue is a fire... There is a scathing indictment of the tongue as being at the bottom of slander, vilification, and speaking in double standards: *from the same mouth come blessing and cursing.* See Matthew 12:36, 37 on the dangers of speech.

Comments

In this and succeeding chapters James cites one example after another of those things which threaten the harmony of community life. The damage that can be caused by a loose tongue comes in for particular denunciation especially when the damage is caused by teachers. The role of a teacher would indicate that community structure seemed to have had an office of teacher (just as later the office of *presbyter* is mentioned – 5:14).

It is almost as though the tongue is personified and takes on an independent existence, whereas the tongue only reflects the thought/words of the mind. So by calling attention to the tongue as the instrument of the mind, James is really condemning the individual person whose inner thoughts are being expressed through the words spoken by the tongue – a member that no one can tame/control. In this James reflects Psalm 34:13; 39:1; 62:5 – the tongue is used to bless God and to destroy human beings created in God's image (Mtt. 12:36, 37 on the dangers of speech).

3:13-18: False and true wisdom

...who is wise and understanding among you? by their good life let them show their works in the meekness of wisdom... The criteria for judging a *good life* is both works and speaking wisdom in meekness.

...if you have bitter jealousy and selfish ambition in your hearts... this wisdom is not as comes down from above...there will be disorder and every vile practice... There is a practical description of wisdom that emanates from vested interests and selfish motives.

...but the wisdom from above is first pure, then peaceable, gentle.... without uncertainty or insincerity... The characteristic features of true wisdom (see also Mtt. 5:7) are given and are seen as practical efforts towards establishing relationships and building up community life (ethics).

Comments

The passage brings out that just as faith has to be manifested in works, so also wisdom must be spoken in meekness – still giving advice to teachers. The passage brings out the ethical/behavioral implications of expressing faith through works and proper talk. This ethical dimension comes close to the teaching from the Sermon in the Mount – *you will know them by their fruits* (Mtt. 7:16), and Paul's teaching on the fruits of the Spirit – *love, joy, peace, patience, kindness, goodness, faithfulness, gentleness, self-control* (Gal.5:22). The stress is on true wisdom being properly expressed and measured by its contribution to community life and fostering relationships. See also Matthew 5:9 - *blessed are the peacemakers.*

4:1-17: Against friendship with the world

...what causes wars and what causes fightings among you? Is it not your passions...you desire and do not have, so you kill...you covet and cannot obtain, so you fight... An analysis of the unrest in the community, an analysis that would apply to the community in any city.

...you ask and do not receive, because you ask wrongly... The analysis for unrest continues, focussing on what the persons ask.

...friendship with the world is enmity with God... The author's ultimate statement of why there is unrest (see also Mtt. 6:24 – friendship with the world as enmity toward God).

...God opposes the proud but gives grace to the humble...submit yourselves therefore to God...resist the devil...draw near to God... The author's ultimate remedy for unrest; a reference to Proverbs 3:34. A common teaching and understanding was that God exalts the humble (Ps. 18:27; Mtt. 5:4; Lk. 1:52), and puts down the proud.

...do not speak evil against one another...who are you to judge your neighbour?... The author's exhortation to observe ethical norms in one's relationships.

...you do not know about tomorrow... This teaching comes close to the teaching of Jesus (Mtt. 6:25-34).

...whoever knows what is right to do and fails to do it, for them it is sin... Further ethical teachings that speaks against a pacifist attitude. There is a wide definition of sin: not just what is done, but also what is not done.

Comments

The emphasis on true wisdom at the end of chapter 3 leads into a condemnation of various envies and desires that separate people and make them unhappy. The reference to Proverbs 3:34 sums up the thought in James.

Judging fellow members of the community is condemned (4:11-12) as arrogance/slander and as taking the place of God who is the only judge (see also Mtt. 7:1-5 – against judging others).

5:1-20: Against oppression by the rich, exhortation to patience, and the power of prayer.

...come now you rich, weep and howl for the miseries that are coming upon you...   This is a re-iteration of woes against the rich whose wealth, and the usage of that wealth, was seen as the basic problem of oppression of the poor (cf. 1:9-11, 2:1-9). Here again there is an echo of the Beatitude on the poor in the teaching of Jesus (Mtt. 5:3ff.; Lk. 6:20, 18:18ff.). There is also an echo of the parable of the rich man and Lazarus (Lk. 16:19-31) and the parable of the rich fool (Lk. 12:16-21).

*...be patient until the coming of the Lord...the coming of the Lord is at hand...*The exhortation to patience indicating that the situation was a difficult one which also gave rise to eschatological thinking. The prophets are examples of suffering and patience (Mtt. 5:12); and the 'patience of Job' is quoted as an example to be emulated. The coming of the divine Judge is imminent (Mtt. 24:33).

...do not swear,,, let your yes be yes and your no be no... The exhortation not to swear echoes the teaching of Jesus (Mtt. 5:33-37), and reflects the

author's insistence on being of a stable mind – *a double-minded person is unstable in every way* (1:8).

...is anyone among you suffering? Let them pray... The passage (5:13-18) is an exhortation to offer prayer in all circumstances.

...is any among you sick? Let them call for the elders of the Church, and let them pray over them, anointing them with oil in the name of the Lord... An early practice in the church is being re-iterated. The use of 'elders' may reflect a pastoral office; also the use of 'church' is indicative of an identifiable body/structure.

...confess your sins to one another, and pray for one another, that you may be healed... This re-iterates the common belief that sickness/ illness was a result of sins. The combination occurs several times in the ministry of Jesus: e.g. Mark. 2:1-12. The effectiveness of prayer is illustrated in the example of Elijah praying for rain (I Kings 17 & 18).

...whoever brings back a sinner...will save their soul from death and cover a multitude of sins... The exhortation is to be concerned with, and implement, the evangelistic task.

Comments

This chapter opens with a very pro-poor and anti-rich section. There are warnings to the rich, the self-indulgent, the contentious, the proud, the deceitful – the rich *who have withheld the wages of the labourers by fraud... who have lived on earth in luxury and pleasure...* Their gold and silver will not save them from punishment by fire (see Mtt. 6:19 against laying up wealth where it can be destroyed). It shows how strongly wealth and riches were opposed in the new Christian community which emphasized giving up of all that stood in the way of God's mission (Mtt. 8:18-21; 10:1ff.; 16:24ff.; 19:23ff.).

The appeal to *be patient until the coming of the Lord* (5:7-11) is related to the understanding that the poor will get little justice in this word at the hands of the rich. The emphasis on the *coming of the Lord* – eschatological expectations – distinguishes

James as a Christian writing. This is a call to patient suffering/passive acceptance of suffering which was characteristic of early Christianity in the period of persecution.

The emphatic negative attitude towards oaths/swearing (5:12) is close to the teachings of Jesus in the Sermon in the Mount (Mtt. 5:33-37). It also brings out the teaching in Jesus and James that a person must have a stable mind in order to be found trustworthy.

James emphasizes prayer for the sick and *anointing with oil;* this was a liturgical act which was practiced in the early church (also practiced today) and regarded as a sacrament. Today it is often referred to as 'extreme unction', i.e. prayer and anointing before death. After the Protestant reformation, extreme unction was removed from the list of sacraments; however, prayer and anointing are still practiced by many.

The mention that the *presbyters/elders of the Church* were to perform the act of anointing indicates that the term presbyter does not refer to just a senior member of the community, but to a person specially assigned the duty – i.e. an ordained person. The tradition is that Peter and Paul did healings (Acts 3:6, 5:15, 14:8-10, 28:8; see also Mk. 6:13 where anointing and healing were part of the duties of the apostles), there was a special *charism* of the Spirit for healing (I Cor. 12:9, 28, 30); following this tradition, it became part of the presbyter's/elder's duty to anoint and pray for the sick. There have been many echoes of Jesus' teachings in James, so the anointing of the sick could also be thought of as a continuation of the mission entrusted to the disciples by Jesus.

The prayer for healing is coupled with the forgiveness of sins: this was the common belief that disease/illness was the result of sin, so confession of sin and forgiveness was part of the cure of the disease/illness (the example of Job where his friends asked him to repent in order to be relieved of his suffering. Jesus portrays Himself as a "physician" – Mtt. 9:112; Lk. 4:23. Profanation of the eucharist results in illness, weakness and death – I Cor. 11:29-30).

The closing verses in James (5:19-20) introduces a new topic – the pastoral and evangelistic concern/task of bringing back those who have *wandered from the truth* (a contrast from Hebrews which does not hold the possibility of a 'second repentance'). Here too, James, echoes the teaching of Jesus – every effort must be made to bring back the lost (see Lk. 15 for three parables dealing with bringing back and forgiving the lost). The person who makes the effort is also rewarded with forgiveness.

The letter/writing does not close with the customary epistolary ending of greetings and benediction, but the concern for the return and forgiveness of the lost is an appropriate pastoral ending for a writing that has been, in many ways, so stern and admonitive in nature.

*

A liberation theology perspective on the Epistle of James

In her commentary, *The Scandalous Message of James: Faith Without Works Is Dead*, Elsa Tamez uses Latin American liberation theology to bring out exegetical, hermeneutical and homiletical perspectives when dealing with the Epistle of James. Since her insights are an interesting contribution to the study of James, especially using the methodology of liberation theology of analysing/approaching the text from the contemporary socio-political context, a brief description of her perspectives are given below:

1. In referring to the difficulty to include the Epistle of James in the canon, Tamez suggests that the letter was "intercepted" because it would have been seen as subversive since it talks against the rich and the exploitation of the poor by landowners of that time and so kept out of the canon for a long period. James was a document that called into question some of the basic social practices of the time, probably even practices that were followed by Christians, especially Christians who did not find an expression of their faith in works and concern for the poor and those in need. The letter was addressed to a situation where there was suffering, exploitation

and oppression, so any writing that spoke against the accepted practices of the rich and gave a voice to the oppressed, would have been put down – intercepted – and not given recognition. Tamez also feels that the challenges raised by James have been "intercepted" throughout history when groups have questioned the inclusion of James in the canon, including Luther who during the Reformation called James *an epistle of straw.* Since the church is probably the largest and richest landowner today, Tamez suggests that the message of James may probably be interpreted today as a "Marxist-Leninist infiltration in the churches", and therefore, as in early Christianity, the concern for the poor and oppressed people and a call to action to exercise the 'option for the poor' as a means of expressing one's faith, would again be "intercepted" by those with vested interests, whether in the church or in larger socio-political groups.

2. Tamez suggests three hermeneutical perspectives which must be taken together to see the total message/impact of the Epistle of James.

The first is the ***angle of Oppression-Suffering.*** Tamez suggests that the first group with whom the author of the Epistle identifies himself/herself (1:2 – *my brothers*), is the oppressed-suffering people. The poor within the community, and in society in general, are oppressed and dragged before tribunals (2:6-7); the poor peasants are exploited by the rich farmers who accumulate wealth at the expense of the workers' salaries, there are rich merchants who have no concern for the poor (5:1-4); even widows and orphans are oppressed (1:27); there are those in the community who do not have clothes to wear and food to eat (2:15ff.); some are reduced to the status of visitors to the worship service and are not given proper seating (2:2ff.).

The second group are the rich, referred to three times (1:10-11; 2:6b, 7; 5:5-6) and each time in a negative manner, in the context of judgment and an unfavourable verdict, and as a description of their customary oppressive behaviour. For James, the great champion of the poor, this was scandalous oppression with poverty as the result: the rich dress elegantly (2:2), they drag the poor to courts to extract taxes from them

(2:6), they are anxious to accumulate and acquire even more wealth (4:13; 5:3), they live luxuriously (5:5), they condemn and kill the just person (5:6). It would seem that though the original community might have consisted of the lower and poorer strata of society, as the community expanded and probably as support for mission work was required, the resources of the rich were tapped and they were also admitted to the community. However, it would seem that James did not look in favour at this move, but faced with the development, James insists that the vocation of the church, i.e. its mission, is the poor who are *rich in faith and heirs of the Kingdom* (2:5).

The fact that the letter is addressed *to the twelve tribes in the Dispersion* (1:1) is itself the vocabulary of oppression-suffering in that it expresses a displacement from one's homeland and a situation of alienation/foreigners leading to marginalization and poverty.

Hence the first hermeneutical perspective is that of the **angle of the Oppressed-Suffering people.**

3. The second hermeneutical perspective is the **angle of hope**. In James, there are many signs of hope expressed as 'joy', 'rejoicing' because of the proclamation of the end of oppression, end of corruption, end of injustice. The poor and oppressed rejoice because of the promise of liberation and its anticipation. This call to rejoice begins with the greeting: rejoice (1:1 - χαιρειν), be happy, be joyful; from the beginning of the epistle, the author brings a word of happiness and joy/hope for those who suffer oppression. Joy is also a result of *praxis* (1:25-27) – doing something good that makes a difference to others and to oneself. This is referred to as *the royal law* (2:8ff.) and summed up as *you shall love your neighbour as yourself.* James gives the concrete examples of the suffering of the prophets, and the patience of Job, all of whom were declared happy (5:10-11); the oppressed and weak who follow their example are declared blessed.

In addition to χαιρειν the other Greek word used in James to express the same angle of joy, pleasure, happiness is 'blessed' (μακαριος), used three times (1:12; 1:25; 5:11). In 1:2-4, the author writes, ...*count it all joy...when you meet various trials...* referring to a variety of oppressions and persecutions that strengthen the spirit and brings an integrity to the person, and community, who is faithful. There is also the eschatological joy of knowing that at the end of time the oppressed will be favoured, so there is rejoicing in anticipation of the new social order that is coming soon (1:9-12; 5:1-6, 8-9). There is also the encouragement of, and hope for the poor, to know that God is in solidarity with them – the God who heard the cry of slaves and liberated them from Egypt is the same God even in the present because in God *there is no variation or shadow due to change* (1:17), so it is that *has not God chosen those who are poor in the world to be rich in faith and heirs of the Kingdom which God has promised to those who love God?* (2:5). Finally, in the hope perspective, there is judgment against the rich and the imminent coming of the Lord (5:1-6). The tone of the passage is prophetic – there will be justice – but the thought and style are apocalyptic – final judgment – an act of God that will put an end to the present time and inaugurate a new world order; James simultaneously denounces injustice and announces its end. James re-enforces the thought of imminence with *the coming of the Lord is at hand...behold the Judge is standing at the doors* (5:8-9). The reassurance of this judgment means hope for the end of oppression and the crying of the poor – the proclamation of the last judgment is a proclamation of justice for the poor and oppressed.

Hence the second hermeneutical perspective is that of the **angle of hope.**

4. The third hermeneutical perspective is the **angle of Praxis.**[5] In a situation of oppression and exploitation, only identifying the oppressed, the oppressors, and proclaiming hope is not sufficient; *praxis* is needed, i.e. believers are to do something with regard to addressing the situation and bringing about changes. James is

particularly concerned about Christian communities being signs of God's reign/kingdom where the poor are taken care of and injustice righted. James posits three challenges that call for *praxis* undergirded by unconditional and sincere love among members of the communities, and even extending beyond the communities into wider society.

A. The first challenge is **patience**: at the core of *praxis* is patience because it is a difficult attribute in the face of persecution. Patience is too often viewed as being passive and submissive because nothing else can be done. But such an interpretation smacks of fatalism, and James was not calling for this type of patience. He was calling the communities to a "militant patience", i.e. a patience that is very active and heroic and watches for the opportune (*kairos*, καιρος) moment, like the military in battle waits patiently to strike a telling blow. In fact the Greek words (μακροθυμια – patient perservance/ persistence, 5:7, 8, 10-11; ὑπομονη – patient steadfastness, 1:3-4, 12; 5:11) used for patience in James are strictly military terms used for being on alert. Thus James calls communities to have a militant patience – to be on alert for opportune moments rather than a negative submission to forces of oppression.

B. The second challenge is **integrity**: In James, the core of *praxis* is a personal and communal integrity: consistency in hearing, seeing, believing, speaking, and doing. At a time when the church was called upon to be a sign of God's reign/kingdom, it had to be a model different from that of the world. Therefore James exhorts the communities that they should be persons of integrity, sincere, transparent, consistent in everything they do; they should be sure of themselves, resolute, decisive (1:5-8; 5:12). They are not to show favouritism toward the rich, not to seek the important places in the church (2:1ff.), they are not to be envious, jealous, argumentative (3:1ff.), and not to be hypocrites speaking badly of one another (4:11ff.). From the beginning of the letter, James focuses on integrity (1:2-4) holding that integrity comes from having gone through a painful experience. The painful experience or *various trials* brings about an experience of wholeness and integrity within oneself and in the community. God is the ultimate model of integrity and everyone must strive to follow God's values that leads to integrity (1:5ff.); all should act as God acts (1:17). Faith and practice must go together in order to be an integral and whole person (1:2-4, 8; 2:9-20; 4:8): a person *is justified by works and not by faith alone...faith apart from works is dead* (2:24-26). Here *works* is understood as those liberating actions that effect justice – the social works that the prophets demanded of the people and the demands made by the Law given at Sinai – James brought out the unity between faith and works as part of the necessary consistency in believing, hearing, saying, and doing, so a concrete example is given linking faith with the practice of justice (2:14-17). Wisdom is also linked to integrity: anyone lacking wisdom should ask God (1:5); those who have wisdom will show it by their deeds (3:13-15) so that *the wisdom from above is first pure, then peaceable, gentle, open to reason, full of mercy and good fruits, without uncertainty or insincerity* (3:17).

C. The third challenge is **effective prayer**: Prayer is seen as a fundamental practice in the life of an individual and in the life of the community; prayer is mentioned several times in the letter for it is only through prayer that the Christian identity of the oppressed people becomes visible. However, there are inappropriate prayers and ways of praying (1:6 – pray but without doubt; 4:3 – you do not receive because you ask wrongly); but the cries of the oppressed are the prayers that God hears and answers (5:1-6); James concludes the letter with a call to earnest and fervent prayer in all situations of suffering and joy (5:13-18). There is concern in the letter also that the right to pray is not held/given only to *the elders; everyone should pray for each other* (5:16) – a practice of self-introspection and communal purification – a practice that requires the highest degree of integrity. Prayer will be a comfort when suffering oppression and will give hope for the future that injustice will not always prevail.

Hence the third hermeneutical perspective is that of the **angle of *praxis*** involving patience, integrity, and prayer.

The above briefly outlines one approach from the perspective of liberation theology to the Epistle of James, especially the perspectives brought to bear on the text by Elsa Tamez in her commentary, *The Scandalous Message of James.*

*

Conclusion

At the end of this brief study of the Epistle of James, it has been seen that 'the epistle of straw' posed a challenge, and continues to pose a challenge, to Christian communities: the challenge to follow the values taught by Jesus and urged by James – integrity of word and deed, to work for justice, confront acts of oppression, care for the needy, and to be honest/fervent in prayer. This ancient letter written by a person concerned with the poor and oppressed people of that time challenges Christians today to examine their own stand and perspectives on wealth, poverty, justice, integrity of relationships, and a call to *praxis*. James clearly brings out that poverty is the result of acts of oppression and injustice. This is a message that was not looked on favourably in the early centuries, and it remains a message that should make Christians uncomfortable in situations of oppression, greed, economic, class and caste distinctions, and injustice. The forces in the early church that saw in the epistle the challenges that it poses were stronger than those who would keep the epistle out of the canon, and so, even though late, James found a place in the canon of the New Testament. The message of James must challenge Christians to *praxis*: seeking to be *perfect and complete, lacking in nothing* (1:4), *resisting the devil…and drawing near to God* (4:8); being *doers of the word, and not hearers only* (1:22); seeking to exercise pastoral care among members of the community in care for the poor (2:1ff.), in prayer for one another (5:13-18), and in supporting one another in crisis (1:19-21; 5:19-20). James, *a servant of Jesus Christ*, was concerned about the oppressed Christian communities of his time; today, his message must be re-visited and revived in the light of socio-economic-political-religious contexts.

***

Select Bibliography for Section II

Adamson, J. B. *James: The Man and His Message*. Grand Rapids: Eerdmans, 1989.

Brown, R. E. *An Introduction to the New Testament*. Bangalore: Theological Publications in India, 2000.

Davids, Peter H. *The Epistle of James: A Commentary on the Greek Text*. New International Greek Testament Commentary. Grand Rapids: Eerdmans, 1982.

James, Arthur. "James" in Brian C. Wintle (General Editor), *South Asia Biblical Commentary*. Udaipur, Rajasthan: Open Door Publications, 2015, pages 1732-1738.

Kee, H. C. And F. W. Young. *The Living World of the New Testament*. London: Darton, Longman & Todd, 1966.

Kummel, W. G. *Introduction to the New Testament* (Revised Edition), translated by Howard C. Kee. London: SCM Press, 1975.

Moo, Douglas J. *James*, Tyndale New Testament Commentary. Downers Grove: Inter Varsity Press, 2007.

McKnight, Scott. *The Letter of James*. The New International Commentary on the New Testament. Grand Rapids: Eerdmans, 2011.

Mitton, C. L. *The Epistle of James*. Grand Rapids: Eerdmans, 1966.

Nystrom, David P. *James*. New International Version Application Commentary. Grand Rapids: Zondervan, 1997.

Tabor, James D. *The Jesus Dynasty: A New Historical Investigation of Jesus, His Royal Family, and the Birth of Christianity*. New York: Simon & Schuster, 2006.

Tamez, Elsa. *The Scandalous Message of James: Faith without Works is Dead*. New York: Crossroad Publishing Company, Special Revised Edition, 2002.

SECTION III

The First Epistle of Peter

Chapter I

Introduction to I Peter

Background and purpose, Authorship, Date.

Background and purpose

The First Epistle of Peter was addressed to the *exiles of the Dispersion in Pontus, Galatia, Cappadocia, Asia, and Bithynia* (1:1. Present day Turkey) who were threatened by persecution. The first part of the letter – 1:3-4:11 – has to do with matters of Christian conduct in the light of having taken baptism; the second part deals with an appeal to stand firm in the face of *the fiery ordeal which comes upon you* (4:12). This clearly refers to the threat of persecution in the area of Asia Minor, but the author does not attack Rome as such like the author of Revelation, although the author does refer to Rome as "Babylon" (5:13) and *your adversary the devil prowls around like a roaring lion, seeking someone to devour* (5:8) – both certainly alluding to Rome; yet the author also calls upon Christians to recognize the emperor and government officials (2:13-17), probably reflecting different contexts for each part of the letter. The second part of the writing sees the period of suffering as a time of judgment for the church (4:17) during which the faith of Christians will be tested. The author expects the end to come in a little while (5:10), but does not see the conflict with Rome as the end-time perhaps because the author is described as *an elder* (5:1) and so feels the pastoral responsibility of advising fellow Christians to keep the peace and to avoid unnecessary conflict with Rome.

In the overall picture, I Peter is a moderate writing as compared to Revelation giving rise to the speculation that I Peter was written to Christians in Asia Minor to correct the disturbing effects that Revelation had produced in the area. This move of a more moderate attitude towards Rome reflects the period of the late first/early second century when the church was trying to work out a way of co-existence with the empire.

It is not clear as to whether Christians were being addressed in the cities mentioned or the geographical areas or the Roman provinces; the general consensus is that the writing is addressed to Christians (both Jewish and Gentile Christians) in the area of Asia Minor – Christians were being addressed as members of the true people of God who live scattered throughout the empire as strangers since their home is in heaven (1:1, 17; 2:11). In this sense, the writing is relevant for all Christians in all ages.

The purpose of the writing is presented as a message of comfort and admonition in the face of persecution, hate, suffering slander; Christians are to *stand firm in the true grace of God* (5:12). Further, Christians are to hold fast to the Christian faith by proper behaviour and not allow themselves to wander into error (4:1-11). Suffering is to be regarded as the divine testing before the appearance of Christ (1:6; 4:12ff.).

The concept of the *people of God* (2:9-10) is yet a further purpose in the writing: the concept serves to link Christians to the history of Israel where the Israelites were known as the *people of God and a holy nation* (Ex. 19:5-6; Deut. 7:6, 14:2, 21; 26:19; Hos. 2:23). Modern scholarship (Elliot, *A Home for the Homeless*) has made a strong case for showing that one of the purposes of I Peter would have been to provide a sense of belonging since they felt that were *aliens and exiles* and probably had little to do with the local inhabitants and so felt a sense of separation (2:11-12) so they were encouraged to maintain good relations with *the Gentiles*. I Peter, therefore, would have reassured them of being within the wider fellowship of Christians and provided them with an identity in continuation with the history of Israel.

In the light of the above purposes, scholars have concluded that those addressed are not the same throughout the letter, for instance, suffering is described as a possibility in 1:6, 2:20, 3:14,17, whereas suffering is described as a present reality in 4:12,14,19, 5:6,8. Also 1:3 – 4:11 does not display the character of a letter with a concluding doxology in 4:11, while Christians are addressed in a concrete situation of suffering from 4:12 onwards; further in 1:3 – 4:11 there are clear indications that those being addressed are newly baptized Christians. These have contributed to a variety of conclusions: 1. that 1:3 – 4:11 is to be regarded as a baptismal homily which was later placed in the framework of a letter by adding the superscription of 1:1-2 and the doxology at 4:11;   2. that the letter is a single writing into which a baptismal sermon was included; 3. that two baptismal homilies (one before baptism and one after) have been combined with the addition of letter formats at 1:1-2 and 5:12-14; 4. that the first part of the letter (1:3 – 4:11) is to those who are yet to be persecuted, and the second part (4:12 – 5:11) is to the persecuted. In the tradition of the early church, I Peter was used in the liturgy of baptismal services at Passover time, i.e. in the period just before Easter when converts were baptized; thus it was referred to as a "Passover encyclical" although the images and terminology of Passover are not directly mentioned.

Taking all of the above into consideration, the background and purpose of I Peter, addressed to Christians all over the empire and especially to those in Asia Minor, seems to consist of two parts: **1. that of a hortatory writing formed from traditional baptismal exhortations, ethical requirements and expectations** (1:3 – 4:10 ending with a doxology in verse 11) **including the possibility of persecution; and 2. that of a hortatory writing to a situation of persecution as an apologetic for suffering and for finding the strength to endure suffering** (4:12 – 5:11). **To these two parts were added an epistolary opening formula** (1:1-2) **and an epistolary conclusion** (5:12-14) **thus giving the composite writing an epistolary framework.**

Authorship

The writer describes himself as *Peter, an apostle of Jesus Christ* (1:1) in the first section of the writing, and in the second section as *fellow elder and witness of the sufferings of Christ…* (5:1); he is associated with *Silvanus and my son Mark* and is writing from *Babylon* (Rome) (5:12-13). The prescript points to Peter, one of the disciples of Jesus (Mk. 3:16-19 and par.), and the reference to being a witness of the sufferings of Christ is an attempt at authenticating the apostolic origin of the writing. According to tradition, Peter was well qualified to talk to *exiles in the Dispersion* (1:1), if the expression referred to Gentile Christians as he was one of the first to preach to the Gentiles (Acts 2-5, 10, 15). However, the expression is better understood as referring to Jewish and Gentile Christians, i.e. all Christians, living outside Palestine.

The reference to *Silvanus* (5:12) is probably a reference to the same person associated with the Pauline mission (Acts 15:22-32; 15:40-18:5; I Thess. 1:1; II Thess. 1:1; II Cor. 1:19), and the reference to Mark (5:13) is probably a reference to the person from Jerusalem (Acts 12:12) who appears elsewhere as a fellow-worker with Paul and/or Barnabas (Acts 13:5, 13; 15:37, 39; Col. 4:10; Phlm. 24), but never in connection with Peter. So the mention of these names does not necessarily point to Peter, the disciple, as being the author. The only supporting point is that in the tradition of the church, Paul and his fellow-workers ended up in Rome, where Peter was already present; so **the mention of *Babylon* (a symbol used for Rome in other New Testament writings) as the place of origin may be accepted.**

The following points speak against the authorship of Peter:

The language of I Peter is cultivated/educated Greek which would not be possible from a Galilean fisherman;

I Peter presupposes Pauline theology – the death of Jesus has atoned for the sins of all (1:18ff., 2:24); Christians are to suffer with Christ (4:13; 5:1), obedience to the civil authorities (2:14ff.); the Pauline formula of ἐν Χριστῷ – in Christ is used (3:16; 5:10, 14). However, presupposing Pauline theology would be questionable where Peter is concerned as he was not certain of agreeing with the Pauline position of freedom from the Law (Gal. 2:11);

There is an early tradition that Silvanus was entrusted by Peter with the task of writing the letter, and since Silvanus was closely associated with the Pauline mission, it would account for presupposition of Pauline theology found in I Peter;

I Peter contains no evidence at all of familiarity with the earthly Jesus which would have been expected given the closeness of Peter to Jesus as reflected in the Gospels, especially the suffering that came from denial of Jesus (Mk. 14:66-72 and par.);

The situation of persecution referred to in I Peter, especially in the places mentioned in the prescript, can be understood only as taking place towards the end of the 1st century under Domitian (same as for the Book of Revelation) especially if I Peter is seen as moderating the strong attack on the empire in the Book of Revelation.

The two sections of the book speak against a single author and lean more towards a composite document put together/compiled in Rome using the name of Peter, perhaps by Silvanus or a group who regarded themselves as heirs of Peter's legacy.

The Epistle of I Peter can therefore be placed among the composite pseudonymous writings of the New Testament.

Place and date of writing

If by *Babylon* (5:13) is meant Rome, then I Peter could well have originated in Rome, the traditional place for the last days and death of Peter. This would attempt to add authenticity to the use of the name Peter. However, it was not until the end of the 2nd century that I Peter began to appear in the list of writings considered to be apostolic and thus accepted as canonical in the Eastern churches whereas it is missing from the Muratorian canon (reflecting the Western church position at the end of the 2nd century. See Vol. I of this series for history of the canon.). This late acceptance into the canon would indicate that there was no early tradition associating this writing with Peter, the disciple of Jesus.

The reign of Domitian (A.D. 81-96) could probably be taken as the time of writing which would account for the references to persecution. The most probable date would be A. D. 85-95 which would provide sufficient time for the writing to become known in the Eastern churches before the close of the 1st century.

Chapter II

Ethical Behaviour, Persecution and Suffering as Marks of a True Christian

Analysis and commentary on the text of I Peter.

As discussed above, I Peter is probably a composite writing, combining at least two documents (1:3-4:11 and 4:12-5:11) brought together in a letter format with much paraenetic material, and as such, a formal outline is difficult. The section-wise break-up offered below is for the purposes of study only and can in no way be understood as the formal outline of the writing.

1:1-3 : Prescript

Peter, an apostle of Jesus Christ (Πετρος ἀποστολος ᾿Ιησου Χριστου)... The name Peter is used without any introduction indicating that the person being named is well-known and needs no introduction (see introductory issues for discussion on Peter as author). 'Apostle' was a title for an office used for the twelve disciples and used by Paul to describe his missionary mandate. The use of the title may indicate the period of early Catholicism (see also Vols. II & III of this series) when the title began to be officially used.

...to the exiles of the Dispersion... The *diaspora* (διασπορα) was the name used for lands outside of Palestine: literally a 'scattering of the seed', it referred to Jews who had shifted their residences to areas/cities outside Palestine. The areas/provinces/cities mentioned cover the geographical area of Asia Minor or modern day Turkey.

...chosen and destined by God...for obedience to Jesus Christ and for sprinkling with His blood... the language of 'election' which was used to understand the relation of the Jews to Yahweh is here used for Christians.

Comments

The opening formula is the same type that is used in other New Testament writings. The writer does not qualify his name other than 'apostle' which suggests that the witness borne in the letter (cf. 5:1) is not so much an eyewitness memory of Jesus' ministry and sufferings, but a testimony of one who has served as a great apostle and is now looked on as a 'pillar' of the church (cf. Gal. 2:9).

The address is *to the exiles of the Dispersion* – a term used in Hebrew scriptures for Jews living outside of Palestine, but here used for Christians indicating the move in early Catholicism to interpret Hebrew scriptures in terms of Christ and Christianity. The use of 'exiles' is indicative that they thought of themselves as being away from their homeland; perhaps even descriptive of being away from their heavenly home. The new 'chosen people' include both Jews and Gentiles thus making 'Dispersion' a very wide and inclusive term.

The cities/provinces mentioned outline the route that would have been followed by the messenger of the letter: from the port of *Pontus* southward through *Galatia*, and then eastward into *Cappadocia*, then westward to the province of *Asia* and finally northward to *Bithynia*. The journey describes a crescent-shaped route.

A noteworthy feature of the opening formula is the mention of the triadic pattern: *God the Father...the Spirit...Jesus Christ.* This would indicate a theological development that is known from the later part of the 1st century.

1:3 – 12 : Salvation and the possibility of suffering

...by God's great mercy we have been born anew to a living hope...and to an inheritance which is imperishable, undefiled, and unfading kept in heaven... An affirmation of the dignity of Christians. The reference to *born anew* (also in 1:23) perhaps indicates a baptismal context.

...in this you rejoice, though now for a little while you may have to suffer various trials... While there is a rejoicing in hope, the warning is sounded that baptism – the beginning of Christian life – brings with it the possibility of suffering.

...as the outcome of your faith you obtain the salvation of your souls... An exhortation given in a baptismal context that salvation is the final outcome of faith.

...the prophets... searched and enquired about this salvation... it was revealed to them that they were serving not themselves, but you... The author sees God's salvific plan starting with Israel's prophets and being fulfilled in Christ with Christians as the beneficiaries.

Comments

The description of salvation and the description of the people are strongly reminiscent of the language used for Israel during the exodus event. The understanding of the exodus event was through complex symbols: freedom, yet resulting in suffering; passing through water understood in terms of baptism. The author of I Peter uses these symbols to depict the Christian understanding of the new life in Christ and the suffering that inevitably follows faith. There is a strong affirmation that Christians are now the inheritors of God's plan of salvation and that this salvation is finally consummated in heaven.

Along with the affirmation of God's plan of salvation, there is also an indication of the possibility of suffering that will result when faith and hope are expressed through baptism (1:3, 23 – *you have been born anew...*). This opening section dealing with faith, and rebirth, becomes the basis for later ethical action. This first section of I Peter refers to the possibility of suffering; in the second section, suffering is actually taking place.

The 'new life' is characterized by *a living hope,* i.e. the sure affirmation that people will inherit salvation, but along the way, they will face suffering when they exercise ethical decisions especially in their faithfulness to God.

1:13 – 2:12 : Holy living

...gird up your minds...do not be conformed to the passions of your former ignorance...be holy in all your conduct... This is the call to holy living – i.e. to change one's ways from what was being followed, to a newness of thinking and acting that comes with baptism.

...you were ransomed from your futile ways...with the precious blood of Christ, like that of a lamb without blemish or spot... The death of Christ viewed as a sacrifice with echoes of the Passover lamb and Day of Atonement.

...He was destined before the foundation of the world... through Him you have confidence in God...your faith and hope are in God... The author makes a reference to the pre-existence of Christ and an affirmation that salvation had always been God's plan for creation.

...having purified your souls... love one another earnestly.... you have been born anew, not of perishable but of imperishable... This is perhaps a reference to baptism seen as a rite of purification. Its effect is to be demonstrated in acts of love.

...put away all malice and all guile and insincerity and envy and all slander... The author cites some of the qualities that no longer have a place in the life of a person after baptism and that no longer have a place in community relations.

...come to Him, to that living stone... Christ is being compared to the building material that ensures the quality and value of the building. The comparison is supported by quotations from Isaiah 28:16, Psalm 118:22, and Isaiah 8:14-15.

...you are a chosen race, a royal priesthood, a holy nation, God's own people...(ὑμεῖς δε γενος ἐκλεκτού, βασιλειον ἱερατευμα, ἐθνος ἅγιον, λαος εἰς περιποιησιν)... The titles by which Israel was known is now used for Christians; this shift reflects the movement in Early Catholicism (i.e. after about A.D. 70) when descriptions of Israel were appropriated by Christians to describe themselves.

...once you were no people but now you are God's people... The author quotes Hosea 1:10, 2:23 which describes Yahweh's relation to Israel.

...I beseech you as aliens and exiles to abstain from the passions of the flesh...maintain good conduct among the Gentiles... The author reflects the strong feeling that Christians are exiles in the dispersion. The *passions of the flesh* would refer to the pre-baptismal condition. There is an exhortation to maintain ethical relations with all people.

Comments

The Christian's concern with faith has also to find expression in deeds of love – ethical/holy living. This means that Christians, can no longer follow their *passions* as they did before baptism: they have been called out of their *ignorance* with a call to be holy just as God is holy. God's holiness is expressed in love, mercy and judgment. Holiness has to be expressed in sincere deeds of love (1:22-25); in the 18th century, in the reformation under Wesley, 'social holiness' was stressed.

The author's progression of thought can be traced: 1:3-12 – new life grounded in faith; 1:13-21 – faith demands holiness; 1:22-25 – the new life and faith give rise to a community bound together in sincere/earnest love for one another. The law of love determines the life of the community – love that is concerned about the welfare of others so what harms others must be put aside (2:1).

The concept of a community – *the people of God* – was rooted in Jewish tradition: Israel as the people chosen by God to bear witness to God through word and through obedience to the Law. Now the titles/names given to Israel are applied to Christians: *you are a chosen race, a royal priesthood, a holy nation, God's own people...* The acceptance of the community as God's people gives dignity, identity and honour to the members.

As a chosen race, the church is in exile (2:11), nevertheless the church is to live in the world and therefore must have its ethical norms to govern relationships: the church is to *maintain good conduct among the Gentiles (those who are not Christians), so that in case they speak against you as wrongdoers, they may see your good deeds and glorify God...* (2:11-12). Christians are to conduct themselves in such a way that their lives become witnesses to God; this is what defines Christian ethics.

I Peter reflects the ethical teachings of the church: 2:1 – 4:11 is a series of these teachings which seem to be exhortations to those who have been newly baptized (1:3; 3:21) – what is now expected of them in their new life including the possibility of suffering for their faith.

The emphasis on ethical behavior/relations as a result of new life and baptism (1:3, 11; 3:21) have led scholars to view the first part of I Peter as a baptismal homily (see introduction, above) and/or reflecting a baptismal liturgy used especially in areas where there was the threat of persecution. The references to the exodus event and Passover imagery suggest that this could be part of the Easter Vigil (Saturday night) when candidates were prepared for baptism which would take place early on Easter Sunday.

2:13 – 17 : Obedience to authorities

...be subject for the Lord's sake to every human institution...emperor, governors... The exhortation is to be obedient to civil authorities so that *by doing right you should put to silence the ignorance of foolish people.*

...live as free people, yet without using your freedom as a pretext for evil...live as servants of God... the author couples freedom with socio-ethical responsibility.

...honour all people. Love those in the community. Fear God. Honour the emperor. The author combines love and ethical behaviour as marks of good citizenship.

Comments

The author has dealt with faith and the new life that follows faith as the basis of ethical action, the exhortation now turns to the community as the place in which the new life is nurtured; a series of exhortations follows dealing with various relationships such as government, slavery, marriage, family. This code of conduct probably reflects pre-Christian codes that were well known and used elsewhere in the New Testament (see Vol. II in this series for the use of *haustafeln* – household codes – in Ephesians – 5:21-6:9 – and Colossians – 3:18-4:1). There is no call to change the existing order, even if it is unjust, but only to call Christians to ethical behavior that exemplifies the patience and self-giving of Christ.

This section (2:13-17) deals especially with Christians in relation to the authorities/government and the call to obey those in authority. There does not seem to be a situation of persecution/suffering as in the call to obey the authorities there does not seem to be antagonism between Christians and the State. Obedience to the government/authorities was seen as *God's will* (2:15) and therefore Christians were exhorted to live in harmony with all.

There seems to be a passive accommodation to authorities rather than any aggressive/violent behavior. In this sense, I Peter is moderate in its response to situations of persecution/suffering as compared to Revelation which talks of destruction. Christians are urged to *honour the emperor* whereas only God *is to be feared* (2:17).

2:18 – 3:12 : Responsibilities within the household and in society

Servants, be submissive to your masters with all respect... The second area of ethical behaviour deals with the relationship between servants/slaves and masters. Servants/slaves should be respectful of their masters *not only to the kind and gentle but also to the overbearing.*

...if when you do right and suffer for it...you have God's approval... Christ also suffered for you, leaving you an example... The exhortation is to servants/slaves to bear their sufferings patiently because Christ also suffered.

...when He was reviled, He did not revile in return; when He suffered He did not threaten...He bore our sins in His body...by His wounds you have been healed... The reference to the Suffering Servant passage (Is.

52:13 – 53:12) shows how Hebrew scriptures was re-interpreted in terms of Christ.

...you were straying like sheep, but have now returned to the Shepherd and Guardian of your souls (ἐπεστραφητε νυν ἐπι τον ποιμενα και ἐπισκοπον των ψυχων). This portrays the image of Christ as the Good Shepherd (Jn. 10) – a popular pastoral image. Interestingly the word *episcopos* (bishop) is translated 'guardian'.

...wives, be submissive to your husbands...so that some may be won... by the behaviour of their wives... The behaviour of the wife, and the relationship maintained by her is seen as a means of evangelism.

...let not yours be the outward adorning with braiding of hair, decoration of gold... Women were exhorted to refrain from outward ostentation and to concentrate on *the hidden person of the heart with the imperishable jewel of a gentle and quiet spirit which in God's sight is very precious.*

...as Sarah obeyed Abraham... The example of Abraham and Sarah is given as a model to be followed.

...likewise you husbands, live considerately with your wives, bestowing honour on the woman...since you are joint heirs of the grace of life... An exhortation to the husbands indicating that the husband-wife relationship was thought of as a two-way process so that they become *joint heirs.*

...have unity of spirit, sympathy, love for one another, a tender heart and a humble mind... A final exhortation in the household code – values which characterize a Christian.

Comments

The first section of the passage (2:18-25) shows how closely the portrait of the Suffering Servant (Is. 52:13 – 53:12) had been taken over and integrated into the Christian understanding of Christ's suffering. This reflects the apologetic for suffering developed especially when persecution became widespread, after A.D. 80 in the reign of the Emperor Domitian.

The exhortation to the slaves ends on a pastoral note that Christ is their Shepherd and Guardian. This is a pastoral image taken over from John's Gospel (ch. 10) and the commission to Peter to *feed my sheep* (ch. 21). It is interesting that the master's responsibility to the slave is not given as in other household codes. However, as in the letter to Philemon, no clear statement is made with regard to the abolition of slavery, rather Christians seem to have conformed to the convention of the day, a position that many centuries later was used as justification for slavery. It should be noted that slavery is not being defended as a divine institution; the concern here is to bear witness to God within the social structures of the day.

The passage on responsibilities within the household and community ends with a call to exhibit Christian values in all relationships and quoting Ps. 34:13-17 as the promise of a blessing from God. Perhaps the passage is again reflecting baptismal liturgy where these values were emphasized as being required of a Christian. The point is that the pattern/model of conduct is Christ himself – *when He was reviled, he did not revile in return....*

The ideal wife is pictured as being submissive to her husband and avoiding ostentatious ornaments and clothing. The context, and model, of the time was the conduct of wives of those in authority: their life-style, their jewelry and their clothing. Therefore, the exhortation was not to be a 'second class citizen', or being submissive as a sign of inferiority, but there is a theological motive – to be a means of evangelization, being instrumental in winning over a husband who is not a Christian. Thus the author moves from understanding the role of a wife in the social context to a theological interpretation of her role as an evangelist. The Christian was thus called upon to bring a new understanding and to transform relationships.

In a similar vein, there is a proper code of conduct in the instructions to the husbands – he is to *live considerately* with his wife and to honour her *as a joint heir*, i.e. they are equal partners in the household and so they transform a husband-wife relationship into a Christian and theological model of equality before God.

The context of I Peter is a situation that has the potential for conflict so the section on ethical behavior in the new life ends with a plea for love and humility. The pattern for love and humility is to be found in the example of Christ who humbled himself and suffered.

3:13 – 4:6 : Preparedness for suffering

...who is there to harm you if you are zealous for what is right?...even if you do suffer you will be blessed... A beatitude is given for those who may suffer wrongly reflecting the Sermon on the Mount, *blessed are you when people revile you and persecute you and utter all kinds of evil against you falsely on my account...* (Mtt. 5:11).

...always be prepared to make a defence to any one who calls you to account for the hope that is in you...do it with gentleness and reverence; and keep your conscience clear, so that, when you are abused, those who revile your good behaviour in Christ may be put to shame... This is an exhortation to defend the faith – *the hope that is in you* – but it should be done with respect.

...Christ died...the righteous for the unrighteous... The reference to Christ is given as an example of innocent suffering.

...He went and preached to the spirits in prison... This reflects the traditional belief that after death, Christ preached to those in hell to give them a chance to repent. This is reflected in the Apostles' Creed: *He was crucified, died, and was buried; He descended to the dead...*

...in the days of Noah...eight persons were saved through water. Baptism which corresponds to this... The reference is to those who would not repent which led to the destruction of the world through flood (Gen. 6-8). The saving of Noah and his family from the flood waters is likened to the act of baptism strengthening the understanding that the writing/homily was part of a baptismal liturgy.

...since Christ suffered in the flesh, arm yourselves with the same thought... The apologetic for Christ's sufferings as a model for the suffering of Christians.

...doing what the Gentiles like to do... The list of behavioural patterns refers to *the time that is past,* i.e. before baptism. The word *Gentiles,* as in other places in I Peter refers to those who are not Christians, or to those who have not yet accepted baptism.

Comments

The section continues to talk about defending the faith in true humility i.e. bearing witness not in arrogance, but in gentleness and reverence (3:13-15). The type of evangelism being advocated here is not an aggressive proclamation of the Gospel, but a quiet witness that puts people to shame.

The warning is also given that humility could lead to undeserved suffering. Probably the reference is to a time when Christians were brought before magistrates for questioning and also beaten but their good behaviour put the accusers to shame. However, this innocent suffering is to be seen in the example of Christ's sufferings who himself stood before the Roman procurator for questioning and then suffered the cross.

Christians were exhorted to put aside the pattern of the old life – *licentiousness, passions, drunkenness, revels, carousing, and lawless idolatry...wild profligacy* (4:1-6). These describe the behavior of those involved in the rites of the mystery cults and so uncompromisingly rejected by the church.

The reference to the flood in the time of Noah and the saving of his family was interpreted as a symbol of baptism – they were washed from the evil that had resulted in the destruction of the world; similarly Christians are cleansed by the waters of baptism (3:20-21). This further strengthens the case for the first half of I Peter having a baptismal background.

This section contains two texts which are important for the belief that Christ descended to the dead to preach there: 3:18-20 and 4:6. There are references to Christ's descent to hell in other passages in the New Testament, though not absolutely clear, e.g. Romans 10:7; Ephesians 4:8-9; Philippians. 2:10; Colossians 2:15; there are several 2nd century texts which also emphasize this belief; finally the belief finds its way into a clause in the Apostles' Creed: *He descended to the dead.* I Peter is the clearest expression of this belief – that Christ's death also had an effect on those who had died earlier, that it was for salvific purposes to give those who had died earlier the opportunity to hear the Gospel and repent.

4:7 – 11 : General exhortation and doxology

...the end of all things is at hand... The eschatological dimension is introduced.

...hold unfailing your love for one another, since love covers a multitude of sins... The ethical exhortation to uphold members of the community in love – a love that is willing to forgive.

...practice hospitality ungrudgingly...employ your gift for one another... whoever speaks, as one who utters oracles of God...whoever renders service, as one who renders it by the strength which God supplies; in order that in everything God may be glorified through Jesus Christ... The final general exhortations to ethical behaviour are given and the norms for ordering of the Christian life.

...to Him belong glory and dominion... The doxology which brings to an end the first part of the writing or the section that is set in a baptismal context with advice on ethical behaviour after baptism.

Comments

I Peter does not show an overemphasis on eschatology and end-times, however, the concern is not totally forgotten. Ethical behavior and right relationships are important in the light of the nearness of the end (4:7) because this will be the basis of judgment (2:12; 4:5-6).

There are final exhortations to right conduct with love as the main controlling motif – with love as the basis, there will be *gifts used for others, ungrudging hospitality, rendering of service, and glorifying God* (4:8-11). Love that is unselfishly shared leads to forgiveness and building up of the community. In a hostile world, it would be love that would bind the community together and strengthen the resolve to support one another and to bear witness.

All of the above ethical exhortations become understandable and meaningful in the context of a baptismal homily/liturgy where the new converts are instructed in the *new life* and the values that must characterize it.

4:12 – 19 : Exhortation when suffering begins

...do not be surprised at the fiery ordeal which comes upon you to prove you... The exhortation to endure suffering sets the tone for this section of the writing.

...rejoice in so far as you share Christ's sufferings... The exhortation is given to endure suffering because it means a sharing in Christ's suffering. In this way, suffering was justified and beatitude pronounced – *if you are reproached for the name of Christ, you are blessed....*

...let none of you suffer as a murderer...thief...wrongdoer...mischief-maker... The author makes it clear that only innocent suffering is a sharing in Christ's sufferings, otherwise it becomes a license for wrong conduct.

...time has come for judgement to begin with the household of God... The warning that judgment begins within the community – a reflection of the Sermon on the Mount (Mtt. 7:1-5) on self judgment first before judging others.

Comments

In the final section of I Peter (4:12 – 5:11) the author adds a letter dealing with the crisis in which the readers find themselves – *do not be surprised at the fiery ordeal which comes upon you…* (4:12). This section is set very much in the context of a specific situation of suffering/persecution which was a present reality rather than generalizing a situation that was still to come as in the first section of the writing.

The exhortation is that even in suffering Christians should rejoice since they suffer for Christ and share in Christ's sufferings (4:12-19); further, Christians throughout the world suffer with them (5:9) and God will provide the strength to endure (5:10). However there is the warning that suffering in itself is not a virtue; only innocent suffering can be condoned (4:16); to suffer for one's own wrong doing is not to share in the suffering of Christ.

5:1 – 11 : Exhortations to older and younger people and general exhortations

…as a fellow elder and a witness of the sufferings of Christ as well as a partaker in the glory that is to be revealed… The writer refers to himself/herself as an *elder,* possibly an office in the church. *Witness to the sufferings…*possibly an attempt at authenticating the writing, and *partaker in the glory* – a situation that is yet to come.

…tend the flock of God… The pastoral charge which also reflects Jn. 21 – *feed my sheep.*

…not for shameful gain but eagerly… Possibly the offices were paid occupations so this would reflect a situation of the late 1st century. The model for the shepherd is *Christ, the chief shepherd.*

…younger be subject to the elders… clothe yourselves, all of you, with humility… Exhortations for maintaining right relationships in the community. Obedience must be shown by those under the authority of the elders.

...humble yourselves...cast all your anxieties on Him, for He cares about you... The exhortation to completely trust in God and the affirmation that God cares for God's people.

...the same experience of suffering is required of your fellow Christians throughout the world... The acknowledgement of suffering/persecution taking place all over the empire reflecting the period of the reign of Domitian – A.D. 81-96.

...after you have suffered a little while, the God of all grace...will restore, establish and strengthen you... The affirmation that suffering is only temporary.

Comments

In this final section, the author deals with the crisis in which the readers find themselves – a situation of suffering which they find hard to explain/understand. However, they are to rejoice when they suffer for Christ and thereby glorify God (4:12-19); they are not alone as Christians all over the world (empire) are also joined with them in suffering. However, the suffering is only for a short while after which there is glory.

I Peter helps in understanding how early Christians tried to live in the world as *holy people* without being assimilated by the world; they were constantly reminded that their adversary was *like a roaring lion seeking someone to devour;* they were under obligation to transform the world through exhibiting love, humility, hospitality, and undergirding their ethical principles in the light of Christ's example.

5:12 -14 : Concluding greetings

...by Silvanus... It may be that Silvanus served as the amanuensis – the person writing the letter on the dictation of the author – or it may be that Silvanus was the person with whom the letter was sent.

...she who is at Babylon sends you greetings... The usual symbol for Rome was Babylon (as also in the Book of Revelation), so it could be that the writing originated/was compiled in Rome.

...my son Mark... There is a tradition that Peter was related to Mark (Acts 12:12) – see Introduction, above. Mark is usually associated with Paul (Acts 12:25, 13:5, 15:37).

Comments

The two persons mentioned at the end of the writing – Silvanus and Mark – are usually spoken of in association with the Pauline mission. Tradition has it that they both ended up in Rome during Peter and Paul's imprisonment there and were useful to both the apostles.

In the final exhortation, the author reminds the readers of the purpose of the writing: *exhorting and declaring that this is the true grace of God; stand fast in it* (5:12). The writing was a compilation of a baptismal homily/liturgy in which Christians are exhorted to follow the ethical values of the *new life,* and the exhortation to stand firm in the faith in the face of suffering/persecution.

***

Select Bibliography for Section III

Beare, F. W. *The First Epistle of Peter,* 3rd ed. Oxford: University Press, 1970.

Brown, R. E. *An Introduction to the New Testament.* Bangalore: Theological Publications in India, 2000.

Clowney, Edmund P. *The Message of I Peter.* The Bible Speaks Today, Leicester: Inter Varsity Press, 1989.

Cranfield, C. E. B. *The First Epistle of Peter.* London: SCM Press, 1950.

Elliot, J. H. *A Home for the Homeless.* Philadelphia: Fortress Press, 1981.

Gnanakan, Chris. "I Peter" in Brian C. Wintle (General Editor), *South Asia Biblical Commentary.* Udaipur, Rajasthan: Open Door Publications, 2015, pages 1741-1748.

Goppelt, I., *A Commentary on I Peter.* Grand Rapids: Eerdmans, 1993.

Green, Gene I. *Jude and II Peter,* Baker Exegetical Commentary on the New Testament. Grand Rapids: Baker, 2008.

Grudem, Wayne A. *I Peter.* Tyndale New Testament Commentary. Leicester: Inter Varsity Press, 2009.

Kee, H. C. And F. W. Young. *The Living World of the New Testament.* London: Darton, Longman & Todd, 1966.

Kummel, W. G. *Introduction to the New Testament* (Revised Edition). translated by Howard C. Kee. London: SCM Press, 1975.

Lucas, Dick and Christopher Green. *The Message of II Peter and Jude.* The Bible Speaks Today. Leicester: Inter Varsity Press, 1995.

SECTION IV

The Epistle of Jude

CHAPTER I

Introduction to Jude

Background and purpose, Authorship, Addressees, Date, and Place of writing.

General Background and purpose

In the earlier writings of the New Testament – Paul's letters, Gospels – the attempt was to preserve and communicate the gospel and its implications to those outside Palestine. As the community expanded, foreign influences began to find their way into Christian thinking and teaching, and leaders had to define very clearly what was to be considered as truth and what must be rejected as error. This hardening of the Christian stand can be seen starting from the early letters of Paul to the fairly firm stand in the Pastorals and then to the rigid stand against false teaching in II Peter and Jude. This is reflected in the history of the church where the orthodox position is defined over and over again as a reaction to emerging heresies. The false teaching that the author of Jude combats so vehemently seems to have reached an advanced stage, hence the setting seems to be in the early 2nd century. It is significant that the short writing of Jude has greater dependence on interpretation of events/incidents in the Hebrew scriptures and Jewish apocryphal writings than many of the longer books in the New Testament.

The writing's understanding of 'faith' also undergoes a change: for most of the New Testament writers 'faith' was an expression of trust in, and commitment to God as a response to the message of the Gospel; whereas in Jude (and in the Pastorals) 'faith' is understood as "sound doctrine", "sound words", "truth entrusted to you" (I Tim. 1:120; Tit. 2:1; II Tim. 1:13, 14) placing an emphasis on 'faith' as right understanding about God and Jesus. This can come about only by right teaching – a body of truths passed on to Christians by those who proclaimed the gospel and who were recognized apostolic authorities (II Peter 1:1; Jude 3). This shift in meaning reflects the period of Early Catholicism (between A.D. 90 to 150), and especially at the beginning of the 2nd century.

The general context seems to be that the letter was written to combat libertine Gnostic thinking which held that Christians were totally emancipated from the Law and so could go to any extreme: they became like animals (Jude 10), they turned Christian fellowship into an excuse for indulging in fleshly desires, carousals etc...(Jude 14-19). This was recognized as a threat to the Christian way of life and ethical conduct. Jude was written to address such a situation and to call Christians to hold fast to faith, prayer, love and hope (Jude 20ff.). A further purpose was to combat the questioning that had started regarding Christ's return and the 'last times' (17-23).

Unlike its related writing (e.g. verse 4, 6, 7, 8, 9, 11 are parallel to II Peter 2:1, 4, 6, 10, 12, 15. See section on II Peter, below, for further details of the literary relationship to II Peter), the letter of Jude found early acceptance in the canon of the New Testament. At the beginning of the 2nd century Jude was placed among the "doubtful writings", probably because of the strong use of apocryphal literature which itself was under question. However, it does indicate that Jude was not an uncontested writing nor was it classed among the false/pseudo writings. By the end of the 2nd century, in the Muratorian canon, Jude was fully accepted as apostolic and authoritative (see History of the Canon in Vol. I of this series). In the 16th century, Luther raised the issue of canonicity again, and by his criteria that a writing must preach Christ, Jude was placed after "the true, certain and chief books of the New Testament" since it did not preach Christ. However, the Council of Trent (1546) reaffirmed the canonical status of Jude and the writing has been subsequently accepted by other Protestant reformers/reformation movements.

Authorship

The writing describes the author as *Jude, a servant of Jesus Christ and brother of James* (1). Since *James* is mentioned without qualification, it could only refer to a well known personality, probably James, the brother of Jesus, who was a leader in the Jerusalem Church (Acts 12:17, 15:13, 21:18; I Cor. 15:7) (in a study on the relatives of Jesus, Bauckham shows that members of the family were dominant forces among Christians both in Galilee and Jerusalem, and that the churches in Asia Minor which were evangelized by the Jerusalem mission still owed allegiance to the family) and is associated with the epistle of James (James 1:1; Gal. 1:19; 2:9; I Cor. 15:7). James and Jude are mentioned in the list of the brothers of Jesus (Mtt. 13:55; Mk. 6:3), however, nothing further is known about Jude from the New Testament.

The author was presumably a Jewish Christian since there are references to Jewish apocalyptic thought/writings which the author cites from Greek translations of these works. The writing is in polished Greek not expected of a Galilean. This coupled with the fact that there is no reference to the earthly Jesus which would be expected if the author was a brother of Jesus, makes it extremely unlikely that the Jude mentioned in the writing is actually the brother of Jesus. The most common suggestion as to why the author did not identify himself as the brother of Jesus rather than as a brother of James, is probably because although Jude is mentioned in the list of the brothers of Jesus, but in proclaiming Jesus as Messiah, family relationships are transcended (Mtt. 12:46-50; Mk. 3:31-35; Lk. 8:19-21; Jn. 7:1-10). So obviously the author wants the writing to appear only as having been written by a person who is in authority and has an acceptable position in society and the church.

The literary association with II Peter (see the section, below, on II Peter for the literary relationship) also places the writing after the apostolic age and closer to the start of the 2nd century. Further, the contents and warning regarding false teachers, the use of 'faith' as a body of beliefs *which was once for all delivered to the saints* (3), and the *predictions of the apostles* (17) point to later developments in Christianity belonging to the period of Early Catholicism. So the supposition that the writing comes from a brother of Jesus is extremely improbable. All that can be inferred is that the name of this brother of Jesus, and James and the family relationships, was still sufficiently well known at the end of the 1st century so as to give credence to a writing in his name. Since the Epistle of James was classed as a pseudonymous writing (see relevant section on authorship of James, above), and if *brother of James* is a reference to the author of that epistle, then it is all the more fitting that **the author of the Epistle of Jude must also remain pseudonymous.**

Addressees, Date, and Place of writing

The epistle is addressed *to those who are called, beloved in God the Father and kept for Jesus Christ* (1). This very general address indicates that the letter was for all Christians although the contents suggest that the readers were Jewish Christians familiar with the interpretation of Hebrew scriptures. The literary association of Jude with James and II Peter makes it possible that the letter was first written to Christians in Asia Minor (from Jewish and Gentile backgrounds) who were facing persecution, the threat of false teachings, and misinterpretation of the understanding of freedom from the Law. Given its association with other writings, especially II Peter, and that without doubt Jude exhibits the concerns of the period of Early Catholicism, the date of writing is probably between **A.D. 100 and 120. The place of origin cannot be determined.**

CHAPTER II

Jude

Warnings against False Teachings and Heresies regarding the Person and Work of Christ, with Special Reference to Christ's Second Coming; Insistence on sound doctrine; An analysis and commentary on the text of Jude.

Verses 1-2 : Opening formula

Jude, a servant of Jesus Christ and brother of James... The author describes himself (see authorship issues above).

...to those who are called, beloved of God... A general address for all Christians. *Beloved of God* – a designation for Israel (Deut. 32:15; 33:5, 26) now taken over by Christians.

Comments

The opening formula (1-2), places the writing in the literary genre of a letter written to address a troubled situation but which may have widespread implications, hence *to those who are called...* without a specific address.

In the opening formula, Jude claims authoritative status as the *brother of James.* Probably in the Jerusalem Church and in the mission activity of that community, the family connections were still respected and looked up to as authoritative (see Authorship issues, above).

The taking over of designations which were descriptive of the relationship between Yahweh and Israel – *beloved of God* - suggests a period towards the end of the 1st century, the time of Early Catholicism when the church began to define itself, especially in the light of the death of the apostles (for details, see Section V, below).

Verses 3-4: Purpose of writing

...eager to write to you of our common salvation...I found it necessary to write... An expression of the understanding that all the addressees are included in the understanding of salvation. The author regards himself as having the right to expound this *common salvation* since he claims an authority of *the brother of James.*

...to contend for the faith which was once for all delivered to the saints... 'Faith' used as a reference to a body of beliefs that have been passed on through the saints/proclaimers of the Gospel.

...admission has been secretly gained by some...who pervert the grace of our God into licentiousness and deny our only Master and Lord, Jesus Christ. The infiltration of false teachers and those who come from a background of false teaching. An example of the false teaching is given.

Comments

a. *Our common salvation* seems to indicate that the understanding of salvation is a fixed tradition and accepted by all. Probably this reflects a later date for the writing when beliefs were more clearly defined and accepted as tradition.

b. *Faith* is also being thought of as a traditional body of teaching (doctrinal and moral) that had been handed down by those who proclaimed the gospel and that this repository of faith was not to be changed. The church had to respond to the problem of false teaching by closing ranks and clearly holding on to what had been traditionally taught and delivered.

c. *Some have gained admission...* probably refers to those from outside who propagate teachings and beliefs contrary to what has been handed down. Two examples of the false teaching are described – *licentiousness and denial of Jesus.* Later in the writing these are further elaborated, but even at this point, it would seem that the false teaching has elements of libertine Gnosticism which advocated the freedom to live as one liked as it was only the outward body that was affected and not the inner soul. This problem of outsiders somehow gaining admission into Christian communities with different teachings was a problem in the last part of the 1ˢᵗ century-beginning of the 2ⁿᵈ century (further examples of this can be found in Acts 20:29; II Tim. 3:6; II John 10).

Verses 5-10 : Three examples of punishment for disobedience
I desire to remind you, though you were once for all fully informed... The author takes for granted/presupposes that the readers are well aware of the incidents in the Hebrew Scriptures.

...God who saved a people out of the land of Egypt, afterward destroyed those who did not believe... The first example of punishment for disbelief/disobedience – those who came out of Egypt did not enter the promised land.

...angels that did not keep their own position but left their proper dwelling...have been kept by God in eternal chains... The second example of punishment for disobedience – even angels are punished.

...Sodom and Gomorrah...acted immorally and indulged in unnatural lust...undergoing a punishment of eternal fire... The third example of punishment for disobedience – the destruction of Sodom and Gomorrah.

...in like manner these people in their dreaming defile the flesh, reject authority, and revile the glorious ones... A description is given of the false teachings/immoral behaviour advocated by those who have gained 'secret admission' into the community.

...the archangel Michael did not presume to pronounce a reviling judgment upon the devil... Final judgment is left to God and no one else can pronounce judgment.

…but these people revile whatever they do not understand…by instinct as irrational animals do, they are destroyed… A very severe indictment of the false teachers and those who follow libertine Gnosticism; their thinking and behaviour is self destructive.

Comments

1. The writer assumes that the readers knew what was erroneous in the teaching being attacked, and also assumes that the readers were familiar with Israel's history and folklore so either the writing was addressed to Jewish Christians or to Gentile Christians who were taught about these incidents, or to Christians in general where these incidents would have been part of their background. The writer offers three examples from Israelite tradition in which God punished the disobedient:

   a. The first example is that of the punishment of those who were brought out of Egypt, but who were not permitted to enter the Promised Land due to disobedience (Num. 14) and lack of faith.

   b. The second example is that of the angels (*sons of God*) who left their privileged place in heaven to lust after women (Gen. 6:1-6) so God locked them beneath the earth in darkness till judgment day (I Enoch 10:4-6; chps. 12-13). This example is taken from Jewish apocalyptic writings.

   c. The third example is that of the people of Sodom and Gomorrah who practiced immorality and were punished with destruction by fire (Gen. 19:1-28).

2. These three examples are followed by commentary, *in a similar manner…* showing how the ancient texts are understood and applied to the present situation. The erroneous conduct of the false teachers/ infiltrators is contrasted with the modesty of the archangel Michael who did not blaspheme when the devil tried to claim Moses' dead body, but only rebuked the devil. This story is derived from the Moses legend that had developed after Moses' death as narrated in Deuteronomy 34:1-6 where Moses died in the land of Moab and

God buried him, but no one knows the place of burial; the legend from Israelite folklore was that the devil wanted custody of Moses' dead body but that was not granted. The legend has its origin in the Jewish apocryphal writings.

Verses 11-13: Further examples of disobedience and description of false teachers

...they walk in the way of Cain... The example is given of Cain who was a murderer (Gen. 4:1-10).

...abandon themselves for the sake of gain to Balaam's error... The reference is to Balaam who accepted bribes from the Midianites to curse Israel (Num. 31; Deut. 23:5; Josh. 24:9-10).

...perish in Korah's rebellion... The reference is to the mutiny against Moses and Aaron (Num. 16).

...these are blemishes on your love feasts... Following the examples above, would result in a problem in the observance of the love feast (Eucharist). *Love feast* was the name that was used for the eucharist as it brought the community together.

...they boldly carouse together, looking after themselves; waterless clouds...fruitless trees, twice dead, uprooted...wild waves of the sea... wandering stars for whom the nether world of darkness has been reserved forever... A series of invectives against those to whom the author had referred.

Comments

1. The three further examples of disobedience are taken from developments in rabbinic tradition and writings describing those *who have no share in the world to come:*

    a. The story of Cain as a murderer was further expanded in rabbinic tradition to include all kinds of evil beyond murder. This is also reflected in I John 3:12. He was punished for his evil deeds.

    b. The story of Balaam who was bribed by the Midianites to curse Israel but to whom Yahweh did not listen, so he was killed.

   c.   The story of Korah who led the mutiny against Moses and Aaron and had to pay the price for disobedience and lack of faith.

2.   Following the examples, the author comments/applies the rabbinic traditions to those who follow the present false teachers in very severe language and idioms, showing that the final result would be eternal punishment. Jude's use of rabbinic sources for supporting the argument has often been questioned, but such use is not uncommon in the New Testament and early Christianity (e.g. see Acts 17:28; I Cor. 15:33; II Tim.3:8; Tit. 1:12).

3.   There is a reference to the celebration of the eucharist which came to be called a *love feast* since the community gathered for a fellowship/social meal. However, more than just participation in a meal, the main point celebrated was Christ's presence in the midst of the meal and the hope of his final return. Such a solemn celebration was at the heart of the community, so those who had gained admission had entered the very core of Christian belief and their behavior was defiling the celebration (this is the same sort of situation addressed in I Cor. 11 where Paul categorically states that *anyone who eats and drinks without discerning the body, eats and drinks judgment upon themselves*). The nomenclature of *love feast* faded out by the mid-2nd century when a more liturgical celebration replaced a shared meal which came to be known as the Eucharist.

4.   The strong invective used, however, does not describe the false teaching itself; but only describes the persons in very colourful language (*waterless clouds, fruitless trees, restless waves, wandering stars* – all promise a blessing but fail to deliver), and the punishment reserved for them.

Verses 14-19: Prophecies of Enoch and the apostles

...Enoch... The reference to the mysterious figure who walked with God and was taken up to heaven without dying (Gen. 5:21-24).

...Enoch...prophesied saying, behold, the Lord came...ungodly sinners have spoken against him... The author cites a reference about Enoch prophesying which goes beyond the texts in the Hebrew scriptures.

...grumblers, malcontents, following their own passions, loud-mouthed boasters, flattering people to gain advantage... A description of the characteristics of the false teachers who had entered the community.

...the prediction of the apostles..."in the last time there will be scoffers...." The false teachers were foretold by the apostles, probably in the use of this anachronism, i.e. making it sound as though the present situation was foretold long ago.

...It is those who set up divisions...devoid of the Spirit... The false teachers only achieve divisions and conflict within the community.

Comments

It is part of the style of Jude to recall that the warnings of the coming of false teachers were foretold, indeed going back to Jesus himself: *...if anyone says to you, "look here is the Christ!", or "look there he is!" do not believe it. False Christs and false prophets will arise and show signs and wonders, to lead astray, if possible, the elect* (Mk. 13:21-22). The false teachers who propagate divisive teachings are not controlled by the Spirit of God.

There is reference to a prophecy against the ungodly by Enoch, but the prophecy goes beyond what is known of Enoch in Genesis 5:21-24. This is taken from Jewish traditional material preserved by the rabbis and in the texts found at Qumran (I Enoch1:9). The description of these impious people is a very severe indictment especially in that they are responsible for divisions and confusion within the community and when they want something, they turn to flattery which makes them insincere and untrustworthy.

The writer cites the apostles with regard to a description of the impious people who will come at the last time. However, the citation does not come from any known source in the New Testament. The writer is probably drawing on material that is wider than Christian tradition as was done in the case of the example of Enoch where material was taken from sources wider than that of Hebrew scriptures.

Verses 20-23: Appeal for faith and different kinds of judgment to be exercised

...build yourselves up in your most holy faith... 'Faith' is presented as though it is a body of accepted teachings that needs to be studied, unlike earlier New Testament writings where 'faith' is a dynamic trust and commitment.

...keep yourselves in the love of God...wait for the mercy of our Lord Jesus Christ..convince some...save some...on some have mercy with fear... An encouragement for community members to have concern for others through pastoral and evangelical expressions.

Comments

a.　In contrast to the false teachers, the author's *dear friends/beloved* are to stay faithful to the *most holy faith...pray...keep yourselves in the love of God...and wait for the mercy of our Lord Jesus Christ* and to be effective evangelists, *convince some who have doubts, save some by snatching them out of the fire; on some have mercy with fear...* There is a strong call to an evangelical faith and the pastoral task.

b.　In spite of the strong invective, those who do wrong must still be reached out to – they are to be shown mercy, snatched from the fire. Their corruption and falseness is to be hated, but the person is to be saved – a strong evangelical and pastoral call to believers.

c.　*...hating even the garment spotted by the flesh.* This is a reference to contaminated clothing that should be destroyed (Lev. 13:47-59) as per the Law of Moses.

Verses 24-25: Concluding doxology

...to him who is able to keep you from falling...now and forever. Amen. Jude's concluding doxology is one of the most beautiful in the New Testament and well known in Christian circles.

...to the only God our Saviour through Jesus Christ or Lord... The stress on monotheism – *only God* - taken over from Judaism, and given a Christian orientation – *through Jesus Christ our Lord.*

Comments

There are no personal greetings/personal information at the end of Jude such as found in other letters. Instead, the letter ends with one of the most beautifully phrased doxologies as an affirmation of faith. Possibly the doxology has been adapted from the liturgy and phrased to give hope to the community.

The monotheism of Judaism is strongly expressed – *the only God* – coupled with the Christian modification of such a belief – *through Jesus Christ our Lord.* So even in the closing doxology, there is the influence of Judaism re-interpreted to express a Christian message.

The letter ends in the same way as it began – stressing God's ability to keep and protect believers. The doxology in Jude is one that is well known and loved in Christian circles, stressing God's love, protection, *glory, majesty, dominion and authority* through Jesus Christ. It is an affirmation that God reigns supreme and that false teachers/teachings cannot take the place of God.

***

Select Bibliography for the Epistle of Jude given at the end of Section V.

SECTION V

The Second Epistle of Peter

CHAPTER I

Introduction to II Peter

Background and purpose, authorship, and date.

General background and purpose

In all likelihood, II Peter was chronologically the last New Testament writing; due to its dependence on Jude, II Peter is here treated after Jude and as the last of the New Testament canonical writings. The author of II Peter was forced to combat Gnostic Christians who were misinterpreting Pauline teachings and the Hebrew scriptures (3:15-16) and who were questioning whether the *parousia* would take place (ch. 3); the author warns that those who deny the humanity of Christ are false teachers (2:1). These teachers interpret Hebrew scriptures to their own advantage (1:16) believing that they are free from the Law and so indulge themselves in revelling, dissipation, and carousing (2:13-14). The author is at pains to warn readers that they should not make the mistake of following those teachers for although they promise freedom, they are themselves slaves of corruption (3:17); Christians who are involved in such corruption are worse off than if they had never believed (2:18-21). It would seem then that the struggle with these teachers was not just the false teaching, but the Christian way of life itself – the Christian concept of morality, the morale and unity of the community were all threatened and the author wrote strongly to defend the faith. This shows that the struggle was not just theological differences/speculation, but that the leaders saw in the false teaching a very real threat to the unity of the church/community. This situation, at the end of the 1st

century-beginning of the 2nd century, placed great strain on the leaders to combat false teachings with the re-affirmation of the fundamental truths of the Gospel, otherwise there was the threat of the community being completely submerged in Hellenistic modes of thought which would have perverted the Gospel, and destroyed the unity and ethical conduct of the community. This general background often leads to II Peter and Jude being listed and understood as 'conflict epistles'.

The epistle also serves to instruct its readers about the transfiguration of Jesus of which Peter was a witness; the transfiguration serves as a prediction/representation of the coming *parousia* (1:12-21 and chp. 3). This emphasis was probably a response to the denial of the expectation of the *parousia* being advocated by the false teachers (3:3ff.), characteristic of the Gnostic movement in the early 2nd century.

The above two points – combating false teachers/teachings and concern for re-affirming belief in the *parousia* – bring out the purpose of II Peter and the necessity for its writing.

In spite of the heavy stress on the Peterine authorship of the epistle, II Peter does not seem to have been known, or if known then not recognized, in the 2nd century – important church leaders of that time, and the Muratorian canon, are silent about II Peter (see Vol. I of this series for the history of the New Testament canon). It is only from the 3rd century that it begins to be mentioned, and even after the closing of the canon in the 4th century, the writing was not fully accepted by certain churches. It is only at the end of the 4th century-beginning of the 5th century, under the influence of Jerome and his work on Latin translations, that II Peter began to be accepted.

Authorship

The following issues are usually raised in support of Peter as the author:

> The letter makes the claim that it is written by the apostle Peter (1:1);

> the author speaks as an eyewitness of the transfiguration of Jesus (1:16ff.);

the author makes reference to the saying of Jesus regarding the martyrdom of Peter (1:14);

The reference to *the beloved brother Paul* (3:15ff.) places the author and Paul on the same level of apostolic authority and their writings as scripture.

There is a reference to I Peter: *this is already the second letter that I am writing to you* (3:1). The author regards his death as near (1:13ff.) and so this letter is in the form of a testament of Peter.

In spite of the above strong points of identification, the Peterine authorship of the epistle has been challenged chiefly on account of the differences in vocabulary and style from the first epistle and its dependence on the epistle of Jude. The arguments against authorship by Peter are usually listed as follows:

The literary dependence on Jude is very strong (e.g. 1:5 with Jude 3; 1:12 with Jude 5; 3:2ff with Jude 17ff; 3:14 with Jude 24; 3:18 with Jude 25). Jude is normally dated towards the end of the 1st century-beginning of the 2nd century (A.D. 100-120, see above). The most striking agreements are seen in the portrayal of the false teachers (e.g. 2:1ff. || Jude 4; 2:10ff. || Jude 8ff.; 2:18 || Jude 16) and in the illustrations from the Hebrew scriptures (e.g. 2:4ff. || Jude 5ff.) and other rabbinic and Jewish apocryphal writings. This dependence rules out the apostle Peter as the author of II Peter as Peter is traditionally believed to have been martyred in Rome in the persecution under Nero, about A.D. 64-66, much before Jude was written.

The large sections quoted from Jude's interpretations of Jewish apocryphal literature indicate a tradition that stemmed from the Jerusalem community and venerated by those Christians for whom *the brothers of the Lord* were authorities. There is no indication of the struggle between Paul and the Jerusalem leaders (James and Peter – see Gal. 2:9, 11), instead the writing reflects a later tradition, especially in Rome, in which both

Peter and Paul are regarded as 'pillars of the Church' (*our beloved brother Paul* – 3:15; I Clement 5:2-5). So by referring to Peter's experiences as normative, and Paul's writings as scripture, II Peter is like a link bringing together the two major factions of the Church in the period of Early Catholicism.

The conceptual world and rhetorical language are strongly influenced by Hellenism which rules out Peter or any of his helpers/pupils who may have written under his instructions. The Hellenistic vocabulary/concepts include: *the divine power* (1:3), *virtue* added to *faith* (1:5); *knowledge* (1:2, 5, 6, 8; 2:20); *participation in divine nature* (1:4, 16) – from the language of the mystery religions. There is direct evidence of those who deny the *parousia* (3:4) echoing the writings of church leaders at the end of the 1st century which show that the questioning of, and skepticism regarding the *parousia* was an issue from about A.D. 90-150. II Peter therefore is aimed against a movement which bears essential features of early 2nd century Gnostic thinking.

There is also a reference to a collection of Pauline letters, *our beloved brother Paul wrote to you according to the wisdom given him…there are some things in them hard to understand which the ignorant and unstable twist to their own destruction, as they do the other scriptures…* (3:15-16). Since the concept of scripture was difficult to define at this time, II Peter holds that *no prophecy of scripture is a matter of one's own interpretation…those moved by the Holy Spirit spoke from God* (1:20). Since not everyone has the Spirit, the explanation of Scripture was reserved for those in the ecclesiastical teaching office which did not develop till after A.D. 70. Accordingly, II Peter reflects a period later than Peter and more into the period of Early Catholicism.

The consistent stress throughout the writing by appealing to events (as per the Gospels) in which Peter was involved, raises the suspicion of pseudonymity. This, coupled with relating the writing as a "testament" of Peter (1:12-15; 3:1ff.), and the reference to I Peter, *this is now the second letter that I have written to you* (3:1ff.) – as an appeal to the apostolic authority of Peter, *the guarantor of the tradition* (1:12ff.), further strengthens the suspicion of pseudonymity.

The silence of the 2nd century church leaders in referring to, or in acknowledging II Peter, resulting in its ambiguous place in the canon, indicates that the Peterine authorship of the writing was not automatically accepted. The first attestation comes from Origen and Eusebius in the 3rd century who list II Peter among the "disputed" writings. It is only in the 4th century that II Peter began to be recognized, and its final inclusion came from the influence of Jerome in his translation work.

In the light of the reasons given above, **the apostle Peter or his associates, are today, not regarded as being the author of II Peter. The writing is listed among the pseudonymous writings of the New Testament, written by someone giving advice on the prevailing situation of false teaching and loss of hope in the *parousia*, and written in the name of Peter to give the writing both authenticity and authority.**

Date

There is no fixed point, such as a reference to a historical event/person, for a dating to be fixed with any degree of certainty. The writing's dependence on Jude (almost word for word) would suggest early 2nd century (i.e. after the date for Jude, A.D. 100-120, see above) and the references to a Gnostic development regarding the *parousia* would suggest a date in the second quarter of the 2nd century. The references to the First Epistle of Peter (3:1) and to the collection of Pauline writings, which were already being regarded as scripture (3:15-16), would further strengthen the thinking that the date would have to be between the end of the 1st century and by the middle of the 2nd century. The thinking regarding the *parousia* which changes from the normal New Testament christologically based eschatology to an apocalyptic which Jews and Gentiles treasure and preach (3:7, 12-13) shows that II Peter reflects later thinking. Thus **II**

Peter can be dated between A.D. 120 to A.D. 140 and would become the last of the written documents in the New Testament canon.

II Peter is addressed *to those who have obtained a faith of equal standing with ours*...(1:1), and to those who know the Pauline letters and I Peter, so probably to Christians in Asia Minor, but more possibly **it is addressed to Christians everywhere; its place of writing cannot be determined with any exactitude.**

CHAPTER II

Warning against False Teaching and a New Understanding of Hope

Analysis and commentary on the text of II Peter.

1:1- 2 : Prescript: Introduction and greetings

Simon Peter, a servant and apostle of Jesus Christ... An unusual reference to both the Jewish and Greek names of Peter.

...to those who have obtained a faith of equal standing with ours... An affirmation that all Christians share the same faith with Peter as the spokesperson. 'Faith' is here seen as a body of beliefs to be accepted.

...grace and peace be multiplied to you... This is verbatim from I Peter 1:2.

...knowledge (ἐπεγνωσει) of God and of Jesus our Lord... The Greek word translated as 'knowledge' is literally 'full/complete knowledge'.

Comments

a. The prescript is the only part of the writing which suggests that a letter format is being used. The reference by title/description to *Simon Peter...servant and apostle...*is not usually used either in the Gospels or in other New Testament writings. Simon Peter, an original companion of Jesus *(servant and apostle)* is portrayed as the spokesperson for all Christians. The detailed description, and stress on Peter, strongly suggests a pseudonymous writing.

b. In the prescript and introduction, the place of the readers is not specifically mentioned; they are generally reminded of all the good things which they have received and of their standing – they have *obtained a faith of equal standing with ours....* This is one of the reasons why the writing is included among the 'Catholic Epistles'.

c. The 'full/complete knowledge' that is added to *grace and peace be multiplied* in the greeting, is a theme that will recur later in the writing as a means of combating false teachers/teachings.

1:3-11 : Privileges, character and admonitions

...His divine power...things that pertain to life and godliness, through the knowledge of Him...glory and excellence...His precious and very great promises... The style is baroque (adjectives and adverbs used in abundance) in that it heaps one phrase on another in abundance (1:5-7).

...supplement your faith with virtue, and virtue with knowledge, and knowledge with self-control, and self-control with steadfastness, and steadfastness with godliness, and godliness with affection and love for all... A list of virtues which must characterise the Christian life as *holy and godly* (see ch. 3:11ff).

...they keep you from being ineffective or unfruitful in the knowledge of our Lord Jesus Christ... The author's insists on the necessity of cultivating Christian virtues and of fully knowing Christ.

...whoever lacks these things is blind and short-sighted and has forgotten that they have been cleansed from their old sins... A reminder of the faith in which the believers stood and an admonition to remain faithful.

...be the more zealous to confirm your call and election...so that there will be richly provided for you an entrance into the eternal kingdom of our Lord.... The exhortation is to remain faithful because of the eternal reward in the future.

Comments

This section of II Peter is the first example of the baroque and very literary Greek style of writing and vocabulary/idiom. The phrases linked together, and tumbling over one another, is certainly not the style of the earlier writings of the New Testament. The point being made is that Christians who do not make progress in the understanding of their faith are liable to become blind and forgetful; there has to be a continual progress/growth in faith.

The word 'knowledge' is used several times in the passage stressing that the believer's understanding cannot remain stagnant, but must continually grow and expand into fuller and fuller understandings of God's salvific action.

The practical aspect of faith has to be supplemented with virtues – virtue (moral/ethical behaviour), knowledge, self-control, steadfastness, godliness, love. These characterize a Christian in a situation where these values are despised/disregarded. Such values that are cultivated also help Christians to recall what God has done in Christ and the sacredness of the Christian's call. The author will return to this practical aspect as *holy and godly* living in 3:11ff.

1:12-15 : Author's impending death

...I intend always you remind you of these things...I think it right, so long as I am in the body, to arouse you by way of reminder, since I know that the putting off of my body will be soon, as our Lord Jesus Christ showed me...after my departure you may be able at any time to recall these things. The author indicates that he/she is expecting death in the near future, and so is preparing his/her legacy for the readers.

Comments

1. Speaking as Peter, the author indicates that death is near – whether by old age, illness, or martyrdom is not clear – and so he/she stresses that he/she wants to leave a reminder/refresh the readers' memory/ to remember the truth so that they may recall the true teachings after his/her death.

2. In a reference to John 21:18-19 there is again an appeal to a situation in the life of Jesus in which Peter was involved. The Johannine passage talks about being dependent on others in one's old age; it

does not indicate the manner of Peter's death even though it says, *this He said to show by what death he was to glorify God.* Does the Johannine text indicate that Peter was to die an old man dependent on others to lead him around? However, the strong tradition of the church is that Peter was fleeing from Rome when he met Jesus going in the opposite direction, and Peter asked Jesus, *?Quo vadis, Lord? – where are you going?;* Jesus replied that he was going to Rome to die in Peter's place. This made Peter so ashamed that he turned and went back to Rome to die a martyr's death at the hands of Nero, requesting that he be crucified upside down as he was not worthy to be crucified in the same way as his Lord.

As is common in II Peter the interpretation of scripture is different from the tradition of the early church as is known from the end of the 1st century (e.g. the above Johannine reference to Peter's death), indicating that Peter cannot be the author and that the writing comes from a much later date, probably into the 2nd century, when there was no one who could verify/authenticate the Gospel record/interpretation. Further, the section of John's Gospel in which Jesus supposedly speaks of Peter's death (chapter 21) is known as the Epilogue to the gospel and was probably added around or shortly after A.D. 100 (see introductory issues in John's Gospel in Vol. III of this series), adding to the pseudonymity of II Peter.

3. The reference to Peter's impending death is much like II Timothy which talks of Paul's death (II Tim. 4:6ff.): each of the writings, II Peter and II Timothy, appeals to an apostolic authority; each is concerned with the appearance of false teachers in the community; each assumes a deposit of teachings referred to as 'faith'; and each are concerned for the preservation of the true faith which the readers had heard from the apostles.

1:16-21 : Author's reminder of the transfiguration of Jesus and the dependability of the prophetic word

...we did not follow cleverly devised myths...but were eyewitnesses of His majesty... The author appeals to a historical event in support of his/her teachings – the transfiguration of Jesus.

...He received honour and glory...the voice was borne...by the Majestic Glory...we were with Him on the holy mountain... A recounting of the transfiguration which was such a powerful experience that even the mountain is referred to as 'holy'.

...we have the prophetic word made more sure...you will do well to pay attention to this... The author sees the transfiguration as an authentication of the experience which was foretold by the prophets of old.

...no prophecy of scripture is a matter of one's interpretation, because no prophecy ever came by the impulse of humans, but humans moved by the Holy Spirit spoke from God. The affirmation that prophecy and scripture comes from God and not open to human interference.

Comments

a.	There is probably a reference to the interpretations of scripture by the false teachers – a concocted story or *cleverly devised myths* – and to which the author takes objection. The author focuses on a historical event (as opposed to a *cleverly devised myth*) to support his/her argument and to which he/she was an eyewitness – the event of the transfiguration (Mtt. 17:1-8; Mk. 9:2-8; Lk. 9:28-36) where the voice from heaven proclaims Jesus as God's son. The transfiguration serves as a source of assurance of who Jesus is, and as an assurance of his coming again.

There are several questions that come up from the appeal to the transfiguration of Jesus:

A.	Is the reference trying to stress the presence of Peter at an important event in the life of Jesus thereby trying to authenticate the question of authorship? If so, the overstress only leads to a greater suspicion of pseudonymity.

B.	Only three disciples were eyewitnesses: James (dead by this time), John (either dead or far removed from the writing), Peter (the date places the writing much after the life time of Peter). Hence it would seem that the appeal to the transfiguration was made when the original eyewitnesses were not around to authenticate the event or its interpretation.

C. How does the transfiguration guarantee the *parousia* which was the issue with the false teachers/teachings? No other New Testament writing interprets the transfiguration in this way, nor does the event as recorded in the Gospels use the event to refer to the *parousia*.

D. Is the appeal to the transfiguration by an alleged eyewitness a means of establishing the priority of Peter over Paul (see 3:15-16, below) ? Paul could claim to have seen the risen Christ (I Cor. 15:8), but not the transfigured Jesus, thus giving Peter an edge over Paul which may be the reason for II Peter not appealing to the appearance of the risen Lord to Peter mentioned in I Corinthians 15:5 as this would place Peter and Paul on equal footing as the risen Lord appeared to both. By the end of the 1st century, Peter and Paul were both hailed as leaders, so this may have been an attempt by the Peterine group to assert the priority of Peter over Paul.

E. Is the appeal to the transfiguration an attempt to thwart the arguments of the gnostic visionaries who frequently referred to the 'risen Christ' whom no one had seen, as a way of questioning the resurrection? In chapter 2, the author takes up the whole question of the resurrection and *parousia* as an answer to the false teachings of the Gnostics.

b. *The prophetic word made more sure* is probably a reference to the Hebrew prophets, especially to Elijah who appears with Jesus on the *holy mountain* as a representative of the prophetic tradition in Judaism.

c. The most famous text in II Peter is 1:20-21 – *all prophecy of scripture is not a matter of one's interpretation…rather people moved by the Holy Spirit spoke from God.* The reference is perhaps to the prophets who did not speak of their own understanding, but claimed that they were the messengers of God's word using the formula, *thus says the Lord*; the text has been employed in this way to defend the divine inspiration of all scripture and to challenge the rights to private interpretations which was an issue during the period of Early Catholicism; it could also be a challenge to Paul's writings which are left open to various kinds of interpretations (3:15-16), which would again try to set up the priority of Peter over Paul. The author writes with the authority to speak the truth about Christ as he/she was an eyewitness to God's revelation of Jesus in the transfiguration. The author, therefore, claims to be rooted in history, prophecy and revelation.

2:1-22 : Warning regarding false teachers/teachings and severe polemic

...false teachers also arose among the people, just as there will be false teachers among you... This is a reference to the false teachers/prophets in Israel and the warning that there will be false teachers again in the community. The false teachers are not identified (this is done later in 3:3-4), only the polemic against them which would fit any situation.

*...(false teachers) who will secretly bring in destructive heresies...many will believe their licentiousness...they will exploit you with false words... their destruction has not been asleep...*A general description of the false teachers/teachings which will be made more specific later.

...God did not spare the angels...God did not spare the ancient world... the Lord knows how to rescue the godly from trial... This gives the examples of those who were punished by God, and the examples of those who were rescued from punishment by God taken from Jude.

...bold and wilful, they are not afraid to revile the glorious ones...like irrational animals...born to be caught and killed, reviling in matters of which they are ignorant, will be destroyed... A severe polemic against the false teachers.

...they count it pleasure to revel in the daytime...they are blots and blemishes, revelling in their dissipation, carousing...eyes full of adultery, insatiable for sin...they entice unsteady souls...hearts trained in greed... accursed children!... A description of the character and behaviour of the

false teachers which finally spells their own destruction, like *Balaam... who loved gain from wrong doing.*

....the last state has become worse for them than the first... In the final judgement against the false teachers, they will be punished so severely that it will not be worthwhile.

...the dog turns back to its own vomit, and the sow is washed only to wallow in the mire. The behaviour of the false teachers is like animals who can only follow their instincts and are not able to improve or emerge from their base behaviour.

Comments

The author ended Chapter 1 with reference to the divine veracity of scripture and chapter 2 adds to that direction by comparing the opponents to the false prophets who troubled Israel, and defending also the author's interpretation of the transfiguration as a prophecy of the *parousia.*

The polemic against false teachers is taken over completely from Jude using a major part of that short writing excluding the non-canonical references to the body of Moses and the prophecy of I Enoch (Jude 9, 14). In the triad of those punished by God (Jude 5-7), II Peter 2:4-8 uses the examples of the angels and Sodom and Gomorrah, substituting the flood for the wilderness wanderings.

II Peter 2:5-9 lists those who were spared God's punishment – Noah and his family of seven other persons from the flood; *righteous Lot* from Sodom and Gomorrah. These are used as examples of the proof that God knows whom to punish and God knows how to rescue the godly from trial.

II Peter 2:10-16 echoes Jude 8-13 except that II Peter stresses several aspects of the character of the false teachers not found in Jude. They had escaped from the world when they found Christ, but now have gone astray so that they are entangled in a web from which they cannot escape – *their last state has become worse than the first.*

It would have been better for these false teachers not to have known the way of righteousness than to turn back after knowing it. As an illustration of this, two animals despised by the Jews is given: a quotation from Proverbs 26:11 about a dog returning to its vomit, and from Semitic sources, a pig that had been washed clean returning to the mire. The point being made is that, like despised animals, the false teachers would never be able to extricate themselves from their base, instinctive natures.

3:1-10 : The day of the Lord

This is now the second letter that have written to you...aroused your sincere mind by way of reminder... The author insists on a link with I Peter, bringing out that the purpose is to bring to mind earlier teachings.

...remember the predictions of the holy prophets and the commandment of the Lord and Saviour through your apostles... The author sees the situation as having been foretold by the Hebrew prophets who are held in veneration, and places the authority of the apostles on the same level as that of the prophets.

...scoffers will come in the last days...saying, "Where is the promise of His coming?..." The problem with the delay in the *parousia* which gave rise to doubts about when and whether it would take place.

...they ignore the fact...by the word of God heavens existed long ago... an earth formed out of water...the world that then existed was deluged with water and perished... The appeal to God as Creator and therefore in control; a further appeal to the destruction of the world by flood in the time of Noah (Gen. 7 & 8) (see also 2:5ff.).

...the heaven and earth that now exist have been stored up for fire... The first destruction of the world was by water (the flood); the second and final destruction would be by fire.

...with the Lord one day is as a thousand years, and a thousand years as one day... An apologetic is offered for the delay in the *parousia* which was causing a problem; the apologetic calls for a new criteria for calculating time.

...The Lord is not slow about His promise as some count slowness... but is forbearing...not wishing that any should perish, but that all should reach repentance... The concern for the delay in the *parousia* continues this time offering an apologetic which keeps the offer of salvation open.

...but the Day of the Lord will come like a thief...the earth and the works that are upon it will be burned up.... There is a stress on the fact that the exact day/time of the Day of the Lord (*parousia*), and the destruction of the world by fire, cannot be predicted.

Comments

The author appeals to the first writing – supposedly I Peter – as an authentication of what is being written. This stress on appealing to the first epistle and its alleged connection with the apostle Peter raises the suspicion of pseudonymity since Peter was long since dead.

The polemic against the false teachers/teachings continues using much of Jude 14-17. The false teaching in this case is clearly identified – problems arising from the delay in the *parousia* and people raising doubts about whether it would happen at all especially since the first leaders who promised/preached an early *parousia* were all dead by this time and the *parousia* still had not taken place (3:4).

The author appealed to the authority of the Hebrew prophets and the prophetic writings which seem to have attained the status of scripture, and to the authority of the apostles, placing both prophets and apostles on the same level, as predicting the *parousia* (*...the prophetic word made sure...1:19*). To the charge that nothing had changed since the foundation of the world, the author refutes the charge by showing that God manifested God's power in creation and in the destruction of the world by water (the flood), and that the same God will judge the world and destroy it with fire including the ungodly and the false teachers which would ensure the *parousia*. The complex sentence structure does not allow for clarity in the author's argument, but has to be carefully considered.

An apologetic is offered for the troublesome question of the non-fulfillment of the Christian hope of the *parousia*: delay in the *parousia* (3:8-10) is seen in the inscrutability of divine 'time' (Ps. 90:4), i.e. divine time cannot be measured in human terms and by human standards (3:8). This line of reasoning brought comfort to many who were troubled by the false teaching that the *parousia* would not take place, and who had no counter argument. However, there is the re-affirmation of the assurance that the *parousia* will definitely take place even though there cannot be an exact prediction (*like a thief* – a commonly used metaphor for the inability to make an exact prediction – Mtt. 24: 15-44; Mk. 13:32-37; Acts 1:7; I Thess. 5:2; Rev. 3:3, 16:15).

A further apologetic is that the delay in the *parousia* is a demonstration of God's patience – making it possible for people to repent rather than to be destroyed. This explains the mention of Noah and Lot who were examples of God's patience thus making it possible for them to escape divine punishment and to be preserved from the flood and from fire.

The image of fire as the destroying medium in the ultimate end (3:7, 12-13) is part of the traditional understanding of divine punishment and the ultimate end of the world (see Vol. III of this series on the Book of Revelation).

3:11-18 : Concluding words of admonition and encouragement

...what sort of persons ought you to be... The admonition and encouragement to remain faithful to the true teachings and to model one's character even when *all these things are to be dissolved...and the elements will melt with fire... We wait for new heavens and a new earth in which righteousness dwells...be zealous to be found by God without spot or blemish, and at peace.* The call to holy and godly living.

...count the forbearance of the Lord as salvation... God's patience is seen as a means of salvation and not as something to be questioned.

...our beloved brother Paul wrote to you....some things in the letters hard to understand, which the ignorant and unstable twist to their own

destruction, as they do other scriptures... Reference is made to the Pauline letters which seem to be regarded as scripture pointing to a period of Early Catholicism and also because the interpretation of the Pauline writings is open to question.

...beware lest you be carried away with the error of lawless people and lose your own stability... The caution/admonition that it would be easy to follow the wrong/false teachers/teachings.

...grow in grace and knowledge...to Him be the glory both now and to the day of eternity. Amen. The concluding blessing and ascription of glory stressing the *day of eternity* – the subject of debate in this last chapter.

Comments

In true apocryphal style, the author sees the dissolution of all things, but having known the examples of Noah and Lot, the readers should live lives of *holiness and godliness* in order *to be found without spot or blemish* when facing the ultimate judgment.

Most of the concluding admonitions and words of encouragement is a summary of what has already been said in the writing, but here written as a final warning to be on guard against the false teachers/teachings (cf. 1:5ff).

II Peter is the only book which refers to the Pauline writings as being authoritative and on being treated as scripture. It is an early reference to the significance and acceptance of the Pauline writings though there seems to be a tongue-in-cheek remark over the difficulties in understanding and interpreting the Pauline writings; this may also be an attempt to show/establish the superiority of Peter over Paul by alleging/expressing a doubt over the Pauline writings.

The final ascription gives glory to Jesus Christ, not only for the present, but also until the day of eternity – a day that is surely coming (3:7, 10, 12-13).

***

Select Bibliography for Sections IV and V

Bauckham, R. J. *Jude and the Relatives of Jesus in the Early Church*. Edinburgh: T & T Clarke, 1990.

Brown, R. E. *An Introduction to the New Testament*. Bangalore: Theological Publications in India, 2000.

Gnanakan, Chris. "II Peter" in Brian C. Wintle (General Editor). *South Asia Biblical Commentary*. Udaipur, Rajasthan: Open Door Publications, 2015, pages 1749-1752.

Green, Gene I. *Jude and II Peter*. Baker Exegetical Commentary on the New Testament. Grand Rapids: Baker, 2008.

Jones, Merlin. "Jude" in Brian C. Wintle (General Editor). *South Asia Biblical Commentary*. Udaipur, Rajasthan: Open Door Publications, 2015, pages 1766-1767.

Kee, H. C. And F. W. Young. *The Living World of the New Testament*. London: Darton, Longman & Todd, 1966.

Kummel, W. G. *Introduction to the New Testament* (Revised Edition). Translated by Howard C. Kee. London: SCM Press, 1975.

Lucas, Dick and Christopher Green. *The Message of II Peter and Jude*. The Bible Speaks Today, Leicester: Inter Varsity Press, 1995.

Moo, Douglas J., *2 Peter. Jude,* New International Version Application Commentary. Grand Rapids: Zondervan, 1997.

Rowston, D. J. "The Most Neglected Book in the New Testament", *New Testament Studies,* Vol. 21 (1974-1975), pages 554-563.

Ecclesiology in the New Testament

CHAPTER I

General Background and Context

The various traditions of the church hold that by A.D. 70 the best known of the Twelve Apostles were dead; the best known of those other than the Twelve, Paul, was also dead. Yet in the sub-apostolic era (the time immediately after the apostles or the apostolic era), the communities founded by these Apostles continued, and several documents of the New Testament were written in their names after their deaths suggesting a claim to apostolic adherence rather than to an objective designation of apostolic writing. The following chapters will therefore examine the images, in some of the New Testament documents, as samples of the various structures and understandings of the church left behind by the apostles, in an attempt to grapple with the inevitable problem of continuance/continuity and succession raised by the death of the apostles. This will be done using the texts of the New Testament and not from the perspective of ecclesiology in systematic and/or historical theology.

The sub-apostolic era/period has often given rise to much debate – when exactly did it begin? When did the eye-witnesses – *one of those who have accompanied us during all the time that the Lord Jesus went in and out among us...one of these must become with us a witness to His resurrection* (Acts 1:21-22) – cease to exist? The earliest thinking, brought out by Clement of Alexandria, was that just as Jesus appointed disciples, later recognized as apostles, so the apostles appointed presbyter-bishops to succeed them; consequently there was an orderly succession of authority in the early church which was broken by the emergence of false teachers/teaching which argued against the appointed authority. Hence in the earliest thinking, the sub-apostolic period was the one immediately after the last of the eye-witnesses to the resurrection had died, from about A.D. 70/80 till A.D. 100/110.

In the 18th and 19th centuries, the Hegelian method of thesis-antithesis-synthesis was applied by F. C. Baur and his school of thought bringing out that the thesis was Jewish Christianity represented by James; the antithesis was a pro-Gentile Christianity represented by Paul; and the synthesis was an intermediary Christianity represented by Peter. This method necessitated the late dating of some New Testament writings like Acts and the Epistles of Peter.

In the 20th century, many scholars like Walter Bauer felt that the sub-apostolic period represented the time when there were many diverse teachings and that finally there emerged, in the early 2nd century, a teaching, accepted in Rome and spreading eastwards, which became known as orthodoxy. Another view was that the sub-apostolic period was when Christianity was associated with the mission centres – Jerusalem as the earliest centre, then moving to Antioch, Corinth, Ephesus, Rome. Some of these centres, like Jerusalem and Rome could be associated with a more conservative Christianity closely allied with Judaism (Jerusalem with the Jewish Christianity represented by James – Acts 15; Rome with a Peterine version); whereas other centres like Corinth, Ephesus and cities in Asia Minor (Paul and John) were probably more allied with new movements, new ways of thinking and expression and therefore more liable to lapse into false teaching/syncreticism since there was no yardstick to act as a controlling criteria. This identification of 'conservative' and 'volatile' expressions would account for many of the New Testament writings being addressed to specific churches and cities.

Perhaps the best way to understand and define the sub-apostolic period (the period immediately after the apostles – from about A.D. 70/80 to A.D. 100/110; after this date it would be known as the post-apostolic period) is an examination of the writings in the New Testament that appeal to apostolic authority which are an indication that the Apostles left behind sufficiently strong heritages on which their communities could survive even without their physical presence. The New Testament evidence also suggests that different communities preserved different aspects of each Apostles' teaching, e.g. one aspect of Paul's thought is preserved in the letters to the Romans, Corinthians and Galatians (that Jew-Gentile relations are difficult in one community – Acts 28:25-29, Rom. 11:11-26, Gal. 2), while another aspect is preserved in Ephesians and Colossians (that the Jew-Gentile divide has been broken down and all are reconciled in one body – Eph. 2:11-22); one aspect of Peter's thought is preserved in Mark's Gospel while another aspect is preserved in the Peterine Epistles (I Pt. 1:13-2:10 – the Gentiles to go through the same exodus experience as the Israelites, moving toward a promised inheritance). Perhaps the only known Apostle to survive, in tradition, beyond the 70's of the First Century, was John, the son of Zebedee; the writings associated with John (John's Gospel, the Epistles of John, and the Book of Revelation) preserve yet another strand of apostolic heritage.

All of these are diverse documents showing that there is no 'one image/model' of ecclesiology in the New Testament, yet all are held together providing for a richness of diversity and tradition in the New Testament which must not be minimized in importance or even rejected, but studied and used as a guide, as an encouragement, as a corrective for traditions, and a challenge for community organization and witness.

CHAPTER II

Jewish and Gentile Influences
in the Ecclesiology of Matthew's Gospel

Introduction

This section on the highlights of the various ecclesiologies in the New Testament starts with Matthew's Gospel, the writing that the church has placed first in the canon, not because it was written first (see Vol. I in this series for Introduction to the Synoptics especially Matthew's Gospel), but probably because of two reasons: 1. It was the most widely distributed and used of the Gospels; and 2. It forged a middle path among the Gospels that would make it acceptable to both Jewish and Gentile converts and to other components of the newly emerging social entity called Christians. In the last two/three centuries of critical biblical scholarship, although Mark's Gospel has held centre stage with focus on the Synoptic problem, nevertheless, Matthew's Gospel continued to be more widely used in the everyday life of the church (e.g. the Matthean version of the Lord's prayer in liturgy) and as an introduction to the teachings of Jesus loved and used even by those of other faiths (e.g. the Sermon on the Mount). In Luke and John there are sequels to their writings (Acts; the Epistles and Revelation) which present the life of the community after the resurrection whereas this is not the case with Matthew and therefore, as will be seen below, the post-resurrectional era has been interwoven into the account of Jesus' ministry, and unlike the Jesus of the other Gospels and Acts, he does not go away by ascending into heaven (Mk. 16:19; Lk. 24:50-51; John 14 & 16: Acts 1:9), but remains eternally present with his followers until the end of time (Mtt. 28:20).

A further example of this blending of pre and post resurrection narratives is that the adversaries of Jesus' own lifetime are also the adversaries of the later Matthean community – the post A.D. 70 situation when the Temple had been destroyed and the Sadducees (priests) who were important players in the death of Jesus gave way to the Pharisees of rabbinic Judaism at Jamnia (the rumours about the disciples stealing the body of Jesus which *story has been spread among the Jews to this day* – 28:15. By the time Matthew's Gospel was written, the Pharisees were the only effective sect of the Jews that were left). A further blending can be found in 16:18 when the author uses the word *ecclesia* (ἐκκλησια – to be called out) for the new community that had come into existence – a word that was used only towards the end of the first century to refer to the church. Another example of this blending is that in Jesus' own lifetime, his ministry, and the commission to the disciples, was to *go nowhere among the Gentiles, and enter no town of the Samaritans, but go rather to the lost sheep of the house of Israel* (10:5-6), but this is blended with the gradual understanding that Jesus' mission had to include all the nations (28:19) – a blending of particularism/exclusiveness with universalism/inclusiveness.

Towards a Matthean ecclesiology

In the introduction to Matthew's Gospel (see Vol. I in this series), it was noted that 'Matthew' was probably a Greek speaking Jewish Christian with perhaps a background from the tribe of Levi which would account for his knowledge of the Hebrew scriptures and his desire to see that they were fulfilled; the esteem for a perceptive scribe in 13:52 may be autobiographical as may also be the use of the personal name 'Matthew' in the list of the disciples (10:1ff.) whereas the other Gospels use the tribal name of Levi. Given this background, his harsh treatment of the scribes and Pharisees opposed to Jesus must have been a reflection of the frustration he felt at their blindness and unwillingness to see that Jesus was not a contradiction to their religious values, but that *Jesus was re-interpreting the Law in a way that would preserve those values in a changed situation*: *think not that I have come to abolish the Law and the prophets; I have come not to abolish them. For truly, I say to you, till heaven and earth pass away, not an iota, not a dot, will pass from the*

Law until all is accomplished (5:17). The Pharisees had their origin as a liberating movement seeking to make the Law relevant through the oral tradition, but by the time of Jesus, the oral tradition had become as rigid as the written law, while at the same time also being so flexible that it began to suit vested interests rather than the interest/upliftment of the people. The Matthean Jesus who says over and over again, *you have heard it said, but I say to you....*(5:21, 27, 31, 33, 38, 43) is preserving the purpose of the Law making it relevant to, and contemporary with, the needs of the time. This placed greater demands on people than the legalist position of the Pharisees which placed boundaries on what God required and how God acts: *whoever then relaxes one of the least of these commandments and teaches others to do so, shall be called least in the Kingdom of Heaven; but whoever does them and teaches others to do them shall be called great in the Kingdom of Heaven. For I tell you, unless your righteousness exceeds that of the scribes and Pharisees, you will never enter the Kingdom of Heaven* (5:19-20). The demands of Jesus are far greater than the demands of the Mosaic Law as interpreted and enforced by the Pharisees.

All of the above points to the Matthean tradition having its **origin in a mission to the Jews and then gradually including the Gentiles.** The Matthean community would have been closer to a form of Hebrew Christianity associated with Peter – a community loyal to the Temple and Judaism, but learning to go beyond those boundaries to include the Gentiles – they observe the Sabbath (24:20), Jerusalem is the *holy city* (27:53) even though the Temple is forsaken and desolate (23:53), and the Jewish element in the community reacts with surprise at the entry of the Gentiles: *truly, I say to you, not even in Israel have I found such faith. Many will come from east and west and sit at table with Abraham, Isaac, and Jacob in the Kingdom of Heaven, while the children of the Kingdom will be thrown into outer darkness...* (8:10-12); similarly, in the parable of the vineyard rented to tenants (21:33-43), the Matthean addition that *the Kingdom of God will be taken away from you* (Jews/Judaism) *and given to a nation producing the fruits of it* (the Gentiles).

Matthew proclaims **a Jesus, though accepted by some Jews, yet is more acceptable to others who see a fulfilment of scripture**: Jesus begins his ministry in Galilee rather than in Judea – a fulfilment of Is. 9:1-2: *Galilee of the Gentiles – the people who sat in darkness have seen a great light...* (4:12-17); the healing on the Sabbath resulting in the Pharisees' plot to kill Jesus (12:9-21) – a fulfilment of Is. 41:1-4, *...I will put my spirit upon Him, and He shall proclaim justice to the Gentiles...and in His name will the Gentiles hope.* These are pointers that the Jewish component of the Matthean community had to learn to live with the Gentile component without envy or discrimination. It is this mixed community that is referred to as "the Church", a designation used for God's people in Deuteronomy 23:1 when describing those who must be kept out of the community of Israel in order to ensure purity, but by calling it *my Church* (16:18), Matthew indicates that the entry of the Gentiles does not mar the purity of the community. The words being placed on Jesus' lips make Jesus the ultimate interpreter of the salvific plan of God for all people – Jew and Gentile alike.

The Jew-Gentile relationships are also reflected in the infancy narrative in Matthew. The child is *Emmanuel – "God with us"* – and is first revealed to Joseph, a just Jew, and he obediently accepts it (1:18-25). Joseph symbolizes the Law-observant Jewish Christians of Matthew's community who by accepting Jesus made it possible for the good news to survive and spread. A second revelation is given to the *magi* who can find Jesus only when the scriptures are interpreted to them (2:1-5). These symbolize the Gentile converts who have learnt their Christianity through the interpretation of scripture in the Matthean community. There is a third group in the infancy narrative of Herod (the Great), the chief priests and the scribes of the people (2:3-5, 20), who are capable of interpreting the scripture but who want to kill the child; they symbolize the Pharisee rabbis of Matthew's time (probably those who formed the Jewish Council/Sanhedrin at Jamnia after the fall of Jerusalem and destruction of the Temple in A.D. 70) from whom the kingdom is taken away.

The Matthean hostility towards the unrepentant scribes and Pharisees has its result in ***persecution and calumny:*** there are hints at the illegitimacy of Jesus (1:18-19), references to persecution of Christians by synagogues/Jewish sources and Gentiles (5:10-11, 10:17-18, 22-23, 24:9), and anti-resurrection propaganda (28:15). Christians are abandoning the community due to these situations (13:21, 24:10); there are internal conflicts (10:8, 41, 17:20, 23:34) about disciples, prophets, wise persons each with different charismatic gifts; in times of persecution, the Holy Spirit speaks through persons (10:19-20), but there are abuses of this gift (7:22-23, 24:5, 11).

In his commentary on Matthew, J. D. Kingsbury shows that *the Matthean community was a mixed group of rich and poor.* Luke writes of small sums and copper coins whereas Matthew inflates these details in his narratives to large sums and gold and silver; Joseph of Arimathea was described as a rich man (27:57; Luke omits his economic status); the Lucan Jesus is harsh on the wealthy but has blessings for the poor (6:20-25), the wealthy barn-builder should have given his money to the poor (Lk. 12:13-21), the poor Lazarus and the rich man have their roles reversed in heaven (Lk. 16:19-25); whereas in Matthew though riches can choke the word of God (11:22), and the rich will find it hard to enter the kingdom of Heaven (19:23), nevertheless with God all things are possible (19:26); and if the rich are *poor in spirit* and *hunger and thirst after righteousness* they can be included in Jesus' beatitude (5:3, 6), a beatitude for which there is no corresponding curse against wealth and riches. There is also a pastoral nuance in dealing with these mixtures: misbehaving charismatics should not be thrown out because such a purge might damage good members, but the situation should be tolerated until divine judgement thereby exercising patience and mercy (13:24-30, 36-43).

The Matthean community is *exhorted to be good citizens* with regard to payment of taxes: the narrative of the coin in the fish's mouth (17:24-27). This was a tax to support the Temple and paid only by Jews; after the destruction of the Temple, the tax continued to be imposed on the Jews and went into the Roman treasury. The narrative indicates that Jewish Christians still considered themselves to be good Jews.

The Matthean community has also to deal with *the issue of Church authority:* Matthew rejects the Pharisaic claim of precedence (23:5-7), but the principles of authority are upheld: *the scribes and Pharisees sit on Moses' seat; so practice and observe what they tell you, but not what they do; for they preach but do not practice* (23:2-3). Authoritative judgement is not new to Matthew – the 12 disciples are to sit on thrones in judgement (19:28) – but the ultimate authority comes only from Jesus. Peter as the rock on which the church is built with the power to bind and loose on earth and so in heaven (16:18-19) with the imagery of the keys of the kingdom being given to Peter is akin to setting up Peter as the chief rabbi like the main administrator in the Davidic kingdom (Is. 22:22). In all these instances the power and authority is given by Jesus but it reflects a strong sense of organization and authority in the Matthean community, nevertheless a community that rejects the use of rabbinic titles (23:8-11), lest an exaggerated view of authority begins to be exercised, instead authority had to be tempered with humility: *the one who is greatest among you shall be your servant, whoever exalts themselves will be humbled, and whoever humbles themselves will be exalted* (23:11-12).

The Matthean sermon on the Church – Matthew 18

Chapter 18 of Matthew's Gospel has often been called the Sermon on church order and life. It is set in the context of teaching the disciples, including later Christians – teaching which is placed back on the lips of Jesus but which reflects the later church situation, i.e. this purported teaching of Jesus anticipates and gives direction for dealing with the prevailing issues that the later church would face because of the very fact that it was a structured organization and exercised authority.

The dispute concerning greatness (18:1-5) serves as the preface to this sermon. This concern among the disciples may have arisen when thinking about the ultimate arrival of the kingdom; yet Matthew also speaks of the kingdom of the Son of Man in this world (the rest of the chapter deals with issues pertaining to present life on earth), so here is a dispute which would have meaning for the church where inevitably there would arise a concern for authoritative positions; the point being made is to discern what becomes important in a religious society where there is authority and who exercises this authority. The image/vocabulary of 'kingdom' immediately raises issues of prestige and power – issues that Jesus regarded as a temptation to reduce the Kingdom of God to the level of a kingdom of this world (4:5-10). Sociology teaches that in an organized society, religious or otherwise, the issues of who exercise authority would sooner or later become of prime importance because the person with the greatest authority is the primary figure in the group. However, Matthew would argue otherwise: that the sociological norm cannot be allowed to be dominant in the presence of Jesus. In Jesus' values, the humble are more important than the powerful, as dependence on, and obedience to God is what makes one open to God's rule. So the example of a little child is given – a child who symbolizes dependence and who is without power. The point being made is that in the Kingdom of Heaven, it is God who has the power/authority, and closeness to God, and therefore greatness in the Kingdom, comes from the degree of dependence on, and submission of power to God. Thus the sociological value system of this world is turned upside down in the value system of the Kingdom of Heaven – not power, but the lack of it is what makes a person great. This is the first point that any teaching on church order and life must make; therefore the issue concerning greatness in the Kingdom serves as the preface to the sermon/teaching.

The section that follows deals with the condemnation of scandals and temptations (18:6-9), even attitudes that can cause someone to stumble (σκανδαλιζομαι = scandal; to cause to stumble), would be appropriate for a church congregation; such scandals existed in churches found elsewhere in the New Testament, e.g. Romans 8:13, I Cor. 1:11ff, 8:13, 11:19, but they are absolutely condemned.

The parable of the lost sheep (18:10-14) also has congregational/ pastoral implications for by most standards, the success of any organization is the extent to which they take care of the majority, so better to let one person go rather than lose the 99 supporters. But Jesus came to save the lost (10:6, 15:24) and so there is a different value teaching to the disciples – pastoral care is an obligation towards even one member who needs encouragement not further scandal. This again is part of the upside down values of the Kingdom.

The next section in the sermon is clearly adapted to, and speaks to a church situation: procedure for correcting a fellow member (18:15-18), the access to heaven (18:19-20), the frequency of forgiveness (18:21-22). The fellow member who refuses to be corrected is to be brought before the church for disciplinary action – a process designed to prevent misuse of power by a single authority which could be a danger in any structured community (possibly a community decision is to counter the absolute authority given to Peter in 16:18-19; somewhat akin to the movement from exclusivism to inclusivism seen in 10:5-6 and 28:19). If the fellow member refuses to be corrected, they are to be treated as a *Gentile and tax collector*. Matthew was written to a mixed community in Syria, so it is these two categories that are of particular interest in Matthew's gospel – Jesus' final instructions to go to the Gentiles (all nations – 28:19), and Jesus' interest in a tax collector called Matthew, one of his disciples (9:9, 10:3), show that the unrepentant person may still be the subject of outreach and concern – love and not authority should be primary in dealing with a member; when all efforts fail, only then are the categories *Gentile and Tax Collector* applied – the two categories that were hated by the Jews. Further it is the community that takes the final action, not an individual – a community in prayer where whatever is agreed upon is granted. The bringing in of the community in disciplinary action shows a development in Matthew from a single, exclusive authoritarian structure to an inclusive community centred model. This interpretation is again highlighted by the issue raised by Peter, probably the acknowledged 'head' and a lesson as to how the 'head' is to exercise authority – how many times to forgive (18:21-22); the answer is to forgive an unlimited number of times. This is confirmed by the parable of the unforgiving servant (18:23-35) that invokes divine judgement on those who refuse to forgive.

This collection of varied ethical teachings has been brought together here and given a perspective that makes it very suited to an established church, especially in the context of the disciples being the representative body, and Peter as the rock on which the church is built (chapter 16). Matthew connects ecclesiology and Christology in such a way that the values of Jesus are preserved in a structured set-up (the church, 16:18,

18:17-20) even if there are other structures and values that surround it, the church will be a society that is distinct from other societies. All this teaching has a very real application to church life – when the churches listen to Jesus speaking to his disciples in this way, they keep alive his spirit, and then will be fulfilled the saying that *"where two or three are gathered in my name, there am I in the midst of them"* (18:20) and when these values have been put into practice then the Kingdom of God would have become a reality.

Strengths and weaknesses

There are two great strengths in Matthean ecclesiology:

1.   *A high respect for the Law and authority.*

In the healing of the paralytic (9:1-8) in the alleged breaking of the Law – *this man blasphemes* – Jesus' authority to forgive sins was questioned, but then it would seem that the Matthean community is reflected in the conclusion in that *they glorified God, who had given such authority to people.* The Matthean sermon on the Church (chapter 18) and the selection of Peter are also indications that a collective authority was being proposed to be exercised in a democratic way with a pastoral concern of love being the criteria.

2.   *Matthew preserves the pastoral attitude of Jesus in interpreting the Law and exercising authority.*

If only the first strength of Matthean ecclesiology is taken then it would result in a weakness that becomes authoritarianism and legalism, but combined with the second strength, the voice of Jesus is heard, so that it's not just *you have heard it said* which would be equivalent to the law (authoritarianism and legalism), but also *I say to you…* which would keep the Law from becoming absolute.

Matthew enumerates the vehicles through which this authority is to be exercised: Peter, the disciples, the whole community, but all get their power from Jesus. This dependence on Jesus was necessary as a corrective, otherwise the figures of authority would become like the scribes and Pharisees – a law, and an end, unto themselves. In this way

Matthew corrects any attitudes in the church which may have been building up or which he could foresee would be a cause of trouble if there was too much adherence to the law and authority.

The strong sense of Jesus' continued presence in the church (28:20 – *I am with you always...*) is reflected in the five great sermons in Matthew's Gospel (see the Analysis and Commentary in Vol. I of this series) which is the means whereby Jesus remains present in a community that is willing to live by his commandments: *Jesus went about all the cities and villages, teaching in their synagogues and preaching the gospel of the Kingdom, and healing every disease and every infirmity* (9:35). Therefore without the component of the teaching and presence of Jesus, the Gospel could not become absolute even in the church – the church must be the place where the teaching of Jesus is lived out in everyday life. This is also a way in which Matthew blends the pre and post resurrectional situation: the on-going life of the church (post- resurrection) is dominated by the presence of Jesus in and through his teachings (pre-resurrection).

All this implies that the one evangelist to use the word *church* (ἐκκλησια) and to present Jesus as building the church on a human foundation (Peter), perhaps to reflect historical tradition, nevertheless foresaw the possibility of the human institution becoming its own authority in a self-sufficient way creating its own teaching and law, and therefore Matthew had to counter this danger by insisting that teaching, preaching, mission, had to be done in Jesus' name because he was eternally present and so the community could not conform to Pharisaic rabbinical structures (Rabbi, Master, Father for human authority) which Jesus had opposed in His lifetime. Matthew has institutional structures, law, and authority, but uniquely Jesus' voice is not stifled and remains normative, only then *this gospel of the Kingdom will be preached throughout the whole world, as a testimony to all nations...*(24:14).

CHAPTER III

A Reflection of the Pauline Influence in the Ecclesiology of Luke-Acts

Introduction

Paul was noted for his missionary activity and the spread of the church especially in the region of Greece and Asia Minor. Yet within 20 to 30 years of his death (ca. A.D. 64), the New Testament reflects at least three different strands of Pauline thought that had emerged – 1. Luke-Acts; 2. Ephesians-Colossians; 3. The Pastorals. Although all three strands eventually trace their origin back to Paul (the Apostolic authority that brought them into the canon), it is not certain where the readers were geographically located (see Vols. I & II of this series for an Introduction to these writings) or whether they knew each other. In the strain reflected by Luke-Acts, Christian history in Acts is divided into almost equal eras of Peter (upto the Council's decision in Acts 15) and Paul (after Acts 15 – taking the mission to the Gentiles from Jerusalem to Rome) fulfilling the mandate that Acts sets for itself – *to the ends of the earth* (Acts 1:8). Yet the author of Acts never mentions that Paul wrote letters nor does the author show any knowledge of the Pauline letters which became the basis of Christian theology. In the strain of Colossians-Ephesians, Paul is regarded as an authority who can address the community as an *apostle and prophet upon whom the Church is founded* (Eph. 2:20); the author of Ephesians knew of many Pauline letters and draws on them in the formulation of thought. Thus, though the authors of Luke-Acts and Ephesians-Colossians have moved beyond Paul's thought they are nevertheless dependent on Paul, thus the Pauline heritage/influence continued even after his death.

Another issue where Paul is both reflected and superseded is that of the Jew-Gentile relationships. In Acts, the last words of Paul to the Jews are: *you shall indeed hear but never understand; you shall indeed see but never perceive,* *for this people's heart has grown dull, and their ears heavy of hearing, and their eyes they have closed; lest they should perceive with their eyes, and hear with their ears, and understand with their heart, and turn for me to heal them. Let it be known to you then that this salvation of God has been sent to the Gentiles; they will listen* (Acts 28:26-28). In Ephesians, the relationship between Jew and Gentile seems to have been resolved peacefully: the wall of hostility has been broken down, those who were once far off have come near, Jew and Gentile are reconciled in one body to God through the cross (Eph. 2:1-22). The different communities addressed by these works – both communities that respect Paul – have very different views about Jew- Gentile relations, and both are at a historical distance from Paul in Romans who argues that the Gentiles were converted to make the Jew jealous, and that ultimately the Jew will be converted, and that the Gentiles are like a wild olive branch grafted onto the true olive – Israel (Rom. 11:11-26).

In the Pastorals there is yet another strand of the Pauline heritage/ influence. There is a disquiet among the communities by the demands of the Judaizers. The author sees a structured church as the answer and therefore insists on the appointment of church officials with their qualifications – an insistence lacking in Luke-Acts and Ephesians-Colossians.

In the undisputed letters of Paul (Romans, I & II Corinthians, Galatians, Philemon – see Vol. II in this series especially the section on the Pauline understanding/presentation of the Church), the *ecclesia* sometimes means the total (universal) church and sometimes the local congregation reflecting the peculiar character of the eschatological community; the individual believer stands within the congregation, and the individual congregations are joined together into one Congregation – the church. At first the *ecclesia* does not denote individual congregations, but the total 'people of God' – the fellowship of the chosen, elect, at the end of days – the eschatological congregation. This means that the individual congregations are the present visible manifestations of the eschatological Universal Congregation (I Cor. 10:32, 11:22, 12:28, 15:9; Gal. 1:13). The local church as a manifestation of the total, universal church is probably meant in the expression occurring in the prefatory greetings of letters: *to the church (of God) in* ,τη ἐκκλησια του Θεου τη οὐση ἐν....I Cor. 1:2; II Cor. 1:1), or in the references to "house churches" (Rom. 16:5; I Cor. 16:9; Col. 4:15; Philem. 2). 'The Church' is therefore simultaneously thought of as a visible local congregation in the world and having to deal with the issues of the world – *the church in Corinth, the church in Ephesus etc...* – and as the invisible, Universal, eschatological Congregation (expressed in the Nicean-Constantinopolitan Creed as the "*One, Holy, Catholic Church*"). The eschatological Congregation is present in the cultic gathering (I Cor. 11:18) in which Christ is confessed as Lord (I Cor. 12:3; Philip. 2:11), and where the Lord, through the presence of the Spirit, bestows *spiritual gifts* (I Cor. 14) so that *if an unbeliever or outsider enters....they will worship God and declare that God is really among you* (I Cor. 14:24-25).

It must also be noted that in the undisputed letters of Paul, the church is a "charismatic" community, i.e. having no definite structure or liturgical pattern though Paul insists that worship should be orderly (I Cor.14:26-33). The letters that reflect a more structured liturgy and church order (Ephesians, Colossians, the Pastorals) are held to belong to a period later than Paul.

Another major issue in the undisputed letters of Paul was *the place of Jews and Gentiles in the Church*. Jewish Christianity was represented by the earliest church in Palestine as it had not separated itself from Judaism and the concept of the eschatological Congregation of the Jewish people (see Acts where the disciples are closely associated with the worship of the Temple; later followed by Paul who always goes first to the synagogue in the City where he is visiting). This Congregation took for granted that a non-Jew, desirous of joining the Congregation had first to submit to the laws of Judaism, i.e. had to become a Jew. In contrast to this, and in the presence of Hellenistic Judaism (i.e. Judaism outside of Palestine which had also incorporated influences of other religions), there arose Hellenistic Christianity which did not require the person to first become a Jew. This Hellenistic Christianity or Gentile Christianity represented by Paul achieved recognition at the Jerusalem Council (see Acts 15 in Vol. II of this series), but the so-called Judaisers still persisted in insisting on the precepts of Judaism being followed before admission to Christianity. Their mission personnel had penetrated Pauline areas of ministry and caused trouble (see the Corinthian Correspondence and Galatians in Vol. II of this series). In the undisputed letters of Paul, he struggled with this problem of Hellenistic Christianity acknowledging the ethical demands of the Law yet rejecting the validity of the Law as a means of salvation; Paul came up with the concept of justification by faith (see Vol. II of this series). Further, in the eschatological Congregation, this world's distinctions have lost their meaning, therefore *there is neither Jew nor Greek, there is neither slave nor free, there is neither male nor female, for you are all one in Christ Jesus* (Gal. 3:28). This indifference to worldly distinctions also extends to *let each one remain in the state in which the call of God encountered them* (I Cor. 7:17-24), a differentiation that does not mean a sociological programme for change, but one which has validity and takes place only within the eschatological Congregation. Thus for Paul, and his interpretation which he refers to as *my gospel,* Jews and Gentiles have an equal place in the church.

The Body of Christ is a major metaphor which Paul uses among many other images to describe the eschatological character of the church: *new covenant* (I Cor. 11:25; II Cor. 3:6ff.), *the Israel of God* (Gal. 6:16), Abraham as the father of those who have faith (Rom. 4; Gal. 3), in the church all promises find their fulfilment (Rom. 15:4; I Cor. 10:11). The most characteristic image is that of "the Body of Christ" used to express the unity of the church and the foundation of this unity (Rom. 12:4-8; I Cor. 12:12-31). The expression of the church as a "body" was developed from the classical Greek tradition which used this image to describe an organically developed and compact community where all the parts have equal importance and work together to present a unity – the organic role of the image of the body. The individual is taken into the "body of Christ" by baptism (Rom. 12:4-5; I Cor. 12:12-13; II Cor. 1:21; Gal. 3:27), so that further existence is "in Christ". The *en Christo* (ἐν Χριστῷ) phrase is here used primarily as an ecclesiological formula though it also retains its eschatological implications: *if anyone is "in Christ", they are a new creation* (II Cor. 5:17) – both a present reality in the church and a hope for the future when all of creation is renewed.

All these variations occur in writings associated with the Apostle, his own letters and letters written after his death in his name; each church emphasized a different aspect of the Pauline tradition, and therefore needs to be given separate thought to do justice to each situation and how they sought to meet the crisis in the sub-apostolic period that came up with the death of the founding Apostle.

Towards an ecclesiology of Luke-Acts

The author of Luke-Acts shows no knowledge of the Pauline Epistles (undisputed writings or otherwise) but does present a picture of Paul, albeit more moderate than the picture painted by Paul himself in his writings to the Corinthians, Galatians, and Romans. The author of Luke-Acts was not writing a book on Pauline Theology, but presenting a narrative in which Paul plays a major role as a missionary and not as a doctrinal expert. Scholars are not agreed on the recipients of Luke-Acts, except to the extent that there was a Gentile element involved expressed in the basic geographic area mentioned: *you shall be my witnesses in Jerusalem and all Judea and Samaria, and to the ends of the earth* (Acts 1:8). It may even be that the author of Luke-Acts[6] and the communities to which the letters are addressed might not have personally known Paul, but without a doubt for them, Paul was an important figure in God's plan to bring Christ to the Gentiles and to the ends of the earth. So it is interesting to trace how Luke-Acts agrees with/differs from the images in Paul's own writings. Acts uses the word "Church" for local churches, nevertheless "the one, holy, catholic, apostolic" church marks the features of each church. The author does this by using Mark as the basis for the story of Jesus, yet rewriting and reshaping it to suit the Lucan context and understanding; the author follows this up with a second volume concerning early Christianity thereby placing on equal level the proclamation of Jesus and the proclamation of the apostles, especially Peter and Paul.[7] This means that what God had done in Jesus is continued by what God does through the Spirit. Such an understanding leads to a major characteristic in Lucan ecclesiology – the *heilsgeschichte* – the continuation of salvation history from Israel to Jesus to the church; one of the purposes of the Gospel of Luke was to trace a continuation of biblical history with Christianity as the logical and legitimate continuation of Judaism. First, a succession of characters based on Hebrew scripture models are brought forth in the infancy narrative (Zachariah, Elizabeth, Anna, Simeon etc..), the characters are all pious Jews and everything is done according to the Law; then Jesus stands as a continuation and fulfilment of the *Law and the Prophets* (Lk. 16:16) which is seen as ending with John the Baptist and since then *the good news of the Kingdom of God is preached...* With the ascension of Jesus, Luke's Gospel comes to an end (Lk. 24:51), but reappears at the beginning of Acts (Acts 1:1-11) to show that he (Jesus) is the origin of all that follows and therefore the continuity has passed from Jesus to the Church.[8] The relationship between the Kingdom and the church is seen in the question asked of Jesus at the beginning of Acts – *will you at this time restore the Kingdom to Israel?* and the reply that it is *not for you to know times or seasons... but you shall receive power when the Holy Spirit has come upon you; and you shall be my witnesses in Jerusalem and in all Judea and Samaria and to the end of the earth* (Acts 1:6-8): a relationship and commission that places great emphasis on bearing witness rather than on Jesus' coming again; this approach makes the church's existence both explicable and essential until the coming of the Kingdom; it also serves as an apologetic as to why the author is writing a second volume describing the church's existence.

This second volume is called *Acts of the Apostles,* a title which is not quite accurate as Paul, one of the main characters in the writing, is nowhere called an apostle; however, the writing does underline the role played by leaders in the story of the church: leaders like the eye witnesses to the life, death and resurrection of Jesus, His mother and brothers, the women are there in the early community and ensure the continuity with Jesus. Paul was not one of those, but it was believed that he was commissioned by the risen Jesus and later Peter and James certified the correctness of Paul's missionary decision/strategy to go to the Gentiles (Gal. 1:18-20) and convert them without demanding circumcision. *Thus the early stages of the Church life are continuous with Jesus, as well as the next stage represented by Peter and the conversion of Cornelius (Acts 10, 11:1-18), and finally the later stage represented by Paul and his mission to Gentile areas.*[9] If Jesus performed miracles, then Peter performs the same type of miracles followed by Paul; Jesus preached sermons, so do Peter and Paul whose sermons are quite similar – signs of a continuous message and exercise of power. The author of Acts has Paul make provision for the care of communities after he has gone by appointing elders (Acts 14:23); in his farewell address to the elders of Ephesus, he urges, *take heed to yourselves and to all the flock, in which the Holy Spirit has made you guardians* (overseers/ bishops), *to feed* (shepherd) *the Church of the Lord...*(Acts 20:28); thus a continuity beyond Paul is envisioned. This principle of continuity in the *heilsgeschichte* running through, and bringing together, Israel, Jesus, Peter and Paul is well summed up by the words of Acts attributed to Paul in his speech before Felix, the Governor *...I admit to you, that according to the Way* (i.e. the Way taught by Jesus), *which they call a sect, I worship the God of our fathers, believing everything laid down by the Law or written in the prophets...* (Acts 24:14-15).

A distinguishing feature in Lucan ecclesiology is the *role of the Holy Spirit*: it is the connective between the prophecies of Israel and the prophetic activity surrounding the birth of Jesus and the birth of the church.[10] One example of this distinguishing feature in ecclesiology is that Peter is not mentioned after the decision to admit the Gentiles (Acts 15), and that the story stops when Paul reaches Rome (neither of these apostles' subsequent careers or deaths are mentioned), but that is understandable when both figures are being balanced; however, what is more important is that Acts is not interested in the persons, *per se*, but in how they were used by the Holy Spirit as vehicles bearing witness to Christ; it is the Spirit that plays the main role! This idea of the Holy Spirit being the agent of continuity and the connective is later seen in the Pastorals where "Paul" reminds "Timothy", *rekindle the gift of God that is within you through the laying on of my hands; for God did not give us a spirit of timidity but a spirit of power and love and self-control* (II Tim. 1:6-7), and again, *do not neglect the gift you have, which was given to you by prophetic utterance when the elders laid their hands upon you* (I Tim. 4:14). Since Timothy in turn lays hands on others (I Tim. 5:2), the gift of the Spirit is attached to commissioning so that the Spirit enables the person to complete the assigned task.

In Luke-Acts there is a great importance attached to the role of the Spirit. The disciples are discouraged from looking into the sky for Jesus (Acts 1:11) for the gift of the Spirit is to take the place of Jesus on earth. Almost immediately in Acts is the coming of the Spirit on the Day of Pentecost like a *mighty wind* moving over the face of the waters at the time of creation (Acts 2:2; Gen. 1:2). When the church comes into existence through the coming and power of the Spirit, it is a new creation that is taking place matching the first creation; and a renewed covenant comes into existence filling the people with the Holy Spirit (Acts 2:14-17) replacing the old covenant at Sinai. Up to this point, the apostles had not proclaimed publicly what they believed God had done in Jesus due to lack of courage; but now the first missionary movement in Acts is attributed to the Spirit with which the apostles were baptized and empowered to speak (Acts 1:5, 8; 2:33; 4:8, 31). The moving of the Spirit marked entry into the group of believers (Acts 2:38; 8:15-17; 9:17; 15:8; 19:5-6); the Spirit directed missionaries (Acts 8:29, 39); the Spirit directed Peter to the house of Cornelius and was instrumental in the conversion of Cornelius, the first Gentile convert (Acts 10:38, 44-47; 11:12, 15); the Spirit was responsible for the commissioning of Barnabas and Paul on a mission that would convert whole communities of Gentiles (Acts 13, 2,4); the Spirit led Peter, Paul, and James to make the most momentous decision in Christian history – to admit the Gentiles without submitting to the laws of circumcision in Judaism: *it has seemed good to the Holy Spirit and to us to lay upon you no greater burden...*(Acts 15:28); the Spirit prevented Paul from entering Europe on the so-called Second Missionary Journey (Acts 16:6-7); Paul resolved in the Spirit to go to Rome (Acts 19:21); the appointment of *overseers/bishops of the flock of Christ* is a movement of the Spirit (Acts 20:28). Thus, at every important step in the spread of the Gospel, and of how witness was borne *to the ends of the earth*, it was the Spirit at work to guide human agents who would perhaps otherwise choose/decide wrongly.

Strengths and weaknesses

The above analysis has shown that in the ecclesiology of Luke-Acts, two dominant factors have played a role: 1. *Continuity* from Israel through Jesus to Peter and to Paul; and 2. The *intervention of the Holy Spirit* at crucial moments in the history of the church. Both of these factors would have been enormously helpful to the community/readers of Luke-Acts after the end of the apostolic age. In fact, the deaths of Peter and Paul do not even find a place in Acts: Peter's career comes to an end when he confirms the admission of the Gentiles without submitting to circumcision thereby approving the Pauline mission (Acts 15); in Paul's farewell speech to the elders of Ephesus (Acts 20:25, 28) he passes on the care of the flock to them. The chain of *continuity* shows God's plan of salvation being spread to all the earth and when one passes on after having played their role, faith confirms that another will pick up the mantle and God's plan will continue.

This concept of *continuity* gives the Gentiles a sense of pride in their new religion otherwise in the Greco-Roman world, something new would have been viewed with suspicion and dismissed as superstition; by the principle of *continuity,* the new religion is traced back more than 1000 years, and to creation itself, and so considered ancient/respectable by any historical standard. The author connects this *continuity* with Roman history by mentioning Roman emperors and governors in relation to the birth and ministry of Jesus (Lk. 2:12; 3:1-2), Roman officials in the ministry of Paul and Paul's exercise of his Roman citizenship in Philippi and finally in his appeal to Caesar (Acts 13:7; 16:37; 18:12; 23:26; 25:1-2, 10-12). All this shows that even political figures and foreign laws have been touched by the principle of *continuity.* To have had a significant past gives confidence for the future, and the author supplies for Christianity that foundation which would enable it to go forward.

As important as the principle of *continuity* would have been the portrayal of the *Holy Spirit* that intervenes at crucial moments in the history of the movement taking the movement forward into the next stage of God's salvific plan. It is an indication that even the leaders of the movement needed the intervention of the *Spirit* and it relativizes the importance of the apostolic period: the apostles were great instruments of the *Spirit* but other instruments are there, or will be found, to carry on God's plan of salvation; the *Spirit* that brought faith to the Gentiles and brought Paul to Rome is continually in the church guiding it in times of crisis and normalcy; whenever Christians have encountered error, the presence of the *Spirit* has been appealed to for providing true teaching and leadership; when something good and unexpected happens, it has always been attributed to the work of the *Spirit* providing for the good of the church. This legacy of dependence on the *Spirit* for every move in the church is a lasting legacy of Luke-Acts and a yardstick for judging movements in history.

However, this triumphal procession of all set-backs being temporary and then turning out for good (persecution in Jerusalem, imprisonments etc...), of a constantly growing movement in numbers (Acts 2:41; 4:4; 6:1, 7; 8:12; 9:31; 21:19-20), and geographically (Acts 1:8), portrays the picture of a movement in a hugely successful mission; it does not prepare for major defeats that are not recouped. Such a triumphal ecclesiology would leave Christians perplexed when institutions collapse and missions fail, when numbers decrease and other movements/philosophies/ideologies become more popular than Christianity. It often leads to a denial of factual situations – the church cannot fail – rather than a realistic appraisal of the situation and a dependence on the *Spirit* to connect with the past – *continuity* – and to lead into the future exploring new ways and avenues for the mission, especially in situations where Christianity finds itself as a minority and where its existence is at stake. A further weakness in a 'Spirit-dependant/controlled' movement is that decisions are taken out of the hands of human beings: human participation is reduced to only following the Spirit without contributing human intelligence and creativity. This removal of human input from the sphere of development/ growth tends to undermine human decisions and reduce history to simply a working out of fate/predetermined destiny.

Conclusion

From the above, it is seen that the strength of the ecclesiology of Luke-Acts – *continuity* and *the intervention of the Holy Spirit* – can also become its weakness, but in the witness of Luke-Acts, such an ecclesiology serves as a challenge to the present day church to examine the basis of *continuity* and to identify the areas of the *Spirit's* intervention in order to see God at work in the past, to affirm and strengthen the faith that God will continue to work in the present, and in the future, in and through the instruments that God chooses and appoints in, and for, God's own mission.

A Reflection of the Pauline Influence in the Ecclesiology of Ephesians and Colossians

Introduction

Ephesians and Colossians represent a strain of the sub-apostolic period more directly connected to Paul than Luke-Acts (above) or the Pastorals (below). Both the cities of Ephesus and Colossae had a strong Pauline influence in the establishment of the churches/communities there; both letters may have been written within twenty years of Paul's death, and almost at the same time as each other, so they would stand closer to Paul's thought (see Vol. II of this series for discussions on authorship and date) though not to Paul's style of writing, vocabulary, and idiom. In the point under consideration, the question is asked as to how these two writings, standing within the Pauline heritage, contribute towards an ecclesiology after the death of the apostle.

Both the epistles claim 'Paul'[11] as the apostolic authority and the authoritative voice in the *household of God...built upon the foundation of the apostles and prophets, Christ Jesus Himself being the cornerstone* (Eph. 2:19-20). In both epistles, instructions for household relationships *(haustafeln)* are supplied in an authoritative manner different from the Pastorals. In the structure of the churches there are *apostles, prophets, evangelists, pastors and teachers, for the equipment of the saints, for the work of ministry, for building up the body of Christ...* (Eph. 4:11-13). Yet there is no stress on apostolic succession or on the role of "pastors and teachers" though the 'Colossian heresy' (Col. 2:8-23. See Vol. II of this series) would call for a firm response to false teaching, instead, Ephesians and Colossians offers an idealistic view of the church referring to it as the 'body of Christ'. The use of the phrase "body of Christ" in Ephesians and Colossians is imaged as an actual body with Christ as the head (Eph. 1:23, 5:30; Col. 1:18, 24), i.e. as the superior organ – the functional role of each part of the body taken separately. This change in the meaning of the imagery from its use in the undisputed letters of Paul, also contributes to Ephesians and Colossians being placed among the deutero-Pauline writings. Further the absolute, idealistic view of **the Church** offered in Ephesians and Colossians differs from the undisputed letters of Paul where *the Church* refers to individual local congregations (e.g. *to the church of God which is at Corinth* – I Cor. 1:2; *to the churches of Galatia* – Gal. 1:2); this absolute use of **the Church** calls for a different view from the undisputed letters of Paul. In Ephesians and Colossians, **the Church** seems to be more than an earthly reality, for it affects the heavenly powers – the understanding in later theology of a church triumphant (in heaven) alongside a church militant (on earth).

All of this indicates that the ecclesiology of Ephesians and Colossians must be studied separately from the ecclesiology of other strains of Pauline thought.

Towards an ecclesiology of Ephesians and Colossians

In the undisputed letters of Paul, he uses the image of a body and how each part is dependent on the other in order to address the issue of jealousy and gifts of the Spirit in Corinth (I Cor. 12); this diversity of body parts is also used to justify the charisms enjoyed by the Corinthians: *apostles, prophets, teachers, workers of miracles, healers, helpers, administrators, speakers in various kinds of tongues...*(I Cor. 12:22-31). This variety is referred to as *you are the body of Christ* (I Cor. 12:27). This image of the body of Christ is taken over in Ephesians and Colossians and developed in a new way with an emphasis, not on the individual parts that make up the body, but on the body as a whole. By his death, *you who were once estranged and hostile in mind, doing evil deeds, he has now reconciled in his body...* (Col.1:21), and they have been called into one body (Col. 3:15), **the Church,** of which Christ is the head (Eph. 1:22-23; 5:23; Col. 1:18, 24-25). From Paul's reference to Christians as members/parts of a real body, the interpretation of the imagery has shifted to a corporate understanding with Christ as Lord over that body (Eph. 4:4-5). But **the Church** does not become a corporation with administrative and institutional structure, rather in Ephesians and Colossians **the Church** is a growing entity living in the life of Christ himself; the basic error is *not holding fast to the Head, from whom the whole body, nourished and knit together through its joint and ligaments, grows with a growth that is from God* (Col. 2:19). The different ministries are for *the work of ministry, for building up the body of Christ, until we all attain to the unity of the faith...to the measure of the stature of the fullness of Christ...we are to grow up in every way into Him who us the Head, into Christ, from whom the whole body, joined and knit together by every joint...makes for bodily growth and upbuilds itself in love* (Eph. 4:12-16).

In this approach to the church, the theme of **love** is very strong. In the undisputed letters of Paul, the Corinthians are presented as a virgin bride to Christ; this image is expanded in Ephesians to a relationship between Christ and *the Church* and likens the relationship to one between husband and wife; Christ nourishes and cherishes the church: *...husbands, love your wives, as Christ loved the Church and gave Himself up for her...no one hates their own flesh but nourishes and cherishes it, as Christ does the Church...this is a great mystery...Christ and the Church...* (Eph. 5:21-33; Col. 3:18-4:1). The goal of Christ's life and death has become the church, and the Church may be said to be the ultimate goal of God's salvific plan (Eph. 1:22-23, 5:32; Col. 4:12-17).

Another characteristic of ecclesiology in Ephesians and Colossians is **holiness:**... *Christ loved the Church and gave Himself up for her, that He might sanctify her, having cleansed her by the washing of water with His blood, that He might present the Church to Himself in splendour, without spot or wrinkle or any such thing, that she might be holy and without blemish...* (Eph. 5:25ff.; Col. 3:5ff.). The characteristics of **love and**

holiness must go together so that the holiness of Christ may be seen in the Church which is His body being built up in love (Eph. 4:16; Col. 2:19). This results in the Church being identified with the Kingdom of God's Son: *...the Father, who has qualified us to share in the inheritance of the saints in light. He has delivered us from the dominion of darkness and transferred us to the Kingdom of His beloved Son, in whom we have redemption, the forgiveness of sins* (Col. 1:13-14; Eph. 1:21). *God has raised us up with Him, and made us sit with Him in the heavenly places in Christ Jesus...* (Eph. 2:1ff.). Finally, in the Kingdom, God has made known God's plan *for the fullness of time, to unite all things in Him, things in heaven and things on earth* (Eph. 1:10); and as further expressed, *For in Him (Christ) all the fullness of God was pleased to dwell, and through Him to reconcile to Himself all things, whether on earth or in heaven, making peace by the blood of His cross* (Col. 1:19-20).

These qualities almost give to the church a divine character summed up in the doxology: *now to Him who by the power at work within us is able to do far more abundantly than all that we may ask or think, to Him be glory in the Church and in Christ Jesus to all generations, for ever and ever. Amen.* (Eph. 3:20-21).

Strengths and weaknesses

The **first strength** of the exalted ecclesiology of Ephesians-Colossians is that the *body of Christ* imagery personalizes the church and encourages the imitation of the love of Christ for his bride, the church. People, in the final analysis, do not love an institution/structure, but when the image is personalized, it is easier to respond to it in love. The relationship to this personalized image is found in the statement of the author (Paul?) of Colossians: *I rejoice in my sufferings...I complete what is lacking in Christ's afflictions for the sake of His body, that is, the Church* (Col. 1:24). The principle here is that Christ gave himself up for the church (Eph. 5:25), so the apostle follows Christ's example, and after the apostle there will be others, and then still others, and so the church will go on. This happens only when the church is loved in a personalized way, and seen as a continuity with Christ and the apostles and all the personal stories of individuals in history, and not as an institution/structure.

The **second strength** of the exalted ecclesiology of Ephesians-Colossians is the emphasis on *the holiness of the Church*. Inevitably, church members would sin – marriage disputes, incest, immorality, profaning the eucharist etc...; scandals imperil the survival of the church, unless there is an appreciation of the holiness of the church that is not destroyed by individual sins. In spite of human weaknesses, the author of Ephesians could write of the church that it was the spotless bride, holy and without blemish. The concept of the holiness of the church helped members rise above scandals, and other short-comings.

The **first weakness** in the ecclesiology of Ephesians-Colossians is that the emphasis on the holiness of the church could also be a weakness if it begins to hide/silence the faults or to enter into a denial mode, especially of church leaders on the grounds that if faults were made known there would be greater scandal. This harms the inner vitality of the church which then begins to present a weak exterior and unable to stand against issues that hinder the Kingdom. Christians have to learn to deal with the tension that surrounds a spotless church filled with sinners! When the silence is finally broken, and it has to break sooner or later, then the astonishment and disillusionment can be catastrophic.

A **second weakness** in the ecclesiology of Ephesians-Colossians concerns the possibility of reform. It is difficult to think of reforming a spotless bride! If the members of the body are being knit together in growth that comes from God and are being up built in love, then is there a place for defective growths, sickness, and/or for corrective measures? Or does the inherent triumphalism of Ephesians-Colossians not provide for failure? What is the mechanism for the correction of corruption in the church? The emphasis on the holiness of the body of Christ as the spotless bride does not lend itself to reform. To correct this weakness, the church should be seen as the people of God consisting of those sinners, wandering in the wilderness at times, but on a pilgrimage to attain perfection (a typical Wesleyan position!). This corrective image would help to resolve the tension between holiness and the constant need for reform.

A **third weakness** in the ecclesiology of Ephesians-Colossians is that the emphasis on *the* church weakens the role of local churches in ecclesiology. This has resulted in the tendency to speak of a parish or a diocese or a conference or a district rather than the church, and to think of 'church' as the universal entity. But in a very real sense, the believing community finds its identity, not in the concept of the "one holy, catholic, and apostolic church", but when the community celebrates a liturgy in which the word of God is preached and the eucharist lifted up. Without losing the concept of the universal church, the ecclesiology of Ephesians-Colossians also needs to emphasize the holiness of the local church.

A **fourth weakness** in the ecclesiology of Ephesians-Colossians is that the exclusive concentration on the church as the ultimate goal of God's salvific plan in Christ omits from consideration a large part of the world that has not yet been renewed in Christ. Therefore, only in a part of the body of Christ is there cosmic unity. There seems to be only two categories – believers and those who are hostile; but there is a large section in a third category – those who have not yet heard or been affected by the message of the summing up of all things in Christ. This third category exists throughout the New Testament, but becomes more apparent in Ephesians-Colossians.

Conclusion

Ephesians-Colossians makes a huge contribution to the image of the Universal Church and a cosmic Christology with its emphasis on holiness and love which would take the believing community beyond the death of the founding apostle(s) and into the ages to follow. Ephesians-Colossians brings out the distinctiveness of the church's relationship to Christ – love – and the special holiness that flows from that relationship. Even the weaknesses in the Ephesian-Colossian imagery of the church as the spotless bride of Christ can be seen in the renewal of the church each time it goes wrong because of *Him, who by the power at work within us is able to do far more abundantly than all that we ask or think, to Him be glory in the Church and in Christ Jesus to all generations, for ever and ever. Amen.* (Eph. 3:20-21)

CHAPTER V

A Reflection of the Pauline Influence in the Ecclesiology of the Pastorals

Introduction

It is widely accepted in New Testament scholarship that the three letters which constitute the Pastorals – I & II Timothy and Titus – while they may contain some genuine quotations from Paul, have nevertheless, in their present form, been written by an unknown author who has assumed the mantle of Paul's authority in order to meet, or suggest answers to, post-Pauline problems (see Vol. II of this series). In their present form, the letters probably come from the end of the first century, or even into the first quarter of the second century, when some of the concerns expressed in the letters were issues that required urgent answers. The Pastorals, therefore, purportedly envisage a situation near the end of Paul's life (II Tim. 4:6-7) and accordingly, the letters were written by a follower/disciple of Paul as if to present the context of the apostle making provision for the continuation of the work he had begun. These letters, placed in reference to Paul's life, bring out the development that took place in the life of the early church. Paul had spent much of his life as a missionary – preaching and founding churches; now purportedly at the end of his life, the interest is in how these churches/Christian communities were to survive, especially since there were very serious threats from false teachers who could mislead the people (I Tim. 4:1-3; II Tim. 3:1-7; 4:3-4; Titus 1:10-11). In other words, the concern of these three letters is not 'missionary' but 'pastoral', in the sense that their interest is in the internal on-going life, and nurture, of the community. These three letters, therefore, have been rightly called "The Pastorals".

Towards an ecclesiology

The Pastorals very clearly indicate that the answer to the threats to the communities' survival is to be found in terms of structure. Many of the communities founded by Paul during his missionary activity did not have a structure of authority to ensure the nurture of the community and to direct its on-going life and witness. That deficiency was now being set right in the Pastorals and presbyter-bishops were to be appointed (Titus 1:5). The authority vested in these leaders would ensure the nurture of the local communities thereby protecting them from false teachings and disintegration.

It is necessary to understand the background of the terms used in the Pastorals' image of structure: deacon, presbyter, bishop. **Deacons** are encountered in Acts 6 when seven men are elected from the community to serve the meals. The Greek word διακονος *(diakonos)* means 'one who serves'. Phoebe is also mentioned as a deaconess (Rom. 16:1-2) who *has been a helper of many and to me*. Thus it would seem that matters of practical organization such as community meals, house visitation, assistance to the person in-charge etc… (I Tim. 3:8-10) were the responsibility of the deacon/deaconess (although Stephen and Phillip, two of the deacons from Acts 6, were better known for their preaching than for waiting on tables!).

The Greek word πρεσβυτερος *(presbyteros)* primarily refers to age: an elder. The custom of seeking advice from a senior person in the community meant that "elder" or presbyter came to designate a function, and gradually it began to refer to a person of wisdom or special training/competence/ability (today's psychiatrist/psychologist/counsellor) rather than to a person advanced in chronological age. Jewish synagogues had the system of groups of elders who set the synagogue's policy and regulated its life, *viz-a-viz* the community. Christian presbyters went beyond their Jewish counterparts, in that they also had pastoral functions and teaching functions; they were often referred to as 'bishops' – in Greek ἐπισκοπος *(episcopos)* – meaning 'overseer', 'supervisor'. The Dead Sea Scrolls show that the Essene community living on the banks of the Dead Sea at Qumran also had such an office: the 'overseer' had to carry out functions of teaching, admonishing, and administration; they were often referred to as 'shepherds'. Thus it would seem that the titles and functions of the presbyter-bishops were modelled on the organization of a close-knit community like the community of the Essenes at Qumran. The references in the Pastorals (I Tim. 3:1ff; 5:17; Titus 1:5ff) do not differentiate between the functions of the presbyter and bishop as separate offices as found in the later and present church; the words πρεσβυτερος and ἐπισκοπος are used interchangeably; they will be used as a hyphenated word here: 'presbyter-bishop' without prejudice to the later development of these offices in the church.

The question that arises is whether this background helps to understand the functions of the presbyter-bishop in the Pastorals as an answer to how the community was to survive after the death of the apostle and in the light of the critical situation it faced as it entered a period of emerging false teachings. Three areas are suggested:

> The presbyter-bishops were to be the official teachers of the community, passing on the 'sound doctrine' that they had received, and rejecting any new or different teaching. Therefore they were the protectors and preservers of orthodoxy or true teaching, and they could silence false teachers (I Tim. 4:1-11; 5:17; Titus 1:9-2:1). This later found expression in 'Apostolic Succession' – passing on the authority through the laying on of hands (ordination and consecration).

> Since the church was described as a "household" (I Tim. 3:15) probably because it originally met in a family's home, the image of the presbyter-bishop was in terms of a father: taking responsibility for administering the finances and material possessions of the home, and for providing an example in discipline and life-style (I Tim. 3:2-7; Titus 1:5-9).

The close relationship similar to that of a family home, and even religious respectability, were the requirements for approving the character and qualifications of a presbyter-bishop.

These requirements for providing for nurture and respectability reflect the emergence of the communities as closely-knit societies that imposed certain standards on its leaders/public figures. This is somewhat in contrast to Jesus and the group of disciples around him. No longer would it do for the leaders to be from various backgrounds and walks of life that were somehow below acceptance as an established and recognized society/community would not accept fishermen, tax collectors, zealots as leaders/public figures representing the community. Jesus and His disciples had the characteristics of a charismatic group rather than that of an organized, structured society. In fact, neither Jesus nor his disciples, nor Paul himself who is purported to have written these letters, would have been able to meet the requirements that the Pastorals impose on the presbyter-bishops! The charisma to preach, the enthusiasm of a recent convert, the willingness to endure suffering, the absolute trust in God, and often the ability to 'fight' for the Gospel (literally and figuratively) were the marks of an outstanding missionary, but made for a poor residential community supervisor. Charismatic qualities had to be sacrificed for more commonplace qualities that would ensure harmony and continuity in the community rather than controversy and disintegration. In other words, the community had moved from being a loose group of individuals with missionary zeal, to an organized society with responsibility for the on-going life and nurture of the community; there was a movement from individuals, to communities, to societies with structure and organization. In this sociological development, organization of the society in terms of leaders and their qualifications became central to the on-going witness of the church. It is at this point in the history of the church that the Pastorals make their contribution to the church's apostolic heritage.

Strengths of the Pastoral heritage

The principal motif of the Pastorals – the stress on church structure – leads also to an evaluation of the strengths and weaknesses of such an emphasis as an answer to the church's continuity when determining the Pastoral's message for the church today.

Stability and continuity are the marks of an institutional structure designed to preserve the apostolic heritage. Apostolicity is not just personified in the apostle, but a characteristic mark of all those who follow in the footsteps of the apostle and adhere to sound teaching (I Tim. 2:7; 6:20; II Tim. 1:11-14; 3:10-15; Titus 1:9; 2:1). The enemy against whom the advice of "sound teaching" is given are those introducing new ideas described as insubordinate men, deceivers (I Tim. 1:3ff; 4:1ff; 6:20-21; II Tim. 2:16-18; 3:1-9; 4:3-4; Titus 1:10-16). Such teachers *must be silenced, since they are upsetting whole families by teaching for base gain what they have no right to teach* (Titus 1:11). The Pastorals therefore assume a deposit of doctrine which has to be safeguarded by institutional structure. *Hold firmly to the sure word as it was taught* (Titus 1:9) was an essential weapon in a time of doctrinal crises both in the early church and throughout its history. Stringent control exercised by the church on teaching does however run contrary to the democratic values of freedom of thought and expression. But when theological freedom threatens to become anarchy, then the church must have the tools, the ability, and the right not to let itself be destroyed from within.

The orientation towards the pastoral qualities of the presbyter-bishop is a strength meant to ensure a holy and efficient administration. The pastoral office is clearly seen as one that provides leadership to a local community resulting in useful relations and a disciplined life-style (I Tim. 3:1ff; 5:1ff; II Tim. 2:24-25; Titus 1:5-9; 2:1-10; 3:1-2). The era of missionary expansion seems to be over; the era of consolidation seems to have set in. In many ways, therefore, the Pastorals differentiate between a pastor and a missionary: the missionary was to forge new methods and means of expansion; the pastor was to consolidate the local situation and bring stability in a situation that had radically changed.

There is a strength in the church having carefully selected presbyter-bishops who alone can hand on the doctrine safely (I Tim. 3:3; Titus 1:9) with the result that other teachers aroused suspicion. II Timothy. 3:1-9 is a passage that vituperates other teachers who oppose the authority of the presbyter-bishops. The strength lies in the monolithic structure of control: only the presbyter-bishops are authorized teachers. This clearly divides the community into those who are the teachers and those who are the taught; anyone else is kept out.

These strengths, nevertheless, have their weak points as well which should be considered when evaluating the heritage of the Pastorals.

Weaknesses of the Pastoral heritage:

The exclusive stress on officially controlled teaching, introduced to meet the needs of a crisis situation, tended to become the norm or a consistent way of life. A truly pastoral policy required a relaxation of stringent controls when the crisis had passed, and flexibility to adapt to changed situations. The fear of new ideas and official opposition to change could lead to stagnation and irrelevancy. The peril here would not be from new ideas, but a situation of no ideas. A severe limitation in the Pastorals is that the emphasis on preserving 'sound doctrine' does not leave room for encouraging the development of new and constructive insights that would add to the deposit of doctrine/faith.

The qualifications for the pastoral office ensured a sound leadership, but did not leave room for dynamic creativity that would take the community beyond itself into new areas and methods of mission. In fact, Paul himself may not have qualified for a pastoral office since he had new methods and new teachings: Christ is not the end of the Law in contradiction to Matthew 5:18. Galatians 2:4 also indicates that the more conservative element thought of Paul as a threat to orthodoxy. The weakness here is that the Pastorals make no structural provision for on-going mission activity. The emphasis is on holding to the past; there is no encouragement for innovations necessary for an on-going dynamic mission, especially in times of crisis and change.

The strict grouping into the teachers and the taught is not always possible in practical situations. At one time or another, membership in the group becomes fluid – from being part of the taught to being a teacher, and from being a teacher to also learning for oneself. Whereas in the Pastorals the picture presented seems that there are two fixed classes: the presbyter-bishops who are teachers and everyone else – those who are not instructed by the official teachers and who will be deceived by false teachers. This gives little or no encouragement for creative ideas and expressions from the vast majority of the community and does not allow for teaching to come from the bottom up. Such a one-sided situation will become disastrous in any area of the world where the laity are highly educated and quite capable of making a significant contribution towards the overall religious growth of the community.

Conclusion and relevance

The Pastorals were written at a time when the church was established and there was a great need for pastoral supervision to guide the people in sound doctrine. In such a situation, the answer seemed to lie in a structure for church organization and administration to ensure orthodoxy and continuity. The proposed structure answered the needs of the time, but a critical evaluation also reveals weaknesses indicating that what the Pastorals proposed should be evaluated in terms of its situation rather than uncritically accepting it as a norm for all time.

An important lesson that the Pastoral teach is that in a day and age when church leaders are elected by a democratic process of majority votes, the need to have a careful criteria for evaluation of qualifications *viz-a-viz* the post to which the person is to be elected, is of utmost importance, nor do these criteria need to be limited only to those mentioned in the Pastorals. Throughout history, the church has set societal standards for its clergy and leaders in addition to the requirements in the Pastorals (I Tim. 3:1ff; Titus 1:5ff): only men, a theological education, years of experience in the ministry, celibacy (as in the Roman Catholic Church and Orthodox churches and in churches of the Eastern traditions/rites), married only once and not a divorcee (as in some Protestant churches), sexual orientation etc… The right to make such qualifications as requirements has always been a prerogative of the church from the beginning. But since the requirements have to do with public respectability, they can, and should, change in the course of time as values in society shift and new ideas become respectable. It is therefore necessary that from time to time, the church should carefully spell out its criteria for qualifications before the process of election. Failure to do so would not only result in the church's stagnation in terms of ideas, growth and mission, but worse, may ultimately result in corruption and false teaching from within the church by those who are elected to uphold, preserve, enrich, and pass on the faith.

Ecclesiology in the Johannine Writings – I: A Community of Love and a Personal Relationship with Jesus

Introduction

The images of the church in Colossians/Ephesians (*body of Christ*. See above) and in the Peterine heritage (*people of God*. See below) have a strong sense of ecclesial collectivity. The Johannine heritage stresses on the relation of the individual to Jesus Christ – the heritage of the Beloved Disciple, the disciple whom Jesus loved (see Vol. III of this series dealing with John's Gospel). In the study of the Gospel (Vol. III of this series) it was seen that John does have an understanding of ecclesiology as a collective in the symbolisms of the shepherd-flock (ch. 10), and the vine-branches (ch. 15). However, within the collectively of those images/symbols, there is a concentration of the relation of the individual believer to Jesus along with the in- dwelling of the *paraclete*-Spirit in the believer. This chapter will deal with the relation of the individual believer to Jesus, and the next chapter will deal with the in-dwelling of the *paraclete*-Spirit.

Towards an ecclesiology

Ecclesiology in John's Gospel has its roots in Johannine Christology. Only John's Gospel posits an explicitly pre-existent Christ: a presentation of Jesus unique in the New Testament. There are Pauline texts which can be interpreted as referring to the pre-existence of Christ (I Cor. 8:6; II Cor. 8:9; Philp. 2:6-7; Col. 1:15-17; I Tim. 3:16) and although they are rather vague, none of them deal with pre-existence before creation. Pre-existence before creation appears poetically in John 1:1-3: *in the beginning was the Word...the Word was God...the Word was in the beginning with God...;* and also as a claim of Jesus: *Father, glorify Thou me in Thy own presence with the glory which I had with Thee before the world was made* (17:5; and also 8:58 where the reference may be to pre-existence). Pre-existence is the Johannine explanation/way of expressing that divine wisdom and power dwelt in Jesus, God's Son; the other Gospels do not explicitly picture Jesus as pre-existent before creation, and each has its own way of presenting Jesus as God's Son using different pictures/images/symbols but all agree that divine wisdom and power dwelt in Jesus.

A common picture in the early church was that, after an earthly ministry terminating in crucifixion and resurrection, Jesus went to the right hand of the Father and will finally come again in glory to exercise judgement. Using this basic picture, and not excluding the eschatological dimension, John's Gospel presented an alternate model: Jesus had already come down to earth from heaven in glory, so that his pubic ministry constituted judgement – *this is the judgement, that the light has come into the world, and people loved darkness rather than light...* (3:19), but whoever has seen Jesus has seen the Father (1:18; 14:9) and because the Son has life from the Father, so he can give God's own life to the believer (6:57). Christians come into being through faith in Jesus, and they must continue to remain attached to him in order to stay alive (15:4): the picture is of Jesus as the vine and the Christians as branches getting life from the vine. Jesus is the shepherd who tends the sheep that belong to him, knowing them and calling each by name (10:1-6). Therefore the Christian must continue to follow the shepherd (10:27-28) and abide in the vine (15:1-6). This is an ecclesiology particularly shaped by Christology – even though there are collective images of a flock and a vine, this is an ecclesiology that places Christ at the centre with the individual maintaining an on-going relationship to the life-giver.

Ecclesiology in John's Gospel is further expressed in the shift in vocabulary and expression: in the Synoptics, Jesus introduces and proclaims the Kingdom of God – God's rule or reign in the world and many parables start with *...the Kingdom of God is like...* (Mtt. 13:3, 11, 24,31, 44, 45, 47; 21:28, 31, 33, 43; 22:2 and par. See Vol. I of this series for detailed discussion); but in John, except for 3:3, 5, "the Kingdom of God"/rule or reign of God is absent. Rather the allegorical imagery is applied to Jesus himself, e.g. He is the bridegroom (3:29), and most frequently the imagery is the predicate of the sovereign "I AM" sayings: e.g. *I am the bread of life, I am the good shepherd, I am the light, I am the way, the truth and the life, I am the true vine* etc... (6:35, 51; 8:12 & 9:5; 10:7, 9; 10:11, 14; 11:25; 14:6; 15:1, 5. See Vol. III of this series for detailed discussion). In John's Gospel there is no emphasis on the Kingdom of God implying either an entry into a place or accepting a rule/reign; rather the emphasis is on Jesus (Christology) and that the believer needs to inhere in Jesus to be a part of the community.

This is also the case with the sacraments (see Vol. III of this series for further details) in John's Gospel: scenes of the baptism and the commands to baptise (as in Mtt. 28:19) are not found and the reference to Jesus baptizing (3:22) is quickly corrected (4:1-2) so as not to place Jesus on the same level, or even inferior to John the Baptist, who had, prior to Jesus, made a name for himself as a baptizer; similarly there is no account of the institution of the eucharist although there was already a tradition in the church that the eucharist was instituted by Jesus *on the night that he was betrayed* (I Cor. 11:23ff. So also the accounts in the Synoptics). In John, the sacraments are part of the normal, daily life of Jesus and the people – e.g. to be renewed/to be born again (conversation with Nicodemus, ch. 3), to eat a common meal (feeding of the five thousand, ch. 6), to wash in the pool of Siloam (instruction to the blind man, ch. 9), and it is through the understanding of/commentary on these ordinary events that the Christological significance is brought out showing that there is no one particular point of instituting a sacrament, but that all of life and life's events are sacramental because Jesus is present. In John, Jesus fed the hungry and gave sight to the blind, and by the interpretation of these events, Jesus becomes the life-giver – the source of the sacraments – who continues to remain active in and through the sacraments. Thus John's Gospel presents, in a unique way, the relationship of Jesus to the believer (Christology) through sacramental imagery and sacramental interpretation of daily occurrences – the Christian must remain attached to the source of life (15:1-11) and must remain as part of the flock whose name is known by the shepherd (10:1-6).

An interesting point in John's Gospel and the Johannine Epistles is that there is no named apostle as the great hero of the community such as in the Pauline and Peterine Epistles. Rather the figure *par excellence* is a disciple – *the Disciple whom Jesus loved.* The Gospel mentions the Twelve (6:67, 70, 71; 20:24) and that they were *sent* (ἀποστελλειν) *into the world* (17:18) by Jesus, hence the author could hardly have not known that certain leaders were given the title of 'apostle'. The avoidance of the title, therefore was a deliberate attempt to show that what constitutes dignity in Johannine ecclesiology is not the title but discipleship – a status that all Christians enjoy and within that status, what confers dignity is the love of Jesus.

This is also brought out in the contrast between the Beloved Disciple and Peter who was the most prominent of the Twelve by the end of the 1st century/beginning of the 2nd century – the period during which the Gospel and Epistles can be dated. In the Synoptics, Peter is portrayed as the spokesperson of the disciples when addressing Jesus (Mtt. 16:16, 17:24, 18:21), but at the Last Supper, Peter is at a distance from Jesus and so speaks to Jesus through an intermediary – the Beloved Disciple (13:22-26); in the Synoptics, Peter is the only one of the Twelve to follow Jesus into the courtyard of the High Priest (Mtt. 26:69 and par.) but in John Peter cannot follow Jesus into the courtyard until the Disciple arranges it (18:15-16); Peter ultimately abandons Jesus so that at the foot of the cross, no disciple is there (in Mk. 15:40-41 and Mtt. 27:55-56 only women followers are mentioned), but in John's Gospel, one male member of Jesus' followers is there – the Beloved Disciple along with Jesus' mother and other women. Jesus makes His mother the mother of the Beloved Disciple (19:26-27) – the strict Jewish Christianity represented by Jesus' mother is entrusted to the church – the Beloved Disciple. In other words the symbolism implied is reflective of the end of the 1st century when Jewish Christianity was slowly giving way to Hellenistic (Gentile) Christianity and an apologetic, set within the life of Jesus, was necessary to justify the movement (see Vol. III of this series for discussion).

The contrast is continued in the narrative of the empty tomb: Peter and the Other Disciple ran to the tomb, the Other Disciple looked in and finding it empty, he/she believed without seeing the risen Jesus (20:3-10) whereas the narrative does not talk about whether Peter believed. However, in the tradition of the early church, Peter was among the first to see the risen Jesus (Lk. 24:34; I Cor. 15:5). So while traditionally Peter may have been the first of the apostles to see the risen Jesus, the Johannine tradition knows of a Disciple who was even more blessed for having believed without seeing (the beatitude expressed to Thomas, 20:29). When they are together, Peter and the Beloved Disciple see the risen Jesus, but it is the Beloved Disciple who is able to recognize Jesus (21:7-8): love had brought the Beloved Disciple closer to Jesus rather than Peter, the most prominent of the disciples. Martyrdom had made Peter a *pillar of the Church* (from the writing of I Clement 5:2-4 – dated at end of the 1st century in Rome), but the Beloved Disciple was also taken care of by Jesus (21:20-23) – the Beloved Disciple became the on-going witness *par excellence* whose testimony is true (21:24). Without going into the discussion as to whether the Beloved Disciple was a real person or a symbol in all the above examples (see Vol. III of this series for discussion), the Beloved Disciple certainly functions in the Gospel as the embodiment of Johannine idealism: all Christians are disciples and among them greatness is determined by a loving relationship to Jesus and not by function, title, or office.

Finally when offices are recognized in the development of the Johannine churches, they are seen through the prism of Johannine values. There is a question of the on-going care of the congregations/ communities and this is taken up in chapter 21 (which is regarded as an Epilogue to the Gospel and added at a later stage). Earlier statements had made it clear that Jesus alone was the model shepherd while all others were thieves and bandits (10:1-18); the distinctive feature of Jesus' shepherding is not his authority over the sheep, but his love for the sheep and His intimate knowledge of each of them which makes him willing to lay down His life for the sheep. In the Epilogue of the Gospel, Peter is assigned the task of shepherding (21:15-19), a role which, at the end of the 1ˢᵗ century, was already being exercised by presbyters in other New Testament churches and which was being traced back to apostles like Peter and Paul (Acts 20:28; I Peter 5:1-2; I Clement 42:4, 44:1-3). But before Peter is entrusted with that role, he is asked three times, *Do you love me?* (21:15-17). The authority of the shepherd is given only on the basis of love for Jesus because the sheep do not belong to any human church officer, but to Jesus (10:14), and so Peter must meet the Johannine qualifications for shepherding, namely, that the model shepherd must be willing to lay down his life for the sheep (10:11), thus immediately following this Jesus tells Peter by what death he will die (21:18-19); the manner of death is not specified, but in the context of feeding *my sheep, my lambs*, Peter was to die a martyr's death – laying down his life for the sheep, i.e. in Peter's role as shepherd, loving discipleship has been given priority (13:35; 15:13).

Thus it is seen that in Johannine ecclesiology, discipleship finding its expression in love is the important criteria and not offices or titles or any other distinction: a love and a discipleship as exemplified by the Beloved Disciple/the disciple whom Jesus loved; love for Jesus was seen as an on-going element, even among those who never knew him during his earthly ministry. This consistent portrayal of ecclesiology is rooted in Christology – a relationship to Jesus – each believer, branch, must remain attached to the vine and each sheep to the flock; instead of writing about the reign/rule of God, attention is focussed on Jesus in whom the reign of God is perfectly realized, so that inhering in him replaces entrance into the Kingdom. John's Gospel presents a powerfully consistent picture of ecclesiology having its firm roots in Christology.

Strengths and weaknesses

1. The greatest strength comes from the fact that an individual relationship with Jesus is a necessary component of a sound ecclesiology. Other ecclesiologies in the New Testament (discussed in this section, above and below) build upon a collectivity of the church – the church as the body of Christ in which the body/ head controls all the parts (I Cor. 12 and Col. 2:18-19); the parts are

indispensable and dependent on one another in order for the body to function properly and so there is no need for jealousy in the community. But in Johannine ecclesiology, the individual must remain attached to the vine in order to receive life-sustaining status, without reference to the collectivity. There is a stress here on individuality and for the member to receive life from Christ they are to be knit together with him in love. Throughout the Gospel, Jesus was remembered as the one who exhibited love in what he did and was loved deeply by those who followed him.

In addition to providing doctrine and pastoral care, liturgy and sacraments, and a supportive/caring community, the church must bring people into some personal contact with Jesus so that they can experience in their own way what made people follow him in the first place. Any failure to provide this aspect would result in the church becoming an abstract entity and encourage members to look elsewhere for an encounter with the living Lord. This stress on a personal encounter/ relationship is the outcome of an ecclesiology based on Christology.

The weakness in this approach to ecclesiology which stresses on the personal encounter/relationship rather than on the collectivity is that it may result in individualism to the point where a sense of the church/ community is lost. The stress on the personal relationship may also lead to a situation that does not need the church/community in the sense of structure, doctrine, sacraments, liturgy. Church members must receive life from being attached to Jesus, but this life is nurtured within the community and through its structures. Therefore the Johannine stress must be tempered with the correctives in the Pastorals, Colossians/ Ephesians, and the Peterine Epistles that structure is necessary.

2. A second strength in Johannine ecclesiology is its egalitarianism – a sense of equality among the members of the community. As per the above, it was seen that the disciple was the most important category, not titles or offices. In other New Testament churches, appointments – apostles, prophets, teachers etc... (I Cor. 12:28) – are important in the body of Christ, and where these appointments have become institutionalized in the office

of presbyter-bishops and deacons (as in the Pastorals), there is a tendency to give one appointment precedence over another (e.g. apostles are more important than prophets etc...), in imitation of secular societies. Various gospel passages try to correct this situation by addressing who is the greatest in the Kingdom (Mk. 9:33-37, 10:35-40 and par.). However, the question of who is the greatest is not raised in John's Gospel as status comes from the love of Jesus, not from title or office. The figure of the vine and the branches shows that individuals must remain attached to Jesus and that no one is above the other; all draw sustenance and status from being attached to Jesus.

The weakness in a structured church situation is that inevitably there arises an ambition to hold high offices and to wield authority. This is a tacit acknowledgement of how important an office of power had become in the church (and still is today). The Johannine corrective of egalitarianism is to bring about a balance between these two extremes, so that those who do not hold office or wield power still feel part of the community/structure, and those who are positions of power relate to other members in love (Peter as a person in power is instructed three times to *feed/tend my sheep/lambs* – 21:15-17).

3. While the structured nature of ecclesiology can be a strength in that it brings about systematization and order in a human society, it also raises a question regarding the priesthood of all believers: the Johannine equality of all Christians as disciples. A structured ecclesiology tends to place greater importance on the full-time ordained ministry as a separate category of service and inevitably considered more holy. Johannine ecclesiology would, however, place greater emphasis on the sacrament of baptism which relates to salvation and constitutes a person as a child of God which is a dignity that goes beyond any designation/separation of power and authority that is wielded by the ordained ministry. Such an approach to ecclesiology would show that a person's identity as a Christian as demonstrated in the sacrament of baptism is more important than an identity gained from power and authority.

Conclusion

The heritage of the ecclesiology of John's Gospel is distinguished by its emphasis on the relation of the individual Christian to Jesus – an ecclesiology dominated by Christology. While this heritage has its limitations as the ultimate model, its strength lies in the emphasis on love of the disciple for Jesus and therefore a personal relationship – the relationship of love between the Beloved Disciple and Jesus which continues, beyond the age of the apostles, into the on-going times of the life of the community of believers personally attached to Jesus.

Chapter VII

Ecclesiology in the Johannine writings – II: A Community of Love, Secessionists, and the Role of the *Paraclete* in the Community

Introduction

The ecclesiology of the Johannine writings (see the chapter above) was characterized by the personal relationship of the believer to Jesus; a further aspect of Johannine ecclesiology is the role of the Spirit – *paraclete*. Some background of the Johannine community is needed to understand the ecclesiology that emerges.

The Gospel mentions the names of the disciples who follow Jesus and the Christological titles that are given to Jesus (1:35-51), all of which are found in the other Gospels as well, thus indicating that originally Johannine Christianity was not too different from the dominant style of Christianity centred around Jesus. However, in ch. 4, there is an account of the conversion of the Samaritans but not by the original disciples of Jesus but by a Samaritan woman, and Temple worship in Jerusalem is declared as losing its significance (ch.4 – the conversation with the Samaritan woman. See Vol. III of this series). Here John's Gospel departs from the description of the ministry in the other Gospels and is closer to the developments described in Acts 6-8 where Hellenist Jewish Christians separate themselves from the Hebrew Christian majority in Jerusalem who are faithful to the Temple observances; whereas the preaching of Stephen (Hellenist Jewish Christian) proclaimed that God does not dwell in the Temple. In Acts it is these Hellenist Christians – Phillip – not Peter or the Twelve, who are the ones responsible for the conversion of Samaria (Acts 8:4-13). Therefore, the Johannine community would have consisted of not only those from an orthodox Jewish background, but also of those from Hellenistic and Samaritan backgrounds who had no allegiance to the Temple in Jerusalem. In fact, "the Jews" became an expression of those who were opposed to Jesus from ch. 5 of the Gospel onwards, i.e. after the conversion of the Samaritans: "the Jews" hate Jesus because He is making Himself equal to God; there are long debates between Jesus and "the Jews" which grow increasingly hostile reaching a climax in Jesus exclaiming that they are children of the devil (8:40, 44); the narrative of the blind man in Ch. 9 reflects through the medium of the struggles in Jesus' life, the on-going struggles between "the Jews" and the Johannine community (9:22; 15:20; 16:2-3). This opposition by "the Jews" led to a re-iteration and re-affirmation of who is Jesus: he is one with the Father (10:30), he is Lord and God (20:28); there was contempt for anyone who believed in Jesus but who were unwilling to confess it openly for fear of "the Jews" (12:42). The synagogue leaders probably thought that the proclamation of Jesus as God or divine was denying a basic tenet of Judaism – the Lord your God is one. In response, Johannine Christianity over-emphasized the divinity of Jesus: Jesus already knew the answer to a question (6:5-6), Jesus already foresaw that one of the disciples would betray him (6:70-71), Jesus' prayer is only for educating the bystanders to the truth that the Father always hears him (11:41-42), Jesus cannot ask that the hour of his passion pass from him (as do the other Gospels) because it is for that hour that he came (12:27), he cannot be arrested for he is divine, so he has to give himself up (8:59; 18:4-6; 19:10-11); he has power to lay down his life and to take it again (10:18). The entire presentation protects Jesus from whatever could be a challenge to his divinity. The uniqueness of the Johannine concept of the *paraclete* becomes understandable keeping in mind the above highlights of Johannine polemical history.

Towards an ecclesiology

Although early Christians could agree on the importance of the Spirit, there were very different ideas of what was meant by the term. The Greek *pneuma* (πνευμα) is neuter gender and translated as "it" in English versions. This makes it difficult to determine to what extent Peter, or Paul, or Acts considered the Spirit as personal (see discussion of the *paraclete* in Johannine Theology in Vol. III of this series). However, Johannine Christology made an important impact: in the Last Discourse (see Vol. III of this series) the Spirit is to come after Jesus has returned to the Father (14:16-17, 26; 16: 7ff.). The replacement motif is so strong that almost everything said about the Spirit has already been said of Jesus (16:15), so the Spirit emerges as the on-going presence of Jesus while Jesus is absent from earth and with the Father. To describe this concept, John's Gospel and the Johannine Epistles make use of another word for Spirit – the *paracletos/paraclete* (παρακλητος), literally 'one who is called to stand beside'; this enables the *paraclete* to be used as the antecedent for personal pronouns (traditionally translated as 'he' since the *paraclete* stands in the place of a male, Jesus). The forensic and legal contexts from which the concept of *paracletos/paraclete* is taken can also be translated as 'advocate' – to stand beside an accused in court – a legal/forensic term that fits the context of Christians having to defend themselves for their Christological beliefs (described above in the Introduction). Their help and surety was the *paraclete*-Spirit dwelling within them and who interpreted correctly the significance of Jesus (16:13). Indeed, through them and their witness, the *paraclete* was not just the advocate for the defence, but became the prosecutor by *convincing the world of sin and of righteousness and of judgement* (16:8-11). When the disciples are sad because Jesus has said that he is going away, they are consoled by Jesus with the promise of sending one who more than makes up for Jesus' departure – if Jesus was confined to one place and time, the *parclete* dwells within every believer for all times (14:15-17); thus the *paraclete* is a more intimate and enduring presence.

Another role that is emphasized is that of the *paraclete* as a teacher: *...the paraclete whom the Father will send in my name, he will teach you all things, and bring to your remembrance all that I have said to* *you* (14:26). ....*When the Spirit of truth comes he will guide you into all the truth; for he will not speak on his own authority, but whatever he hears he will speak, and he will declare to you the things that are to come* (16:13-14). The *paraclete* will contemporize in each period and in each place the message of Jesus, thus enabling Christians to face the things to come in the future. This approach meets the need of an acute problem: if Christianity is to be apostolic then it must pass on what was received from Jesus by the apostles and therefore Christianity must safeguard tradition; at the same time it must have an element of the contemporary added to the original, thus the work of the *paraclete* will be to see that nothing is distorted and that no false teaching enters into the community to confuse members. In the *paraclete's* role as teacher there is again an emphasis on Christology: the *paraclete* is firmly rooted in the teachings of Jesus.

The above clarifies that in discussing Johannine ecclesiology, the concept of the *paraclete* is another facet of the Johannine emphasis of the relationship of the individual to Jesus (see previous chapter, above): a community of love which emphasizes a personal loving relationship leading to service (...do you love me...feed my sheep/lambs... 21:15-17), and the on-going presence of Jesus in the community through the *paraclete* (John chs. 14 & 16).

Strengths and weaknesses

1. The *paraclete* concept is a strength in Johannine ecclesiology: Jesus came from and was sent from the Father and spoke only what he heard from the Father (5:19-22, 37; 8:16; 12:49; 14:24); the *paraclete* sent by the Father and the Son (15:26; 16:7) speaks only what is told to him by the Father and the Son (16:13); the witness of the community through the *paraclete* is unchallengeable in its Christology: ...*you also are (my) witnesses, because you have been with me from the beginning* (15:27). Thus even after the death of the eyewitnesses, the *paraclete* continues to be the presence of Jesus in the community, the community becomes the witness to Jesus, and the *paraclete* guarantees the correctness of that witness even in the generations to come.

2. The egalitarian nature of the community (brought out in the previous chapter) ensures that in terms of service, all are equal; there is no hierarchal structure: God is worshipped neither in Jerusalem nor on Gerezim but in *spirit and truth* (4:21-24) and *God is a Spirit* indicating that geographically all are equal because God's spirit dwells in every Christian everywhere. The idea that the *paraclete* is given to each person who loves Jesus and thus remains forever (14:15-16) means that chronologically there is equality of all – *blessed are those who have not seen and yet believe* (17:8-9, 20; 20:29). Thus, through the role of the *paraclete* Johannine ecclesiology is without geographical, chronological and status barriers.

3. However, this idealistic picture of the Johannine community and its ecclesiology was marred by what actually happened as reflected in the Epistles of John. The Epistles were probably written about a decade after the Gospel (see Vol. III of this series) and reflect a change in the situation: there is no longer a concern with "the Jews" or other opposition groups, but on secession from within the community, and so serious is this concern that it is described in apocalyptic terms – *you have heard that antichrist is coming, so now many antichrists have come, therefore we know that it is the last hour. They went out from us...* (I John 2:18-19). The author(s) of the Epistles are writing urgently because the "antichrists" are conducting missionary efforts undermining the faith of the community members; the author(s) are hoping to stem this success for the whole world is listening to the false teachers (1 John 4:5), so the warning goes out to the community in a faraway place (II John 7, 10), and there is an abhorrence of Diotrephes who seems to be questioning the community structure which was based on love and service and was trying to set himself up as an authority in an hierarchal type of structure (III John 9-10).

The secessionist teachings addressed in the epistles are never explained in detail, only the objections/refutations to the teachings, but some of the basic issues can be reconstructed: the author considers the secessionists as progressive while the author's(s') position is conservative holding on to what was taught from the beginning (1 John 3:11 ...*the message which you have heard from the beginning...*). The author associates himself/herself with a chain of witnesses reaching back to the Beloved Disciple – *we have heard...we have seen... we have touched...* (I John 1:1-4) and therefore the witness is true. Christologically, the secessionists are also blamed for neglecting the humanity of Jesus (I John 4:2; II John 7). Ethically, the secessionists would see the only sin to consist of refusing to believe in Jesus: the believer who is a child of God is already judged (John 3:18; 5:24) and already has eternal life. Therefore the secessionists would have proclaimed that there is no salvific value in doing good deeds or obeying commandments and that there is no sin provided one believes (I John 1:8, 10). The Johannine Epistles take an objection to such Christological and ethical views showing a bitter schism in the Johannine community. So it would seem that the Johannine community and the secessionists both accepted the presentation of Jesus in the Fourth Gospel, but from the reconstructed polemic of the Johannine Epistles, it would seem that the dispute was over the interpretation of a commonly accepted tradition. "The commonly held tradition" would be a strength in Johannine ecclesiology, but it also led to weaknesses.

4. The evangelist of the Fourth Gospel emphasized what "the Jews" and some other Christian groups denied – the pre-existent divinity of Jesus. Hence the reverting back to *in the beginning...* and an emphasis on both the humanity and divinity of Jesus: *...He was in the beginning...we have touched, heard, and seen...this we proclaim to you.* If the Johannine community members felt deeply enough about the pre-existent divinity of Jesus even to the extent of expulsion from the synagogues on the charge of worshipping another god, and if expulsion made them more adamant so that in describing Jesus they avoided human features, inevitably there would come a time when Jesus' humanity would be downplayed altogether, causing schisms within the community. The author of

the Epistles gives the impression that the secessionists have moved too quickly; it would seem that the author held on to the tradition as it was understood from the beginning, whereas the secessionists probably claimed that they were emphasizing the thrust that gave rise to the tradition in the first place: a weakness in the community that arose from differently held interpretations, and thus an appeal to return to what has been taught from the beginning.

5. Another issue that causes a weakness in Johannine ecclesiology is that polemics and expulsion led to a loss of heritage; expulsion tends to open up a wide gap from the parent body to such an extent that even what was not in dispute is lost, e.g. the Johannine Christians had more in common with the synagogue even after their expulsion on the basis of the pre-existent divinity of Jesus, than with any other religious group that came in from the Hellenistic world: they still held to belief in one God, the Hebrew scriptures, feasts, basic ethics of the Law etc...; but after the expulsion, the Fourth Gospel refers to "their Law" (John 15:25) as though this Law did not belong to Christians as well; the feasts of Passover, Sabbath, Tabernacles etc.. are feasts of the Jews (John 2:13; 5:16:4; 7:2, 10:22) as though these feasts were not also observed by Christians;[12] there is a division between the disciples of Jesus and the disciples of Moses (John 9:28) as if the disciples of Jesus were not also disciples of Moses. In other words, the great common heritage is lost after expulsion and the positions become polarized such as when the parent body and those expelled become two separate religions (Judaism and Christianity); further widening takes place when there is an internal split among the expelled – the proposed history of the Johannine community (see Vol. III of this series) shows that one group of the secessionists joined the Gnostic followers and eventually faded out, another group

joined the mainstream Catholic Church, while the Johannine community itself passed out of existence. Expulsion from the synagogues, and later from the Johannine community, also meant that much history and liturgical value was lost.

The Johannine Epistles, at the end of the 1st century/beginning of the 2nd century, try to recoup some of these losses especially in the light of the acceptance of the Johannine Gospel by the community and by the church at large. Never once does the author(s) of the Epistles deny the insights of, and presentation of Jesus in, the Fourth Gospel, but the epistolary author(s) try to prove to later theologians of the church that the Fourth Gospel which was the focal point of Gnostic commentaries from the end of the 1st century and into the 2nd century and therefore had to be approached with suspicion, was also capable of serving and being accepted by orthodox Christianity. Hence, expulsion from the synagogues/community, while it hardened the differences between Judaism and Christianity and the expelled group from the community, served in a positive way to bring recognition to the Fourth Gospel and to unite the Johannine community with mainstream Christianity.

6. A further strength and weakness in Johannine ecclesiology was that there was extreme hostility towards outsiders, confining love to only those within the community. The adversaries of Jesus, "the Jews", are described in very harsh terms: the devil is their father, a murderer from the beginning, he is a liar and correspondingly they refuse to believe the truth (John 8:43-46, 55); they prefer darkness to light because their deeds are evil (John 3:19-21; 12:35); God has blinded their eyes (John 12:40). When attention turned from external adversaries, "the Jews", to internal differences in the community as witnessed in the Epistles, it is interesting that these same descriptions are applied to the secessionists: they are like Cain who belonged to the evil one and killed his brother (I John 3:12); they are children of the devil who is a sinner from the beginning (I John 3:8-10); they are liars (I John 2:22); their eyes are blinded (I John 2:11); and they have a spirit of deceit opposed to the Spirit of Truth (I John 4:1-6). It is difficult to reconcile this

hatred with the command, *love one another as I have loved you* (John 13:34; 15:12, 17). The commandment to love is important to the epistolary author(s) as well as it is placed on the same level as faith in Jesus (I John 3:23), it is a command from God (I John 2:7-11; 4:21; II John 4-6). There is no demand to love one's neighbour which may include enemies and strangers, as in the Synoptics (Mtt. 5:43, 44; Lk. 10:27-37). Thus is may be seen that the Johannine tradition places no emphasis on love of outsiders; the Johannine ideal is love of God's children who have come to faith in Jesus. So if the community does not reach out in love to the secessionists, it is because the secessionists have gone out from the community and are no longer members or children of God.

In other words, the closeness to Jesus which is the great strength of the Johannine heritage in the Gospel, tended to produce an in-group and most others were thought of as evil and belonging to an outside world. The exception to this are the *other sheep that are not of this fold: I must bring them also...*(John 10:16) – a sign that there were non-Johannine Christians who were not considered evil (probably Christians who came from communities that venerated Peter, Paul, James as their founders – i.e. other churches that are also found in the New Testament). In the Gospel, "the Jews" were the prime example of the world that refuses to believe in Jesus (John 16:8-9); in the Epistles the secessionists belong to the world (I John 4:5). The famous *God so loved the world...* (John 3:16) should not be misunderstood: the giving of he Son, the sending of light into the world produces a division between those who come to the light and those who prefer darkness to light because their deeds are evil (John 3:19-21). Subsequently, in the Gospel, the world and darkness are equated with the realm of Satan, the Prince of this world (12:31; 14:30; 16:11) which is why Jesus does not pray for the world (John 17:9) and his disciples, though in the world, are not of it (John 17:14-18). This attitude carries over to the Epistles where the author speaks of a sin that is mortal and should not be prayed about (I John 5:16-17) in reference to the secessionists refusal to believe and their exit from the community.

It can be concluded that on one hand, love within the community is essential for the survival of the church, and on the other hand, too narrow a Christian focus of love limited to one's own, does little justice to Jesus who was concerned with outsiders – sinners, prostitutes, tax collectors etc...[13]. A further weakness in this limited expression of love leads to a disinterest in ecumenical relations with other ancient communities/churches.

7. Perhaps the most serious weakness in Johannine ecclesiology, and the one most apparent in the Epistles, centers around the role of the *paraclete* in the uncontrollable divisions caused by appeal to the *paraclete*. The thought that there is a living divine teacher in the heart of each believer – a teacher who is the ongoing presence of Jesus, preserving what he taught and interpreting it anew in each generation – is probably one of the greatest contributions made to Christianity by the Fourth Gospel. But the Jesus who sends the *paraclete* never tells his followers what is to happen when believers who possess the *paraclete* disagree with one another. The Johannine Epistles describe what happens when disagreements crop up: they break the *koinonia*/fellowship/community/communion with each other. If the Spirit-*paraclete* is the highest and only authority, and if each side appeals to the *paraclete* as support for their position, then it is almost impossible to make concessions and to work out compromises.

In the divisive context of the Johannine Epistles the author(s) appeal to "tradition" as it was "from the beginning" as partial support for their positions/interpretations, counting on the fact that the readers have been anointed with the Spirit and so can recognize the truth when they hear it: *...the anointing which you received from Him abides in you, and you have no need that anyone should teach you, as His anointing teaches you about everything, and is true, and is no lie, just as it has taught you, abide in Him* (I John 2:27). However, this principle did not work: the secessionists who had been members of the Johannine community were anointed with the *paraclete*-spirit and that anointing which is supposed to be true and free from any lie did not save them from becoming liars, *the one who denies that Jesus is the Christ* (I John 2:18ff.). But how do they become liars when they are guided by the *paraclete*-spirit, the Spirit of Truth? To answer that question the author(s) point out that there is a spirit of deceit as well as a Spirit of Truth and that the believer must test the spirits (I John 4:1-6): the test that is offered is that those who listen to, and obey, the author(s) have the Spirit of Truth, while those who disagree have the spirit of deceit.

There is no way to control such a division in a *paraclete*-Spirit guided community. The Johannine community discovered that as it split up and went out of existence: one group of secessionists drifted to Gnosticism taking the Fourth Gospel with them from which emerged great use by the Gnostics in commentaries and interpretations (from early to mid 2nd century); another group came to terms with non-Johannine Christianity (the strains that developed from Peter, Paul, James etc...) which formed what came to be known as the "Catholic Church", a church that had presbyter-bishops as teachers and finally a single monarchical bishop in each region (a compromise that the Johannine community made since they did not have authoritative structures, but roles based on love). The difficulty in making the shift to authoritative structures seems to be reflected in the author's annoyance with Diotrephes who seems to taking authority upon himself (III John 9-10). The epilogue to the Fourth Gospel (added by a different author reflecting the community situation at the end of the 1st/beginning of the 2nd century), which may represent the last stage of the Johannine writings, acknowledges the authority of a human shepherd (21:15-17), even if that authority is safeguarded in the Johannine tradition by asking Peter *do you love me?*

Thus on the basis of an appeal to the *paraclete*-Spirit, the Johannine community split – the secessionist group to join the Gnostics and eventually fade out; the orthodox group to make compromise with other expressions of Christianity and to be absorbed into the mainstream "Catholic Church". So by the end of the 2nd century, the original

Johannine community of the Beloved Disciple and the *paraclete*-Spirit passed out of existence.

Conclusion

Johannine ecclesiology is an attractive and exciting New Testament study: the personal relation of Christians to Jesus, and of relations among Christians in the community, both characterized by love and abiding in Jesus; the on-going presence of Jesus in each believer through the indwelling of the *paraclete*-Spirit who will teach, guide, bring to remembrance the words of Jesus, and stand beside the believer in times of crisis. However, this ideal picture is destabilized with the coming of false teachers who question the divinity of Jesus and especially his pre-existent divinity, so there is an over-emphasis on the divinity of Jesus avoiding human features; inevitably there would come a time when Jesus' humanity would be downplayed altogether, causing schisms within the community giving rise to the author of I John having to affirm and re-affirm that *we have seen, touched, handled...* When, at the end of the 1st century, there was a move to institutionalize church structures, one group of the Johannine community emphasized an ecclesiology that brought in the dimension of a personal relationship to Jesus cemented by love, and insisted on the in-dwelling of the *paraclete*-Spirit as the on-going presence of Jesus in each believer. However and inevitably, possession of the *paraclete*-Spirit became a dividing factor and those who separated themselves joined Gnostic groups which led to a dead-end. The orthodox group was finally able to come to terms with other expressions of Christianity, and so were absorbed into the "Catholic Church" bringing with them their contribution of the Fourth Gospel. Though the history of the church shows that those who wanted the institutionalization of church structures finally prevailed and alongside the Beloved Disciple (and perhaps even over him) were placed the apostles such as Peter and Paul, nevertheless the community of the Beloved Disciple continues to bear witness that the church must never be allowed to replace the unique role of Jesus and the *paraclete*-Spirit in the life of the believer.

CHAPTER VIII

The People of God in the Ecclesiology of the Peterine Epistles

Introduction

It has been recognized that I Peter, though a later writing (A.D. 85-95 written from Rome by a Peterine disciple. See chapter on I Peter, above), has a close relationship to the Pauline heritage; the date would suggest that I Peter was contemporary with some of the deutero-Pauline writings addressed to Asia Minor. There are also several parallels with the Epistle to the Romans probably because Paul wrote Romans (see Vol. II of this series) as an introduction to his thought in an attempt to find acceptance in the Roman community as he intended to visit there and use Rome as the headquarters for a mission westwards to Spain (Rom. 15:22-29). The community at Rome was more attached to its Jewish origins, probably because of the missionary enterprise of James and Peter, than to the Pauline mission: the Roman community was not strictly Jewish Christianity (James and Peter) nor was it just Gentile Christianity (Paul), but a Jewish-Gentile Christianity which still insisted on preserving aspects of Judaism, perhaps not circumcision, but other observances such as Jewish customs and cult practices (some of the more conservative practices are referred to in Romans especially in chs. 9-11). In any case, it would seem that the Epistle to the Romans won Paul the acceptance of the Roman community and his martyrdom in Rome hallowed his memory, so that by the 90's, along with Peter, he was referred to as a 'pillar of the Church' (I Clement 5:2-5). The Roman community would reflect that there came about a combination of Peter and Paul giving rise to Jewish-Gentile Christianity and that the Epistle of I Peter was an attempt to recapture and preserve the understanding of the church in an attempt to preserve its Jewish heritage.

The Epistle is addressed to *the exiles of the Dispersion in Pontus, Galatia, Cappodocia, Asia, and Bithynia...* (I Peter 1:1. See also Acts 2:9 which shows Jews in these areas), areas north of the Pauline mission, but known for its converts and associated with the mission from Jerusalem (James and Peter). Perhaps Paul's avoidance of a mission in these areas (*...having been forbidden by the Holy Spirit to speak the word in Asia...attempted to go into Bithynia, but the Spirit of Jesus did not allow them...so bypassing Mysia, they came to Troas...* Acts 16:6-8) was because there may have been Jerusalem missionaries already at work there (see the Epistle of James, above, which shows that James was a revered figure in these areas. Also Acts 21:17-26). As a via-media between the thrusts of the Jerusalem mission (Jewish Christianity) and the Pauline mission (Gentile Christianity), I Peter may have been a moderating influence (Jewish-Gentile Christianity) and by doing so, would claim the on-going responsibility for the original mission from Jerusalem by writing from Rome (the traditional site where the story of Peter ends) in the name of Peter.

Towards an ecclesiology

The message to the Jewish-Gentile Christians of Northern Asia Minor forms the ecclesiology of I Peter. Regardless of whether the Epistle was a baptismal homily or a baptismal liturgy (see the discussion on I Peter, above), the message was a reminder of the fundamental way of looking at Christian conversion and at the status of the Christian life. This presentation of 'Christian basics' draws heavily on images/ideas/theological concepts from the Hebrew scriptures: the exodus, desert wandering, promised land etc...and imaginatively reapplied to Christians, thus recalling the Christian's Jewish heritage, and placing the Gentiles within that heritage: if the coming out of Egypt and the desert wanderings made a slave people into God's people, so conversion has made Christians (from Jewish and Gentile backgrounds) into the *people of God*. This reflects that the addressees were well conversant with Hebrew scriptures (whether Jewish or Gentile Christians) and methods of interpretation. Some examples of this are given from I Peter:

> The Hebrews who left Egypt were told to *gird up your loins* for a quick departure (Ex. 12:11), so the recipients of I Peter are told to: *gird up your minds, be sober, set your hope fully upon the grace that is coming to you...*(I Peter 1:13);

> In the desert the Israelites murmured and wanted to go back to Egypt (Ex. 16:2-3), so the recipients of I Peter are warned: *do not be conformed to the passions of your former ignorance* (I Peter 1:14);

> Moses was ordered to tell the people whom God had chosen, *you shall be holy; for I, the Lord your God, am holy* (Lev. 19:2), so the same charge is quoted to the recipients of I Peter: ... *as God who called you is holy, be holy yourselves in all your conduct...*(I Peter 1:15-16);

> Christian life is described as a time of exile with the hope of an inheritance yet to come (I Peter 1:4, 1:17) echoing Israel's desert wandering before it reached the promised inheritance;

> 'Redemption' and 'ransom' were used to describe God's liberation of the people from Egypt (Ex. 6:5-6; Deut. 7:8; Is. 52:3) along with vocabulary that belonged to the Passover (Ex. 12:5-7), so to Christians in I Peter: *you know that you were ransomed from the futile ways inherited from your ancestors, not with perishable things such as silver and gold, but with the precious blood of Christ, like that of a lamb without blemish or spot...*(I Peter 1:18-19):

The imagery drawn from the story of Israel continues into chapter 2 of I Peter, especially imagery dealing with the cult. Drawing on the imagery of a builder and Christ as the stone, the author says, *Come to Him, to that living stone, rejected by people but in God's sight chosen and precious; and like living stones be yourselves built into a spiritual house, to be a holy priesthood, to offer spiritual sacrifices acceptable to God...* (I Peter 2:4-5); later it is made clear that these 'spiritual sacrifices' must consist of good conduct that will bear witness to pagans (I Peter 1:12). I Peter also shows that the author considered himself as a *presbyteros*, an elder, writing to fellow elders about their supervision of the flock (I Peter 5:1-2. See also John 21:15-17 for Peter as a shepherd over the flock) indicating that the presbyter-bishop structure of the Pastorals seems to be in place.

By the re-interpretation of these texts from the Hebrew scriptures, especially as the *people of God,* the ecclesiology of I Peter is developed.

Strengths and weaknesses

1. The issue to be raised was why the imagery of the *people of God* was important for Christians at that time and place. It was often thought that the context for I Peter was persecution under one of the Emperors, Nero or Domitian or Trajan, but recent scholarship has shown that the basic issue may have been alienation and ostracism (J. H. Elliot, *A Home for the Homeless*). In Northern Asia Minor those who converted to Christianity found themselves cut off from others in what was already a sparsely populated area. Their neighbours found them a curious and secretive group so they were warned not to give the pagans reason to hate them, warned to obey the emperor and other authorities, they are not to use their Christian freedom as a pretext for evil, they are to love and honour all (2:13-17). In this way it was hoped that the feelings of alienation and ostracism could be overcome and Christians could be an integral part of the sparse society. Later Roman evidence shows that Christians were considered atheists since they did not worship the local deities, and they were thought to be anti-social since they had closed door meetings and meals. Inevitably such charges/allegations led to Christians being held in contempt and wanting to go back to *the passions of your former ignorance* (1:14); these *passions* are condemned in 4:2ff., and dismissed as *doing what the Gentiles like to do* (4:3) showing the bias of the Roman community (since the letter was written in Rome) which was a product of the Jerusalem mission, as was the mission area in Northern Asia Minor.

I Peter counteracted this alienation by the assurance that Christian converts had found a new family, a new home, a new status that made them a special people with an imperishable inheritance. All the pride of the Israelites as the special people of God was now transferred to Christians who had *tasted the kindness of the Lord* (2:3), and who *once you were no people but now you are God's people; once you had not received mercy but now you have received mercy* (2:10). In other words, Christian converts were being told that they had found something better: *you are a chosen race, a royal priesthood, a holy nation, God's own people...* (2:9).

The strength of such an ecclesiology proclaimed by I Peter rests in the sense that real benefits are gained from a sense of belonging; if people felt that they were getting something worthwhile from the community/church then that community/church would survive: the Israelites went on as God's people even after the deaths of Moses and Joshua, the people of God in the New Testament was surviving even after the deaths of the apostles, especially Peter who is associated with this epistle; the loving care of a shepherd over the flock would have given the new converts a sense of acceptance, identity and dignity. Unless the people had this sense of benefit, they would have gone elsewhere, so the epistle was necessary to reassure them and remind them that in their baptismal experience, they have become a new people.

2. The dignity of *a royal priesthood, holy nation* of I Peter also served to highlight a weakness – the priesthood came to be seen as a group set apart from the community and that it was only those who were ordained who could exercise priestly functions. This was re-enforced by the priests being different: wearing clerical dress, vestments, and perhaps a celibate life style, while the rest of the community forgot that the *royal priesthood* applied to all believers. To set aside a group as being unique and more closely related to God would have created an exclusive group (perhaps based on social standing, gender etc...). When the description of a *royal priesthood, holy nation* was applied to all the *people of God*, then the missionary movement would also have brought about a sense of umbrage that outsiders were announcing that locals were not the people of God.

So, if Christian converts of Northern Asia Minor needed to be reassured of their special status as a support against ostracism and contempt by their pagan neighbours, it can be safely assumed that a strengthened sense of status would inevitably lead to even more hatred and ostracism.

3.   In the statement that *you are God's own people* (2:9), the author of I Peter does not mention that there was a people who had prior claim on that description – the Jews. The whole imagery of the exodus, desert wandering, paschal lamb, promised land etc… is taken over and used to interpret the journey of coming to faith in Christ, however, there is no indication that historically these images came from a period and pertained to a people long before Christ. The intention of the author was probably to show that the Christians were being joined to the existing people of God, Israel, and that therefore the author could appropriate Israelite symbolism without reference to its historical origin. In this sense, the ecclesiology of I Peter comes close to the ecclesiology of Ephesians (there is much similarity between Eph. 2:11-22 and I Peter 1:13-2:10). However, in Ephesians, *you Gentiles in the flesh* (Christians) …*were alienated from the commonwealth of Israel, and strangers to the covenants of promise, having no hope and without God in the world. But now in Christ Jesus you who were once far off have been brought near… Christ has broken down the dividing wall of hostility…and made the two into one, so making peace…reconciling both to God…so you are no longer strangers and sojourners, but you are fellow citizens with the saints and members of the household of God…* (Eph. 2:11-22). Whereas I Peter does not mention Israel or the Jews or the joining of Israelites and Christians into one; I Peter reads as if there were no previous claimants to the title other than Christians. This led in later times to explicitly deny that the Jews were still the people of God for they had been replaced by Christians.

4.   In I Peter, the status of *holiness* is acquired by coming to Christ or coming into the church. There is no reference to holiness existing in outsiders or to reaching out in mission to outsiders to share the

holiness with them. The Christian appreciation for structures and conditions in those of other faiths is totally ignored. In a pluralistic society, this exclusiveness would cause suspicion and tension leading to disruption of the peace of the city/region.

Conclusion

The author of I Peter encouraged converted Christians, ostracized by their families and society at large, to find dignity in their new status as the ***people of God*** and to live as a community of love.

So while the concept of the *people of God,* confers an exclusive status on Christians and a sense of belonging, it must be seen that it is a dignity conferred by God's graciousness and not on the worthiness of the recipients. It has to be recognized that in an increasingly pluralistic society, the *people of God* concept has to be carefully understood and applied.

Today, some groups would try to walk a *via media* by saying that there are two peoples of God or two groups within the one people of God – God's children of Israel and God's children through Christ. However, there are some Christian groups who adamantly refuse to share the title with the Jews, and probably the Jewish position is that they refuse to share the title with Christians.

The caution today must also be noted that the title of *people of God* to one group/set/religion, reduces all others to being a no-people! Such is the exclusiveness inherent in the concept of *the people of God* that the ecclesiology of I Peter must be carefully understood and applied especially in situations of pluralism.

CHAPTER IX

Conclusion

At the conclusion of the study on New Testament ecclesiologies it would be appropriate to re-iterate the opening paragraphs of the Introduction to the Section (see above) where the question was asked about how the communities founded by the Apostles continued after their deaths; several documents of the New Testament claiming apostolic authority were examined suggesting a claim to apostolic adherence rather than to an objective designation of apostolic writing. Thus images in the various New Testament documents, of the different structures and ecclesiologies left behind by the apostles or their followers, were looked at in an attempt to grapple with the inevitable problem of continuance and succession raised by the death of the apostles in the sub-apostolic and post-apostolic eras.

An examination of these writings in the New Testament which appealed to apostolic authority are an indication that the Apostles left behind sufficiently strong heritages on which their communities could survive even without their physical presence. The New Testament evidence also suggests that different communities preserved different aspects of each Apostles' teaching, e.g. one aspect of Paul's thought is preserved in the letters to the Romans, Corinthians and Galatians (that Jew-Gentile relations are difficult in one community – Acts 28:25-29, Rom. 11:11-26, Gal. 2), while another aspect is preserved in Ephesians and Colossians (that the Jew-Gentile divide has been broken down and all are reconciled in one body – Eph. 2:11-22); one aspect of Peter's thought is preserved in Mark's Gospel while another aspect is preserved in the Peterine Epistles (I Pt. 1:13-2:10 – the Gentiles/Christians to go through the same exodus experience as the Israelites, moving toward a promised inheritance). Perhaps the only known Apostle to survive, in tradition, beyond the 70's of the First Century, was John, the son of Zebedee; the writings associated with John with their stress on love (John's Gospel and the Epistles of John), and the hope of Christ's return in glory and judgement (the Book of Revelation) preserve yet other strands of the Johannine apostolic heritage.

It is interesting that none of the New Testament authors insist that the model that they developed should be the standard model and mandatory for all to follow, i.e. there is no evidence in these writings that a consistent or uniform ecclesiology had emerged, including that of the Pastorals which probably has the clearest model of ecclesiastical organization in deacons, presbyters, bishops. The writings were diverse and each was addressed to a different community with an emphasis which would be effective in that particular context, but as seen, each also had limitations/weaknesses that would constitute a danger had the emphasis been taken in isolation and as a norm for all time and all places.

The diversity of the New Testament ecclesiologies has given rise to at least three reactions:

1. Those who reject the evidence that there is diversity in the ecclesiology of the New Testament on the grounds that the New Testament originated under divine inspiration which disregards any human intervention. Therefore there is no diversity but a uniformity in which only God's voice can be heard.

2. Others reject diversity in the ecclesiology of the New Testament on the grounds that the New Testament is a projection of an ideal situation of the 1st century where Jesus had planned out the church and the apostles were united in carrying out His plans; the only ones who differed were the trouble-makers who were condemned in the writings.

Both these are ultra-conservative reactions to the diversity of ecclesiology in the New Testament and totally unsupported by the evidence that has been presented in the above chapters; further, neither reaction is a good way of dealing with the diversity of ecclesiologies while developing a mature Christian approach to recognizing differences.

3.   There are those who hold that the diversities in New Testament ecclesiology are signs of a hardened stance of separation. However, in the writings studied there is no evidence that the positions are so hardened that they result in broken relationships or *koinonia* (fellowship) among the churches, much less a lack of communion and excommunication. In fact, all the writings stress the importance of *koinonia*: the Pauline heritage in Luke-Acts and Ephesians-Colossians stresses the importance of Christian unity as a visible entity; the *people of God* concept in I Peter requires a collective understanding of Christianity; the Johannine heritage stresses love even for the sheep that are not of this fold, and of Jesus' prayer that the disciples may be one; James, Jude and II Peter insist on the importance of Christian unity as a means of combating false teachings and misunderstandings. Therefore, diversity of ecclesiologies in the New Testament cannot be used to justify Christian divisions; ecclesiological divisions cannot be supported on the basis of an appeal to the New Testament.

If the diversity of New Testament ecclesiological differences cannot be ignored or used to justify divisions, then how did these differences help the churches of the sub-apostolic and post-apostolic times, and how does it help Christians today? The above studies in the heritages left behind by the apostles should be seen as strengthening the church, and challenging the church.

Strengthening the Church

Most Christians today belong to a particular denomination because they were born and baptized into it. If they remained faithful to that denomination it is because they found in it a fellowship that brought them closer to one another and to Christ, and that they were able to discern that loyalty to that denomination helped them to be more like the people that Christ expected them to be. Thus church adherence has become a matter of conviction – a conviction that one's own church has remained faithful to the biblical heritage of sound doctrine (Pastorals), of faith expressed in works (James), of love among the community members (John), of belonging to a people (I Peter), of a looking forward to Christ's return (Jude and II Peter), and that within that heritage, there is enough to silence those who propagate false teachings and question the return of Christ. Seen in this way, the heritage left behind by the apostles is a strength that laid the foundation on which the church was built (Apostolic tradition/succession), and continues to be the strength on which the church organizes itself, propagates, and remains faithful to the witness of God's love in Christ.

Challenging the Church

In present day Christianity that is divided into many denominations, there is a long history of how the scriptures were used to prove/justify the denomination's theological and organizational structures. Hence a study of the diversity of the apostolic heritage can challenge the church constructively: to examine the claims made by a denomination as to whether it is faithful to scripture and the diversity represented therein. This is a complex task, but the challenge remains especially before making any absolute claims, and especially in the light of the increasing awareness that there are other ways and means of remaining faithful to the biblical message (the Johannine understanding of "other sheep who are not of this fold"). A church that stressed and stresses the heritage of a sound teaching authority (Pastorals), must be challenged to look at the role of the *paraclete*-Spirit as a teacher dwelling in each believer. A church that stressed and stresses charisms/gifts (Pauline heritage) may need to be challenged by the idea of love among the community (Johannine heritage) and the historical continuity of the *people of God* (Peterine heritage). The governance and theological position of any church must finally be challenged by the Matthean perspective in chapter 18 of the least in the Kingdom.

The variety of New Testament ecclesiologies shows that there is no 'one image/model' of ecclesiology in the New Testament, yet all are held together in the New Testament providing for a richness of diversity and tradition which must not be rejected, but studied and used as a guide, as an encouragement, as a corrective for traditions, and a challenge to contemporarize community organization and witness. In the context of a divided Christianity, instead of reading the Bible to justify a denomination's position, it would be worthwhile to read the Bible to discover where Christians have not been listening: when matters tend to become too structured and formal (Pastorals), one must listen to the call to love (Johannine); when individuals become too high-handed (III John, Jude, II Peter), one must listen to the reminder of the *people of God* (I Peter); when there is too much emphasis on faith as 'only believe', one must listen for the correction that faith is to be demonstrated in works (James). Above all, and running like a thread throughout the whole tapestry, one must listen for the voice of sound doctrine, true teaching, handed down by the apostles in the heritages that they have left behind which has ensured the survival of the church for more than twenty centuries and which will continue to be the strength and challenge for the church in the centuries to come.

***

Select Bibliography for Section VI

See Select Bibliography at the end of each Section in Vols. I, II, III, IV

Barrett, C. K. *Pastoral Epistles.* Oxford: Clarendon Press, 1963.

Brown, Raymond E. *The Gospel According to John,* Chapters 1-12, Anchor Bible, Vol. 29, Garden City, New York: Doubleday, 1966.

__________, *The Gospel According to John,* Chapters 13-21, Anchor Bible, Vol. 29A, Garden City. New York: Doubleday, 1970.

__________, *The Community of the Beloved Disciple.* New York: Paulist Press, 1979.

__________, *The Epistles of John.,* Anchor Bible, Vol. 30, Garden City, New York: Doubleday, 1982.

Brown, R. E. and J. P. Meier. *Antioch and Rome.* New York: Paulist, 1983.

Bruce, F. F. *Stephen, James, and John: Studies in Early Non-Pauline Christianity.* Grand Rapids: Eerdmans, 1979.

Bultmann, R. *Theology of the New Testament,* Vol. I, trans. by K. Groebel. London: SCM Press, 1952.

__________. *Theology of the New Testament.* Vol. II, trans. by K. Groebel, London: SCM Press, 1955.

Cornelius, Paul. "I Timothy" in Brian C. Wintle (General Editor), *South Asia Biblical Commentary.* (Udaipur, Rajasthan: Open Door Publications, 2015), pages 1682-1692.

__________, "II Timothy" in Brian C. Wintle (General Editor), *South Asia Biblical Commentary,* (Udaipur, Rajasthan: Open Door Publications, 2015), pages 1693-1700.

__________, "Titus" in Brian C. Wintle (General Editor), *South Asia Biblical Commentary,* (Udaipur, Rajasthan: Open Door Publications, 2015), pages 1701-1704.

Dunn, James D. G. *Unity and Diversity in the New Testament: An Inquiry into the Character of Earliest Christianity.* London: SCM Press, 2006.

Elliot, J. H. *A Home for the Homeless.* Philadelpha: Fortress Press, 1981.

Fernando, Ajit. *Leadership Lifestyles: A Study of I Timothy.* Wheaton:Tyndale, 1985.

Goppelt, L. *Apostolic and Post-Apostolic Times.* London: Black, 1970.

Hanson, A.T. The Pastoral Epistles. Grand Rapids: Eerdmann's Publishing Co., 1982.

Houlden, J. L. *The Pastoral Epistles.* New York: Harper & Row, 1963.

Kummel, W. G. *Introduction to the New Testament.* London: SCM Press Ltd., 1975.

Theissen, G. *Sociology of Early Palestinian Christianity.* Philadelphia: Fortress, 1978.

__________. *The First Followers of Jesus: A Sociological Analysis of the Earliest Christianity.* London: SCM Press, 1978.

APPENDIX

Summary of Introduction to New Testament Writings

(in canonical order)

Canonical Name	Modern Consensus	Date & Place of Writing
Matthew details given in Vol. I of this series	**Author:** Traditionally attributed to Matthew, the tax collector, a disciple of Jesus. No conclusive internal evidence from the text. Traditional attribution accepted to day or it can be attributed as an anonymous writing. **Comment:** Written in good Greek with evidence of a Jewish background in presenting the fulfillment of Jewish scriptures. So author is probably a Jewish Christian with a Greek speaking background. Most used of the Gospels in the early Church.	A.D. 80 – 85 Traditionally Syrian Antioch which is associated with Matthew, the disciple of Jesus.
Mark details given in Vol. I of this series	**Author:** Identity is nowhere disclosed in the text. Traditionally held that Mark, nephew of Peter, wrote down Peter's memories and the writing was accepted into the canon on that basis. Traditional attribution accepted today although the author remains unknown/ anonymous. **Comment:** Written in poor literary style; accepted as the first of the written Gospels and one of the sources for Matthew and Luke. No biological or chronological interest. Presents down-to-earth reactions of the disciples to various events and teachings of Jesus. The first written interpretation of the words and works of Jesus.	A. D. 65 – 70 Traditionally Rome during the last days of Peter. A non—Palestinian place of origin is also suggested by scholars.

Luke details given in Vol. I of this series	**Author:** Traditionally attributed to Luke, companion of Paul and accepted into the canon on that basis. Author's identity not disclosed in the text. A Gentile writer writing for gentle readership. Traditional attribution to Luke normally held although the author remains unknown/anonymous. **Comment:** Intended to be an orderly account for the most excellent Theophilus. Not biographical or chronological history, but a theological interpretation of history placing the story of Jesus within the framework of world history. Known for the author's special concern for marginalized groups.	A.D. 80 – 90 Traditionally held that the writing originated in Rome as a document for the Roman judge who was trying Paul's case, but it could have been written anywhere outside of Palestine in the areas of the Pauline mission.
John details given in Vol. III of this series	**Author:** Traditionally attributed to John, son of Zebedee, who is also thought to be the beloved disciple or the disciple whom Jesus loved. However, the text does not identify a person. While the identity of the author. remains anonymous, the traditional association of John, the son of Zebedee, as the beloved disciple, who was involved in the process of the writing of the Gospel is still accepted. **Comment:** The writing combines history, philosophy, and theology. The author is selective in his choice of material and in its presentation in order to evoke belief that would lead to life.	A. D. 90 - 100 Traditionally associated with Ephesus and Asia Minor as John is held to have worked in that area.
The Acts of the Apostles details given in Vol. II of this series	**Author:** Traditionally attributed to Luke, companion of Paul especially on the 'we passages' which show the author as a travel companion of Paul, and so accepted into the canon on that basis. Identity not disclosed in the text. Traditional attribution to Luke normally held although the author remains unknown/anonymous. **Comment:** Intended to be a sequel to the Gospel of Luke to the most excellent Theophilus. Not a chronological history, but a theological interpretation of history placing the story of the growth and mission of the Church within the framework of world history.	After A. D. 90 Traditionally held that the writing originated in Rome as a document for the Roman judge who was trying Paul's case, but it could have been written anywhere outside of Palestine in the areas of the Pauline mission.

Romans details given in Vol. II of this series	**Author:** Authorship has never been in serious doubt. The letter to the Romans has, from earliest times, been attributed to the Apostle Paul. **Comment:** Paul did not personally know the community in Rome, so the letter serves as an introduction to Paul's theology and mission plans. A detailed presentation and argument for Paul's theology of justification by faith.	A. D. 56 - 57 Paul was enjoying the hospitality of Gaius in Corinth..
I Corinthians details given in Vol. II of this series	**Author:** There has never been any serious doubt regarding Paul's authorship of this letter. I Cor. 5:9 makes reference an earlier letter which may possibly be found in part or in whole in II Cor. 6:14 - 7:1. **Comment:** I Corinthians is a response to deeply disturbing verbal reports regarding the situation in Corinth, and also answers written questions from the community. One of the first documents to give a theological response to social and community issues.	A. D. 54 - 55 Written during Paul's stay in Ephesus
II Corinthians details given in Vol. II of this series	**Author:** The authorship has never been in doubt, and though a composite document, it has always, been attributed to the Apostle Paul. **Comment:** II Corinthians consists of the following letters (whole or part) dealing with various issues: 1. 6:14-7:1 : "Lost Letter" 2. chs. 10 - 13: Letter of Tears 3. 2:14 - 6:13 & 7:2-16: Letter of Thanksgiving 4. 1:1 - 2:13: Epistolary Formula & exhortation 5. ch. 8 : Instructions to restart the Collection 6. ch. 9 : Urgency to complete the Collection	Compiled in Macedonia or Ephesus, A. D. 57. Suggested dates for letters: 1. A. D. 53 - 54 Ephesus 2. A. D. 55 - 56 Ephesus 3. mid A. D. 56 Macedonia. 4. mid A. D. 56 Macedonia. 5. early A.D. 57 Macedonia 6. mid A. D. 57 Macedonia

Galatians details given in Vol. II of this series	**Author:** The authorship has never been in doubt and has always been attributed to the Apostle Paul. **Comment:** written in response to tensions created in the community by intruders who were propagating that people had to first submit to the laws of Judaism before becoming Christians. Hence the opponents are referred to as "Judaisers" with the main theme as 'freedom from the Law'.	A.D. 55 - 57 Written in Ephesus or Macedonia
Ephesians details given in Vol. II of this series	**Author:** Paul's authorship of Ephesians is seriously doubted. Ephesians is placed among the Deutero-Pauline letters as a pseudonymous writing. **Comment:** Development of Christology and ecclesiology in the post-Pauline context. Shows how Paul's thinking and theological expressions were developed in the post-Pauline era as it moved into wider areas and met new contexts.	A. D. 80 - 100 Asia Minor. There is a close literary relationship with the letter to the Colossians.
Philippians details given in Vol. II of this series	**Author:** At least three letters compiled in the post-Pauline period, hence a pseudonymous compilation. 1. 4:10-20 : letter of thanks for gift received 2. 1:1-3:1a & 4:21-23 : thanks after Epaphroditus' recovery and his return to Philippi; future plans. 3. 3:1b-4:9 : polemic against Jewish and pagan antagonists. **Comment:** The three situations mentioned above are addressed. The hymn on the humility of Christ (kenosis) is one of the best known passages in the New Testament (2:5-11).	A. D. 70 - 90 The individual letters were probably collected and compiled in Philippi after the death of Paul.

Colossians details given in Vol. II of this series	**Author:** Close literary relationship with the Epistle to the Ephesians. As in the case of Ephesians, this letter is also placed among the pseudonymous deutero-Pauline writings. **Comment:** A highly developed Christology (the 'cosmic Christ') and ecclesiology (Christ as the. Head of the Church) is presented. The letter combats false teachings ('the Colossian heresy') that had pervaded Colossae and stresses true teaching.	A. D. 80 - 100 Asia Minor. There is a close literary relationship with the letter to the Ephesians.

I Thessalonians
 	
details given in Vol. II of this series
	Author: A compilation of two originally independent letters. Placed among the deutero-Pauline letters as a pseudonymous writing.
	  1. 2:13-4:2 : First letter with its own thanksgiving and conclusion but lacks address and ending as it has been inserted into another letter.
	
	  2. 1:1-2:12 + 4:3-5:28 : Second letter making no reference to issues of the first letter but stresses ethical teachings and especially references to. the second coming (<u>parousia</u>) - Day of the Lord.
	
	Comment: The first letter expresses joy and thanksgiving. The second letter stresses teachings regarding the <u>parousia</u> and other ethical teachings.
		Compiled in
		A. D. 80 - 100
		
		Compiled in Thessalonica

II Thessalonians details given in Vol. II of this series	**Author:** Compilation and editorial activity carried out after the time of Paul, so placed among the pseudonymous deutero-Pauline writings. **Comment:** Much similarity between the second letter in I Thess. and II Thess.: subject matter is the same. II Thess. is a corrective to misunderstandings/ misinterpretations that might have arisen concerning the Day of the Lord.	Compiled in A. D. 80 - 100 Compiled in Thessalonica

I Timothy details given in Vol. II of this series	**Author:** The theological and ecclesiastical concerns of the Pastorals regarding Church order reflect a situation of the early second century, hence placed among the trito-Pauline writings. **Comment:** Addresses a situation where false teaching has entered the community; calls for a return to the true faith and outlines Church order as an answer to combat false teaching and ensure the transmission of the true/orthodox faith.	A. D. 120 - 140 Any place in Asia / Asia Minor
II Timothy details given in Vol. II of this series	**Author:** The theological and ecclesiastical concerns of the Pastorals regarding Church order reflect a situation of the early second century, hence placed among the trito-Pauline writings. **Comment:** Addresses a situation where false teaching has entered the community; calls for a return to the true faith and outlines Church order as an answer to combat false teaching and ensure the transmission of the true/orthodox faith.	A. D. 120 - 140 Any place in Asia / Asia Minor
Titus details given in Vol. II of this series	**Author:** The theological and ecclesiastical concerns of the Pastorals regarding Church order reflect a situation of the early second century, hence placed among the trito-Pauline writings. **Comment:** Addresses a situation where false teaching has entered the community; calls for a return to the true faith and outlines Church order as an answer to combat false teaching and ensure the transmission of the true/orthodox faith.	A. D. 120 - 140 Any place in Asia/Asia Minor.?

Book	Author / Comment	Date / Place
Philemon details given in Vol. II of this series	**Author:** A genuine letter of Paul putting into practice that about which he had theorized. **Comment:** Letter deals with relationships with special reference to the issue of welcoming back a slave as a beloved brother.	Either A.D. 53-57 from Ephesus Or A.D. 58-60 from Caesarea Or A.D. 60-64 from Rome
Hebrews details given in Vol. IV of this series	**Author:** Early thinking was that it was written by Paul. But scholarship has shown that this is not the case. It is now placed among anonymous writings. **Comment:** Seeks to understand the Christian faith from a background of Judaism using Jewish symbols, history, and theology. Makes a unique contribution in its Christology of Jesus as the High Priest.	A. D. 80 - 90 Alexandria? / Rome?
James details given in Vol. IV of this series	**Author:** A pseudonymous writing by a Jewish Christian using the name and authority of James, a respected leader of the early Jerusalem community. **Comment:** Unmistakably Jewish in nature and stresses that Christianity must be characterized by faith expressed in good deeds. Hence a corrective to an over emphasis on the Pauline position of justification by faith alone.	end of the 1st. century after Paul's writings were well known. Jerusalem?
I Peter details given in Vol. IV of this series	**Author:** A pseudonymous writing in the name of Peter who was an authoritative figure among the apostles. **Comment:** A moderate Christian response to persecution, perhaps trying to find a via media for the church and state to live together. Has a message of comfort and encouragement to endure persecution and suffering.	A. D. 85 - 95 Rome?

II Peter details given in Vol. IV of this series	**Author:** A pseudonymous writing in the name of Peter who was an authoritative figure among the apostles. The writing is closely related to Jude. **Comment:** Written to combat false teachings and expresses concern for re-affirming belief in the parousia (Second coming of Christ). Heavily dependent on the Epistle of Jude.	A. D. 120 - 140 (date after the Epistle of Jude) Place of writing is unknown
I John details given in Vol. III of this series	**Author:** Anonymous writing, but related to the Johannine School of thought, and so associated with the disciple John, the son of Zebedee. **Comment:** Warning against false teachings/teachers and providing an early commentary on the Gospel of John.	A. D. 100 - 110 Alexandria? Antioch in Syria? Most probably Ephesus
II John details given in Vol. III of this series	**Author:** The author describes himself as "elder/presbyter" - an anonymous designation for a person in authority in the line of apostolic tradition. **Comment:** Warning not to allow false teachers/teachings to enter into the community.	A. D. 100 - 110 Ephesus?/Asia Minor?
III John details given in Vol. III of this series	**Author:** the author describes himself as "elder/presbyter" - an anonymous designation for a person in authority in the line of apostolic tradition. **Comment:** To encourage the community to extend hospitality to faithful missionaries.	A. D. 100 - 110 Ephesus?/Asia Minor?

Jude details given in Vol. IV of this series	**Author:** A pseudonymous Jewish-Christian writing. **Comment:** Written to combat libertine Gnostic thinking/teachings. Closely related to II Peter and regarded as the earlier of the two writings.	A. D. 120 - 140 but earlier than II Peter. Place of writing is unknown.
Revelation details given in Vol. III of this series	**Author:** A pseudonymous writing as the claimant John cannot be identified as being in the line of apostolic tradition. Generally accepted that the writing originated in the Johannine School of thought. **Comment:** An apocalyptic writing using all the characteristics of apocalyptic literature such as symbols, figures, colours etc... in order to present a message of hope and encouragement during a time of severe state persecution.	A. D. 90 - 100 Place of writing is unknown. Ephesus?/Asia Minor?